Birth of a Quarry Town
1800s
Lyons, Colorado

Diane Goode Benedict

Applications, Plus

Lyons, Colorado

**Birth of a Quarry Town
1800s
Lyons, Colorado**

By Diane Goode Benedict

First Edition 2002

Lyons Historical Society
P O Box 9, Lyons, Colorado 80540
303-823-6692

ISBN 0-9715714–1–4

Published by:
Applications Plus, P O Box 2567, Lyons, Colorado 80540
Fax: 303-823-5161

Typefaces: Headings, Bodoni Poster, Arial Bold and Body Text, Palatino
Printed by: Thomson-Shore of Dexter, Michigan

To my father,
Joseph Alexander Schipek Goode.
He loved the West with all of his heart and soul.

The cover picture is an early photograph of Lyons circa 1880. The original is owned by Herman O. and Jeanne A. Freudenberg. On the back of the picture is stamped: F. M. Laycook & Co. Photographers; View and Scenic Artists; Hygiene, Colorado. Courtesty of the Lyons Redstone Museum, Lyons, Colorado.

If I had the tongue of Bryan,
I'd give that tongue no rest
In boosting Lyons,
The Jewel of the West.
　　　　___Walter Mason

Acknowledgments

For information, research assistance, and time freely given, I am indebted to the following individuals and organizations.

In Lyons, Colorado:
LaVern Johnson and the Lyons Redstone Museum, Frances Brodie Brackett and the Lyons Cemetery Association, Frank Weaver, now deceased, a Lyons historian and writer. For sharing his love of the country, his large library, and his many suggestions I thank Wayne Werner. Also, thank you to Dennis Moe, Lyons Fire Marshal for the current map of Lyons.

In Estes Park, Colorado:
The staffs at the Estes Park Museum and the Estes Park Library. Especially, those who created the excellent index of microfilms and holdings at the library.

In Longmont, Colorado:
The reference and media staff of the Longmont Public Library, and once again to those volunteers who indexed the many rolls of newspaper microfilms.

In Boulder, Colorado:
Wendy Hall and Mary Jo Reitsema of the Carnegie Branch Library, the Boulder Genealogical Society collection at the Carnegie Branch Library, David Hays at the University of Colorado Norlin Library and Archives, the helpful staff of the Boulder County Record and Clerks Office, and the wonderfully generous people at the Boulder County Coroner's Office.

In Denver, Colorado:
Lance Christensen and George Orlowski of the Colorado State
Archives; James Jeffery and the collection at the Denver Public
Library, Department of Western History and Genealogy; and
the staff of the Colorado Historical Society .

My gratitude is endless to family and friends who read sections of the book and put up with my many questions and need for handholding I am indebted to my son, Robert J. Benedict, Boulder, Colorado, for writing the section, "Geology of Lyons." Without his expertise and patience, I would never have gotten all those strata and stratums straight. Also, for his patience in guiding me through the maze of PageMaker™ manipulations. Thank you for the gentle touch and caring hand of my copyeditor, Lynda Kelling, whose expertise has been invaluable. And to my readers, LaVern Johnson and Frances Brackett, your suggestions and corrections have been so beneficial. Above all, thank you to the people of Lyons both past and present.

Author's Note

I regret any and all errors that may be found in this book. Every effort has been made to ensure that this endeavor is as accurate as possible. I have spent several years researching archives, libraries, census records, courthouses, and coroner's offices, as well as reading newspapers trying to separate fact from fiction. However, as we all know, a fact that is fact to one person, may be fiction to another, over time family histories and loyalties change. If names are misspelled or dates are incorrect, please send any corrections with documentation to: Applications, Plus; "Birth of a Quarry Town"; P O Box 2567; Lyons, CO 80540.

The structure of the book is based upon an accumulation of research of people, places, and things surrounding the development of Lyons during the 1800s. It is my intension to secure in one place some of the material that I have collected.

Family names, stories, and pictures dealing with the first half of the twentieth century are being collected for a future book on Lyons, Colorado and the people who lived and worked in the little town at the Gateway to the Rockies.

Introduction

It has been my privilege to compile the following material concerning the people and places of Lyons, Colorado. These pioneers expressed a spirit of individualism, hard work, and dedication. With their hopes and talents they gave birth to the beautiful little quarry town, Lyons, Colorado.

While documenting the Lyons Cemetery with Frances Brodie Brackett, pioneer descendent and President of the Lyons Cemetery Association, I became fascinated with the people who settled the land. I began to meet the descendents of these hardy souls and to better understand that "something" which draws humans to venture into uncharted territory.

The process revived memories of my father, who loved the West, but never had the privilege of living beyond Michigan. He was born into an Austrian coal mining family, immigrated to the United States in 1907, and worked the mines and farms of Pennsylvania until he was hired as a salesman for Allied Electric in Pittsburgh, Pennsylvania. Unfortunately, his westward movement terminated in the Detroit Metropolitan area where he established a successful manufacturing sales representative firm for electrical construction materials.

In his early years of dealing with wholesalers and municipalities he was able to take an extended vacation each summer. Dad would pack up the Chrysler and gather together my mother, brother, and I to begin the only journey into the West that he would ever make. Our summer treks followed the pioneer trails, the hideouts of the bad men, the celebrations of cowboys and cattlemen, and the cemeteries where they were laid to rest. We wandered and explored through Nebraska, the Dakotas, Wyoming, Montana, Colorado, Utah, New Mexico, Arizona, and Texas.

On these trips I lost my heart to Colorado, so Daddy made sure that I got my wish to attend the University of Colorado in Boulder. I became his storyteller sharing my trips to museums, archives, and cemeteries, sharing the hidden treasures I had found on many mountain hikes. So Dad, you did make it to the West, if only in the guise of your daughter and unfortunately years after those wonderful pioneers who took a chance and fought the heat, insects, prejudices, cold, and short growing seasons. As your mother was, these people were inspired by the hope and promise of a better life, a chance to build a personal "empire," an opportunity to live and challenge the land, the elements, and themselves.

Romantic? Hardly! Women died in childbirth, many children did not reach the age of two years. Crops were lost; livestock died or were rustled by whites and Indians. Land grabbers cheated and gamblers conspired to take their hard earned cash. Still, there was that "something" that drew these men and women to the land; something that was different; something that spoke to their very souls; something that called them to move westward.

My sincere hope is that the following will give the reader a taste of the lives of a few of these pioneers, land developers, and adventurers, those who gave birth to Lyons, Colorado.

Diane G. Benedict
Lyons, Colorado
December 2001

Illustrations and Maps

CONTENTS

FIRST PEOPLE,
TRAPPERS,
AND
THE LOST HUNTER

Birth of a Quarry Town

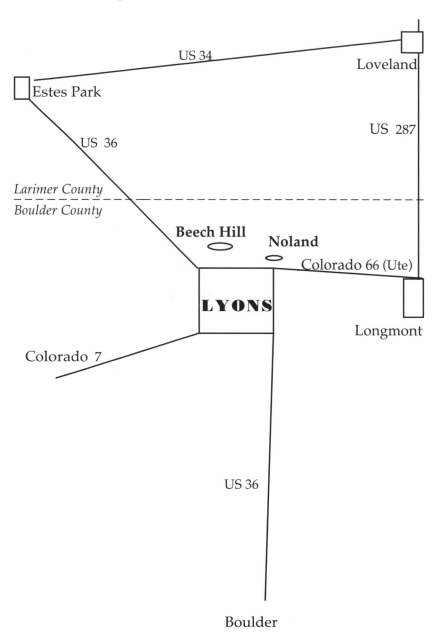

This sectional map is not drawn to scale. It is a representation of the
Front Range in Northern Boulder County into Larimer County.

First People

A shes from campfires, stone tools and weapons indicate that early man arrived in the State of Colorado somewhere between 12,000 and 15,000 years ago. Actual movements and specific tribes of Native Americans living and traveling in the Lyons area, however, have not been documented. Most of what we know comes from oral histories and news articles. These sources talk of Arapahoe, Cheyenne, and Ute, to a lesser extent Shoshone, Pawnee, and Crow, who camped in and around the Lyons area. The river, valley, and bowl-like topography offered a mild climate, good hunting, and plenty of clean water.

The surrounding ridge tops provided excellent lookouts for opposing tribes and later surveillance of the ever encroaching white pioneers. Indian Lookout Mountain up the South St. Vrain received its name from the purpose it served. Further to the southwest is Coffintop, also named by local tribes. They said that the mountain's squared off top looked just like a coffin.

The following are a few of the stories told about the Native Americans in and around the Lyons section.

Chief Niwot and his brother, Neva camped on the South St. Vrain River near Lyons, which seems natural, as the tribes were nomadic and preferred to camp near water. A 100-year-old patient of Dr. William L. Benedict of Longmont, Colorado, name withheld by request, told the story of an Indian that used to visit her grandmother, one of the earliest settlers in the territory.

"Every time he came by, grandma would give him freshly made cookies, then he would leave peacefully. He kept returning; and she kept giving him cookies afraid that she might be scalped if she refused.

3

Well, one day she was tired and had had enough. 'No, I will not give you any more cookies. Just go away.'

The Indian answered her in perfect English, 'Why not? You always have.'

Grandmother was so surprised. She didn't know that this "savage" could speak English, so she asked him who he was.

The man answered, 'I am Chief Niwot.'

Grandma just kept right on giving him cookies."

A news article dated Tuesday January 6, 1948, ran the banner headline, "Skeleton of Indian Found Near Lyons." A human skeleton was unearthed while digging a cesspool at the W. W. Service station at the junction of Lyons and Foothills Highway. Coroner Howe of Longmont estimated the grave to be around 100 years old. The location coincides with a closed meeting of county officials and native elders during the 1970s. Locals say that the purpose of the meeting was to hold a ceremony for an old Indian burial ground and to establish ownership.

In a letter written from Bent's Fort on the Arkansas, May 5, 1844, Solomon Sublette wrote about the Cheyennes camping down near the crossing of the Arkansas only to discover that the large herds of buffalo they needed for food, clothing, and supplies were gone. Angered by the loss, Solomon was told by the elders that all young buffalo would be killed so that the white man could not have them. 'The Indian took only what they needed, why did the whites insist on killing only for the hide, leaving the carcasses to rot in the sun?'

Charles Eagle Plume, a well-known resident of Estes Park was interviewed in 1979. He told of a recent discovery of Indian remains in a cave near Lyons, location not given. They were dated to about 15,000 years ago. He went on to describe the local Cheyennes as a very tall people, athletic, slim, and handsome. The Arapahoes, he related, "were not a very moral people. They were unclean, not very good-looking, and very tricky"

One of the few negative encounters with the Arapahoe was in 1860. William Dewey had purchased property at the mouth of the canyon and had established a successful working ranch. William fearing a possible attack by the Indians had built his house from the abundant field stone on his land. One day a band of young Arapahoe warriors decided to recapture their natural trail up Left Hand Canyon, once unimpeded by the white man's presence. They declared war on Dewey. From within his fortress of stone, Dewey fought the raiding party for four days when suddenly the young braves withdrew, taking their dead and wounded with them.

Warren Smead, a Lyons Pioneer, told many stories about his friendship with the natives. He never had any trouble though the bands were quite numerous and at one time they had had over 500 horses grazing on a meadow near the SE corner of Ute and Foothills Highways, property now owned by Cemex. One of his Indian friends told of one morning that he had laid in wait on a ledge overlooking the approach of two white women debating whether or not to steal some horses. The non-suspecting ladies were Mrs. Susie Miller and Mrs. Alvin Weese. They were moving their cattle up the South St. Vrain into the Lyons area.

Bertha Jane Reese McConnell would tell the story of Indians kidnapping Lillian Hubbell, the daughter of William N. Hubbell, owner of the Estes Park Stage Coach. The ranchers rounded up a posse and rode off into the hills after the band, successfully bringing the young girl back to her family safe and sound.

Mrs. Lee Day, as usual, was frying bacon for the morning meal. Suddenly, she felt uneasy, looking over her shoulder she saw two Native Americans with their heads thrust through the opening for the window. She screamed, threw the frying pan, covering the men with bacon and hot grease.

One day when the Robert Montgomery family came home from a trip to town, they were dismayed to find broken dishes scattered on the floor of their home. A band of raiding Indians had carried off all their possessions leaving behind a mixture of feathers and flour spread from room to room. Another encounter from an Indian raid happened in the late 1800s. This time the Montgomerys were burnt out of their ranch on the Little Thompson. The livestock and hay had been stolen.

A story in a local newspaper told of the "Last Big Raid" in the area. A group of young braves rode south from their campground on the Big Thompson to run off the livestock on Dr. Dow's place [later owned by the Montgomery family]. The doctor saved one of his colts and called together a posse to pursue the thieves. It was reported that the men killed one brave near the Colard ranch up in Spring Gulch and "liberated" the doctor's cattle and horses. No one in the posse was injured.

From the material I have read about this area, there appeared to be little violence between the two groups until cultural differences became impossible for either side to accept. Counting coo while brandishing bow and spear, stealing horses, taking things simply because they were there, and using the white man's clothing for play things was beyond European understanding. On the otherside, Renegades were the major cause of any bloodshed and destruction of the settler's property. These young warriors differed little from present day gangs who lash out in defiance of their elders.

Qualified archeologists had not ventured into the Lyons' section to identify artifacts, teepee rings, and old campfire sites. Much of this was left to amateur collectors, such as Harold Marion Dunning, the author of *Over Hill and Vale,* who lived in Lyons when he was a teenager and Jack Moomaw. During their explorations of the valleys, streams and mountain tops, these men collected Indian arrowheads and other artifacts. Without having followed the strict rules of archeology, scientists consider their collection of little value for identification and location purposes. Part of this record is in the Loveland Museum and another part is stored at the University of Denver Museum leaving for the rest of us a record of Native American movement throughout the valleys, streams and mountains of this area.

Lon Havens, a former resident of Lyons found several tomahawks just east of Lyons near the Longmont Filter Plant on highway 66. Both Lon and Joe Campbell, a Lyons High School teacher reported having found burial grounds on the Little Thompson.

Both Roy Siglinger and Sherman Bohn heard many stories from old timers about the mountain just east of Noland Road. It was said to have been an Indian burial depository. Here they kept their treasures for safekeeping. Young and old searched the mountain. It was rumored that in the1930s a local man had found the cache and taken the loot. Identity unknown. Treasures never seen.

Trappers & Mountain Men

While the West was being invaded by the white man Paris, France was undergoing a revolution; Emily Dickinson, the American Poet was born; and stiff collars became the fashion of the day for men. The American trapper, however, avoided these weighty matters, as well as their prohibitively restrictive clothing. Typically, the trapper and mountain man was more utilitarian, leaving his hair to grow long and wearing a felt or animal skin hat to keep out the cold in winter and the insects in the other three seasons. His clothing was made of wool or leather fringed and thonged, then covered by a pullover, shirt, or a coat-style top worn with a belt. Underclothing was a simple breech clothe if even used. Indian-style trousers were worn with thigh-high leggings to protect against the tall and often lethal shrubs. A buffalo robe or Hudson's Bay blanket was the only protection from the cold and snow. These men lived solitary lives during the hunting and trapping season. Clothing, food, horses, or pack mules were purchased and traded with Native Americans and at the white man's forts.

The Lyons section was part of the Kansas Territory stretching far and wide into unmapped country. The beaver trappers lived and worked side by side with the local "red man" enjoying the solitude and abundant wildlife. In 1839 Trapper Kelly, who roamed the mountains of Steamboat Springs, Colorado, complained about the crowded conditions of mountain living, "Now the mountains are so poor that one would stand a right good chance of starving, if he obliged to hang up here for seven days." Kelly's dream of hundreds of miles of unencumbered and uninhabited open land was quickly being replaced with the inevitable soldier and pioneer on their westward movement.

Some of the mountain men known to live in the region around 1839 included: Jim Baker, Louis Vasquez, John Hatcher; Tom Tobin; Jim Beckwourth; Baptiste Charbooneau, the son of Sacajawea; John Albert; Henry Fraeb; Lancaster P. Lupton, and the young entrepreneur Ceran St. Vrain for whom the rivers around Lyons were named.

Ceran St. Vrain
1802–1879

Ceran de Hault de Lassus de St. Vrain was born in St. Louis, Missouri, the son of a French nobleman. His father Jacquest Marcellin Ceran de Hault de Lassus de St. Vrain married Marie Felicite Dubreuil in 1795. They had ten children of whom the second was Ceran, born May 2, 1802 at his father's estate at Spanish Lake, Missouri. His father died in 1818 when Ceran was only sixteen. After attending St. Louis College, he went to live with Bernard Pratte Sr., who outfitted trapping expeditions in the Missouri River beaver trade, later extending the business into the Santa Fe, New Mexico. At twenty-two Ceran held a responsible position with Pratte, Cabanne and Company supplying trappers and traders.

He moved to Taos, New Mexico and spent most of his life in that area. At twenty-three Ceran was outfitting his own trapping expeditions. On August 29, 1826, he and William S. Williams applied to Governor Narboa for trading passports for New Mexico and Arizona. In 1828 St. Vrain led a trip to the Green River. Because of hostile Indians along the Platte River route, he turned his group south along the Front Range. In order to trap beaver in Mexico, however, you had to hold Mexican citizenship, which St. Vrain applied for and received in 1831.

In September 1830 in Taos, Ceran and Charles Bent became partners. The Bent brothers, Charles and William managing their businesses in Taos and Santa Fe, New Mexico. The trapping business became less profitable and so the men turned to trading with the Mexicans and the Indians. They formed a fur-trading company in the Colorado Territory named Bent, St. Vrain & Company.

Ceran unofficially married Maria Dolores de Luna while in Taos and had his first child, Vicente. Rumor also had him marrying a daughter of Charles Beaubien in 1843. He actually lived with Maria Ignacia Trujillo with whom he had a son. In his later years he married Luisa Branch and lived with her until his death. They had one daughter. He died at his home in Mora, New Mexico, on October 28, 1879.

Fort St. Vrain
1830s–about 1845

Robert Newell, an employee of the Bent, St. Vrain, & Company group was given barter goods and directed to trade with the Cheyennes during the winter of 1836. Fort William, then renamed Fort Bent began about 1830. In 1837 the company built Fort St. Vrain directly west of Gilcrest. The location of the fort was close to the point where the St. Vrain Rivers entered the South Platte. According to a report made by Rufus B. Save, a New Englander traveling in the Rocky Mountain region, the fort was a "large trading post kept by Bent and St. Vrain. Its size rather exceeds that of Fort Platte. At this time, fifteen or twenty men are stationed here, under the command of Mr. Marcellin St. Vrain [brother of Ceran]."

The following year on July 26, 1838, the fort was issued a one-year Indian trading license. The name of the adobe fort changed to Ft. George in 1842 to honor George Bent. That same year Fremont made his first expedition West. The company stayed at the fort where Fremont wrote a description of the surrounding country, but did not describe the post.

Fremont, on his second expedition West, spent the Fourth of July 1843 at the renamed Ft. St. Vrain. Theodore Talbot, a journalist with the group listed the following men at the fort: Marcellin St. Vrain (brother of Ceran), James Barry and the chief trader, Mr. Ward. He described the complex as, "built on an elevated level near the river. It is built of adobes, or unburnt bricks and is quadrangular, with bastions at the alternate angles so arranged as to sweep the four faces of the walls. A tower guards the main entrance further protected by heavy gates. There is a small wicket in one of the bastions occasionally used when trading. The interior or court is surrounded by houses one story high; on one side is the Korall or pen for the cattle and horses. The wall is built sufficiently above the houses to make a good breast-work to their roofs. An Arapahoe war party on their way to the 'Youtas' arrived at the Fort this evening, so for safety we placed our animals in the korall." Water would not be a problem; the large cistern would supply their needs.

Competition became fierce in the trading business. Fort Laramie was built in 1834, Fort Vasquez in 1835, Fort Lupton in 1837, and Fort Jackson in 1838. They were constantly at war with Fort St. Vrain for the Indian trade trying to sabotage their traplines and trade routes.

A letter from Solomon Sublette written from the fort in 1844 indicated that trade was very high during the winter of '43. "I shall leave here in the morning for the South Fork with M. St. Vrain, they have evacuated their Fort on the Platte in the summer and only intend to keep it up in the winter." By the summer of 1845, when Colonel Stephen W. Kearney led his Dragoons to the mountains, the fort was "unoccupied." Francis Parkman in 1846 found the large fort abandoned and fast falling into ruin. The walls were cracked, the heavy gates were torn from their hinges, and the interior overgrown with weeds. That same year a Rev. W. H. Goode reported that a white man with two squaws and a lot of papooses were living in old Ft. St. Vrain.

The obituary of Charles St. Vrain, son of Ceran, gives evidence that Ceran had once lived at the fort with his son.

Denver Feb. 22 FOUNDER OF FORT ST. VRAIN IS DEAD (obituary of son)

"Charles St. Vrain, son of that Ceran St. Vrain who with Kit Carson, Jim Bridger and the Bent Brothers scouted fought Indians, built forts, traded and blazed trails, died at Hastings near Trinidad, Colorado. Tuesday night of the infirmities of age.

He was born at old Fort St. Vrain on Oct. 17, 1844.

He probably heard his father discuss with the Bent brothers, John and Charles and William, the building of the adobe and stone forts, which have since become public monuments. He must have sat goggle-eyed while Carson and Bridger, sitting around the stove in his father's "adobe" home, told of perils on mountain and plain, of fabulous riches awaiting prospectors among the high hills which hadn't been scratched by man.

His was a grand opportunity to live as history was made and to see the results of his father's courage and effort."

— See Appendix II, page 243 for an inventory of supplies purchased by Fort St. Vrain in 1838.

Chester L. Smead, February 27, 1822—January 21, 1915. Courtesy of the Lyons Redstone Museum, Lyons, Colorado.

The Earliest Settlers
In the St. Vrain

The first permanent settlers arrived in the St. Vrain Valley in the 1860s. Many of these pioneers tried mining in the mountains to the west. Copper, silver and gold were found in several places in the upper St. Vrain Canyons, along the Little Thompson, in the Blue Mountain region, Allenspark, Raymond, and south. These men were farmers and ranchers at heart. They soon returned to the plains and with their families established crops and grazing lands. The land lying at the gateway to the Rockies, Lyons, was a Civil War Homestead area. All veterans who applied were give 160 acres of their choice.

During these early years of settlement, Millar Fillmore was President of the United States, California had become a State, Hawthorne wrote *The Scarlet Letter* and later *The House of Seven Gables*, while Herman Melville penned the mighty fight with his nemesis *Moby Dick*. By 1860, the first recorded baseball game was played in San Francisco. Baseball was well on its way to becoming the American pastime with the Cincinnati Reds, the first profession baseball club introducing team uniforms. By the Act of February 28, 1861 Colorado became a new Territory. In the fall seventeen counties were named including Boulder County. *(See 1861 Colorado County Map p.31.)*

Chester L. Smead
February 27, 1822—January 21, 1915

Chester Lyman Smead was born in Atchinson County, Vermont, on February 27, 1822. He moved to Illinois in 1836 and in 1848 married Mary Portwood. The family began their move to Colorado in the fall of 1859, stopping in Missouri until the spring when travel would be easier. They journey ended north of Boulder, where they stayed for a year. This was when Boulder city was made up of a series of tents and one small fort. Later, in 1860, the Smeads settled in Altona just south of the gateway in the St. Vrain Valley. Chester and Mary built their log cabin in 1861 and farmed along the river a mile east of the present Foothills Highway, US 36. A search of Bureau of Land Management records, General Land Office records and the Boulder County Tax Books for the 1800s, indicate that Smead had never filed on his homestead.

Chester Smead, the self-proclaimed first white man of the upper St. Vrain Valley described the country when he and his family arrived. "There was nothing to be seen but tall Buffalo grass, cacti, prairie dogs, wild animals," and the ever present and numerous rattlesnake. He told stories about the 700 Arapahoe Indians that camped on his claim, "but aside from stealing the horses I raised they did little damage and were good neighbors." For reasons unknown, in 1910, Chester's opinion of his fellow humans changed with this announcement placed in the *Old Lyons Recorder*,

> "All hunters and trespassers are warned to keep off my premises under penalty of the law. No trespassers allowed under any circumstances." Nothing further was said.

Chester enlisted his sons, Chester, Marion, Warren and Rufus, along with C. C. Weese, John Weese, and Gouldsbury B. Stanley to dig the Smead Ditch to irrigate his corn, wheat, and garden crops. As testimony to his farming ability, a 1906 *Old Lyons Recorder* states,

"There is a fine display of Wolf River apples at the Lyons Mercantile Store this week, that were grown on the C. L. Smead place. The apples will weigh an average of one pound each."

On February 2, 1880, Marion W. Smead purchased lots 11, 12, 13, & 14 in Section 3 T3N R70W. On June 1, 1896, he added 160 acres from Section 29 T3N R70W, lots 9, 10, 11, & 12.

Emma Bird, as daughters were expected at the turn of the century, returned to the farm to care for her father until the time of his death on January 21, 1915. He was 93. Emma married Charles M. Goddard in 1881; Charles W. Bird in 1890. Mr. and Mrs. Chester L. Smead were buried in the Hygiene Cemetery. The Warren Smead family, also lie at rest in the Lyons Cemetery.

Masheck Sigler Family

Sixty wagons headed out from Memphis, Missouri in 1863 for the great journey into the west. Some turned back, others stopped, and a few continued the six-month trip to Denver, Colorado. The Sigler family became discouraged with the disasters they faced, the loss of their cattle, the constant floods followed by killing droughts, and the ever-present Indians. They left the wagon train to try life east of the Rocky Mountains. In the spring of 1864, Masheck brought his family into the South Saint Vrain Valley. On August 26, 1865, he claimed 160 acres by Land Patent in Sections 21 and 22 of Township 3N, Range 70W and began to farm. The property was just south of present day Lyons and encompassed much of what later was among the large holdings of the Montgomery family. Sigler gave one piece of his land to his son Dalison. This section later became the Al Lane place. Another son, James filed on what became the old Chisholm place.

At sixteen, his daughter Lillian wanted to marry the son of neighboring farmer, Wellington Stiles. The boy was already 20, however, the family approved of the union. To avoid trouble with Colorado law governing the legal age of marriage, the families traveled to Cheyenne for the ceremony. Lillian's firstborn son died at birth. Her second child, Arthur was born in 1883. After the death of her husband, she met and married William N. Hubbell, the owner/operator of the Estes Park Stage Coach.

The Smead's youngest son, Walter was killed in a runaway accident in 1881 while helping the family move from the farm, which they had sold to Robert Montgomery.

William Baker
February 1827–April 6, 1907

According to Leonard Weese in an interview with Lyons resident, Mrs. Kingery in 1936, William Baker came to Colorado in 1859. He traveled from Tennessee in a covered wagon pulled by a team of oxen. *See Christopher Columbus Weese below.* On March 3, 1866, he filed on Section 22 T3N R70W for 80 acres, 1 section south and 3 sections east of the present town of Lyons. William married Mrs. P. J. Franklin on June 20, 1868. They had two adopted daughters, one who married E. S. True a Hygiene pioneer and the other married J. R. Cunningham.

Mr. Baker's house design caused much conversation among the other settlers. Pioneer kitchens were built inside the house, supplying cooking needs and added warmth during the harsh winter months. Why would Bill separate the kitchen from the house and then join the two structures with a covered passageway. Neighbors were sure that it must have been the influence of his southern upbringing.

Because of its location, the stone schoolhouse located on the Montgomery property was originally named the Baker School. The United Brethern and Methodist churches alternated Sundays in the little school.

Christopher Columbus Weese
1845–1916

Christopher Columbus Weese was born in Green County, Illinois. At the age of four years his mother died. He was sent to live with his Uncle William Baker, an Illinois farmer. In 1859 Uncle

William outfitted a covered wagon drawn by oxen and moved west with his wife and young Weese. The two men established a farm near McCall Lake.

In 1864, Christopher became restless and joined the U. S. Calvary to help put down an Indian uprising. Unfortunately, this conflict turned out to be the Sand Creek Massacre. For the rest of his life he was haunted by the memories of those days and his part in the massacre. He had witnessed the murder of an Indian family by one of his superior officers. He had seen women and children slaughtered. He rarely spoke of his experience in the U. S. Calvary.

Several years later Columbus homesteaded 160 acres west of McCall Lake. The property bordered south of the Chapman Switch, north to Dowe Flats, and included the dry land known as Rabbit Hill. In 1880 he married Melinda Jane Baker. She was reputed to be the first white woman in the St. Vrain Valley. This designation is still in dispute, as other pioneer women were thought to be the first in the territory. Nevertheless, life was not easy. One day while Melinda was alone a pack of starving wolves stormed the log cabin looking for food. As the animals began tearing at the buffalo hides that covered the cabin windows, Melinda heated pokers in the fireplace jabbing them through the openings at the attacking wild animals. The wolves left and Melinda continued her life as a pioneer farmer's wife.

The Montgomery Family

The Montgomery family moved from Virginia to Pella, Iowa and worked on a farm from 1860 to 1869. The five Montgomery brothers, William A., Alexander, Frank, Robert Bruce, and Cyrus were the sons of William M. and Mary Elizabeth Dawson Montgomery of Virginia.

When only fourteen years old, Frank came to Colorado. In May of 1860, he signed on as a drover for a group of men heading west. The youngster was without a horse and made the journey on foot. He found work out of Central City as a freighter making runs between there and Cheyenne. With the money he earned, he began to accumulate mining interests in the territory. Later, William A. Montgomery also worked in Central City and

The Montgomery Brothers 1897. Standing from left to right: Cyrus and Robert; Seated from left to right: Alexander, William, and Frank. Courtesy of the Lyons Redstone Museum, Lyons, Colorado.

Black Hawk before homesteading on the St. Vrain. Alexander, the oldest brother, joined a wagon train headed for Leadville, Colorado. Alex also became a freighter driving oxen-teams on a route between Leadville, Denver, Central City, and Jamestown. After his marriage to Emma Peel Ferguson, the couple lived on her family homestead until 1906, when they moved to Lyons. After Emma died in 1918, Alex moved to Colorado Springs to live with one of their daughters.

In 1867, Robert Bruce, nineteen years old, came to Colorado by mule team taking 41 days to reach the Little Thompson where he bought a farm and raised livestock. In 1886 he sold his holdings to buy 80 acres east of Lyons. He raised grain and livestock, as well as maintaining a large apple orchard of over 400 trees. The entire section was known for its excellent production of several varieties of apples and cherries. Produce was shipped into the heartland of the country, as well as further East. Apple Valley, located west of Lyons was named for the many apple orchards that once grew in this area. In a personal interview,

Don Montgomery told me that in 1880 the original Montgomery house was built with only two rooms. As the family grew, rooms and out buildings were added.

In 1869, Cyrus rode the Union Pacific train to Cheyenne continuing overland to Colorado. For many years, he mined at Jamestown. About 1900 he moved to Boulder and lived there until his death in 1935.

Boulder County Land Records show Alexander W. Montgomery recording Section 26, T3N R70W, 40 acres, May 13, 1873 and William A. Montgomery Section 23, T3N R70W, 160 acres, July 14, 1876.

The boys' parents, William and Mary Montgomery moved to Colorado by train in 1874. They lived on a farm in Pella, a small community once located south of Hygiene.

John Reese
January 12, 1831–October 21, 1887

John Reese was born in York County, Pennsylvania January 12, 1831. As a youth he worked on a farm, later serving as an apprentice carpenter. As he traveled West, he made short stops in Ohio and Illinois. Reaching Iowa he purchased a farm and planed to stay. By 1859 the westward-bug bit him again Selling the farm he traveled to Colorado with a wagon train, stopping in Black Hawk to mine gold. In 1862, he moved into the Lyons area.

John married Catherine (Kate) Gifford November 11, 1869 in Boulder, Colorado. She was the first teacher at the Montgomery School (formerly named the Baker School). They had two children, Bertha born in 1870 and Frank born in 1872. John hauled hay to Black Hawk for $40 a ton. In 1871, he became the county assessor. On December 9, 1879 he purchased 160 acres, 80 each in Section 19 & 20 of Twnshp 3 N, Range 70. This is the campus of the present Lyons Middle and Senior High School. In 1885 he was president of the Evans Townsite and Quarry Company. July 16, 1885, John claimed the property at Evans and 3rd street, the present home of LaVern M. Johnson. On July 6, 1886 he purchased an additional 40 acres in Section 19 T3N R70W. An additional 51 acres was added on October 29, 1888 in Sec.30, Lot 1 NWNW 1/4; Lot 2 SWNW 1/4, Doc #5640.

In 1887 John served on the Lyons school board. That year he died after being kicked by one of his farm mules. John's accumulating fortune and community involvement ended abruptly. Kate with the help of her children, Frank, 12 and Bertha, 14, continued the operation of the family farm.

John and Kate's son, Frank Reese remained on the farm, adding 320 acre of the Sites' place. The old Boarding House became his home. Later, he purchased 160 acres to the north of his property, on which stood a stone house built by Mr. Charles M. Cheney. Frank never married. He died in November, 1928.

Reese Street, located North of Main, once part of Nortonville was named for the Lyons pioneer. John Reese is the great–grandfather of LaVern Johnson, president of the Lyons Historical Society. The road surrounding the school campus is McConnell Drive, named after her grandfather, James Albert McConnell.

John Reese January 12, 1831—October 21, 1887. Courtesy of the Lyons Redstone Museum, Lyons, Colorado.

Levi Brackett
1832—1889

Levi Bracket was born in Tennessee in 1821. He spent his early years in Colorado looking for gold. In 1860 he purchased land in Colorado City. Census records show him living in various mining towns.

He moved to Montana, where he spent the next eight years working. He returned to Colorado in 1868. Along with a cousin, Columbus Weese. Levi located in the McCall Lake area.

In 1885 he married Permelia Weese a widow with four children. To this marriage three more children were born. Around 1890 the Bracketts homesteaded on the Little Thompson.When he sold the ranch, the family moved to the Brackett home at McCall Lake. Levi died of heart trouble in 1898.

Levi Brackett. From the collection of Frances Brodie Brackett.

Thomas G. Putnam
(Dates unknown)

In 1885 Edward S. Lyon sold his entire holdings for the townsite, with the exception of his home, to Thomas G. Putnam, a surveyor. Putnam resurveyed the land after discovering that the first map had never been recorded.

—*See* Appendix III, First Property Owners, Lyons.

Charles Bradford
June 7, 1844–January 13, 1929

Charles Bradford was born at Astor, Long Island, New York on June 7, 1844. His father, Eli Bradford served as an American soldier in the Mexican-American War. Of the two children born to his parents, Charles was the only survivor. He was raised and educated in Chicago, Illinois until 1860. He died January 13, 1929 in Lyons, Colorado, from influenza.

During the Civil War Charlie enlisted in Company 1, Third Illinois Cavalry and remained with his troops for four years and eight months. He reached the rank of Quartermaster Sergeant while serving at the front. Later, his unit was sent to Ft. Snelling, Minnesota to help put down an Indian uprising.

Charles headed west in 1866 landing in Central City as a barber. General Grant, then President of the United States visited Clear Creek County stopping to get a shave and a haircut. While he shaved the president they talked about the war, recalling the time that Grant had borrowed Bradford's horse and how he whad been seriously wounded in battle. Charles also had a reminder of the Civil War, a load of sixteen-buck shot that he carried to his grave. In Central City on September 25, 1868 he married Sarah White. She was born in Petersburg, Illinois November 13, 1834.

The next record of the Bradfords can be found in the Land Patent Records. Charles purchased land just west of the present Lyons Middle High School complex in Section 19, T3N R70W, Doc #1278, 160 acres, June 30, 1881; Lot 1, E*NW /14; Lot 2 SWNW 1/4; Lot 3 NWSW 1/4. He began a new career in farming. Later, he sold the property to a Longmont real estate developer, who then divided and sold it in smaller tracts. On the old Bradford Homestead remains a tiny two-story sandstone house with cellar. The Town of Lyons purchased the historically designated building and the 25 surrounding acres. There are plans for restoration.

By 1892 the Bradford Saloon in Lyons, Colorado was in full swing. Here was the place of the famous Kearney/Watt shooting. The 1896 City Directory lists only two of the many saloons in town, the Bradford and the Arcade. The latter was owned by Frank Burk. Several newspapers put the number of saloons during this period as high as 10.

Charlie continued his ventures into different money making schemes. An Old *Lyons Recorder* article dated June 7, 1900 stated that Charles Bradford had purchased 200 Belgian hares from J. M. Merrell in order to go into the rabbit business. However, he didn't have a hare of chance and the venture soon turned into dinner, many dinners. He also raised trout for awhile.

Bradford was known to be kind and generous with the "boys" in town. Records show that he paid for the funeral of Edwin Blanchard Porter who died February 10, 1891. Ed had worked for him for many years. In fact, the Porter family in California shared a letter written by Charles after the death of Edwin telling them what a wonderful man he was. Bradford is also listed as having paid for the burial expenses for Daniel Slaughter, who died August 27, 1923.

Charles was totally involved in the Lyons community. He helped with the building of the original brick schoolhouse. He personally handled the landscaping on the property, putting in the lawn and planting shade trees. He served on the Lyons School Board for 36 years. He was also active in building the Methodist Church in Lyons and was a loyal contributor to its funds and activities.

By 1911, Bradford was known as "Charley, the local banker" cashing up to $35,000 worth of paychecks in his saloon.

His obituary reads:

Birth of a Quarry Town

"The church was packed with all classes of citizens unitied in honoring in death he whose familiar and cheerful face and voice they had learned to love through his many years of outstanding service and citizenship to his nation and community."

William Sites
1834–March 28, 1896

William Sites filed on his homestead January 23, 1885, Bureau of Land Records Document #1718. Section 17, Township 3North, Range 70West, S*SW, SENW, NESW is located east of Lyons. The old milkhouse is now a designated historic site.

A *Boulder Camera* article on January 1, 1893 p1, Boulder, Colorado states,

"Stone Exhibit at the World's Fair

Capt. Sipple and Hon. Wm. Sites have charge of arranging for exhibiting the stone of Boulder County at the fair. There is a move now on foot to get the quarry in this city to donate stone for a handsome column to be placed in the Colorado department at the fair. Also to have enough flagging donated to lay a walk at the grounds 75 feet long and 25 feet wide. The state will pay all expenses after loaded on the cars, and the stone will belong to the parties donating it and can be sold after the fair. Mr. Sites is very anxious that this section should make a good exhibit at the fair, and it is the best opportunity that our stone dealers will ever have to let the world know of the fine quality of stone produced.

We are confident that every quarry owner will see the importance of this matter and willingly do his part toward advertising our chief product. Mr. Sites has a draft of the column and full particulars and will gladly furnish all information. We will have more to say on this subject next week."

The following has been extracted from the Boulder County Estate Files found at the Colorado State Archives; 1313 Sherman Street, Denver, CO 80203:

> File 1533—"**SITES, William** died Lyons 28 March 1896. Administrator of the estate was his daughter, Bessie. The court on 11 June 1910 decided that the widow, Esther J. of Longmont would get 1/2 estate. The children of the marriage would receive each 1/6 of the estate: George, Swansea AR; daughter Jesse, Bakersfield CA; Bessie, Longmont. They divided $1000 estate. Sureties: Esther J., Jesse B. Sites. (Jesse, Mrs. Smith by 1910.) 200 Acre in Section 17, 24 T3N R70W, value $2000. 1/4 share ditch stock, $1000 value."

William Sosey
(Dates Unknown)

William Sosey and his wife Aminata Shinkle Sosey homesteaded 160 acres northwest of Lyons in 1877. On December 26, 1889 he signed Land Patents for Sections 12 & 13 of Township 3N, Range 71W. The property was known as Steamboat Ranch and later the James Lowe Ranch.

Mr. Sosey was a farmer and a carpenter. He worked on the 1881 school building and the Old Stone Church. Fared, his son worked the farm, first having to clear it of boulders and brush. The other son, John worked with Leonard Lyon, son of town founder Edward S. Lyon, on the bottomland cultivating corn and pumpkins.

By 1902 William and Arminta moved into Lyons. In 1904, as so many other pioneers from the area, the Soseys moved to Pasadena, California. Their adopted daughters, Hazel and Olive went with them. John continuedhis education at the University of Michigan and remained there to work for the Kellogg Company. Fred worked for the Pasadena Electric Short Line Railroad. Alice married Leonard Lyon.

The Billings Family

Jabez Pendleton and Elizabeth Lewis Billings. Courtesy of the Lyons Redstone Museum, Lyons, Colorado.

Four Billings brothers, George, Ferdinand, Jade and Norton came by covered wagon to ranch on land along the North St. Vrain River west of what is now Lyons. They lived off the land as ranchers, woodsmen, hunters, sawmill operators, and road builders.

George and his wife Henrietta arrived in Colorado shortly before 1880. They homesteaded in the Button Rock area. George was the first person that Edward S. Lyon encountered on his fateful ride. By 1890 the ranch became known as the Billings Resort and continued in that capacity until 1919 when it was sold to Fred Smith. The Smiths continued to run the resort until it was sold to a group of professors from the University of Colorado at which time it became the Professors Ranch. There were three children, George "Manny", Frances, and Susan.

Ferdinand probably came to the area with his brother George. He married Nellie Wilkins, a widow with four children. They lived on Evans Street when the Town of Lyons was first platted. After the death of her husband, Nellie moved in with Theresa Billings, who lived on Fifth Street.

Jadez (Jabe) P. Billings, his wife Elizabeth, and his brother Norton came to Colorado in 1880 from South Dakota. The couple homesteaded in 1889 west of Lyons up Highway 36. President Benjamin Harrison signed the original deed. On this property Jabez created a hunting and fishing resort, the famous Camp Billings. The camp consisted of cabins and tents. It later became the equally famous, Welch Resort. The couple had two children. George died at Camp Billings when only six years old. Alice grew up, married Ray Woodmanzie, and moved to Detroit, Michigan.

Norton was married in Davenport, Iowa to Elizabeth Browers. They had two children. Etta was born in 1870 at Marshalltown, Iowa. Norman Arthur born in 1874 also born Marshalltown. Elizabeth died in childbirth. The family moved to Deuel County, South Dakota near the Minnesota State line. Norton married Theresa Gilroy in 1878 and they had seven children, Maude Frances Grace Bedell, William, Herbert Thomas, Adeline Adell, Gladys Irene, Hazel Ellowee, and Nina Imogene. Norton held land south of Estes Park in the Fish Creek area. They lived in Allenspark from 1893 to 1897. He and his wife, Theresa held title to land along Old Apple Valley Road west of Lyons.

For an in depth look at the Billings family and genealogy see *They Came by Covered Wagon*, by Frank Weaver. The booklet may be purchased from the Lyons Redstone Museum, P O Box 49, Lyons, Colorado 80540.

—*See Appendix 1 p. 189 for further Genealogical Information on the above families.*

The Disappearance of Aquilla Cook

The Easterner, Aquilla Cook (1833–1868) liked to hunt in the Colorado Rockies. He would arrive in Denver by train, spend several days in the city, then make the trip through Lyons up into the mountains to hunt. In 1868 he checked into the Pacific House, as he had done in years past. Several months later, a Denver newspaper reported that he had not returned to the hotel and his whereabouts were unknown. By May 1869, the *Rocky Mountain News* reported that Aquilla Cook was assumed missing somewhere in the St. Vrain Canyon.

Around 1906, Susan "Sissy" Billings, the daughter of George and Henrietta, was out riding on the family ranch up toward the summit of one of the nearby mountains. The teen-age girl was shocked to find a skull and a few other human bones scattered around a rock. The remains were assumed to be those of Aquilla Cook. A burial is recorded in the Hygiene Cemetery.

No one remembers who or just when, but a relative of Aquilla came to Lyons to erect a monument to the deceased. George "Manny" Billings, Sissy's brother was hired to place the sandstone slab on the exact spot where Cook's remains were found. The marker reads:

Aquilla Cook
Died here
April 20, 1868

The favorite haunt of Mr. Cook was on the North St. Vrain. The most accepted version of his trips into the area is the one told by Clair Billings,

"As near as I can tell Aquilla Cook was just a hunter. He would walk or maybe ride a horse up from Lyons and be gone two or three days at a time."

Little was known about the man from the east before, during, or after his many solitary hunting trips into Lyons.

The mountain where the man lost his life was subsequently named Cook Mountain. It is located near Buttonrock Dam, west of Lyons above the Billings' holdings. The Colorado Topographic Map 0379 by the USGS specifies the location as being in Boulder County 08013 with the summit at 401255N, 1052419W.

WAIT! What about this front page news article in the April 18, 1871 *Rocky Mountain News* Daily Edition. It claims that Mr. Cook's remains were discovered near the creek in 1871.

"The *News* explains a mystery in this [?]; 'Three years ago, Mr. Aquilia Cook, who lived on St. Vrain creek, just within the canon, was supposed to be lost while hunting. The whole surrounding country turned out on [?] to find him, and hunted in vain for several days. His fate was shrouded in mystery until last week when the remains of a man were found on the north branch of the creek about four miles from his home near what is known as the [?] shanty. A gun, powder horn, knife and portions of clothing, which were with the remains were readily identified as those of Mr. Cook. It was said at the time, by some parties that he was not dead but had for unknown reasons left the country."

Two different remains of hunters found up the North St. Vrain. One body found near the creek in 1871. One set of remains found up on a mountaintop in 1906. Was the first really Aquilla? Who was the other man? Had the first man discovered Cook's dead body, taken his gear, and then lost his own life?

The mystery of the second man may never be solved. The mountain is named. The tombstone is reverently set to honor the dead. Both men died while hunting alone.

But who was that second man?

Lyons Ditch Company No. 1

January 2, 1877 construction began on Lyons Ditch No. 1. The ditch was constructed, operated, and maintained to divert water for agricultural purposes. Irrigation was intended for 20 acres of land encompassing Park and the Alley of Evans Street.

Water was diverted out of the North St. Vrain Creek at Meadow Park, continued through the park and east along 20 acres now known as Park and the Alley of Evans Street. The Ditch continued across Highway 66 to the Gordon property, back to the river, with a lateral going along Third Avenue, down the Alley of Park Street to Second and back to the river. It is 2.5 feet wide on the top and about 1.5 feet on the bottom at a depth of one foot. The grade is ten feet per mile with a carrying capacity of 4.25 cubic feet per second. The agreement was set that not more than 100 acre feet of water was to be used per year.

In March 1909, the thirty-one lot owners made a joint offer to purchase the Water Right Decree and Lyons Ditch No. 1 from the Town of Lyons for $25.00. The understanding was that the water would belong to the eighty lots (divided among thirty-one owners). Water was to be sold along with the subject land or the water rights would revert back to the Town. The mayor signed the deed April 5, 1909 and it was recorded April 10, 1909 in book 340, page 88, reception No. 72447 at the Boulder County Court House.

In 1951, Adam and Elizabeth Ford along with Tim Gorter organized incorporation of the ditch. The Secretary of State issued the papers on January 18, 1952. The First Directors Meeting was held April 20, 1952.

Recently, parts of the irrigation trench have been cemented over by the Town of Lyons. The ditch does remain in operation, however, not extending as far as it once had.

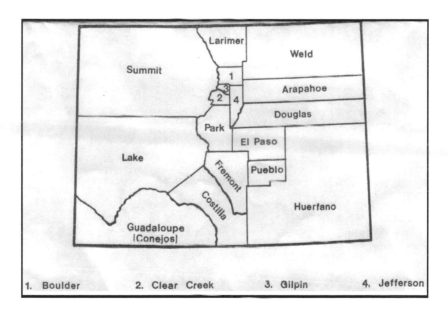

In the fall of 1861, the Territorial Legislature passed a law dividing Colorado into seventeen counties. From the vertical files at the Carnegie Branch Library for Local History, Boulder, Colorado.

ORIGINS

Dora Griffith and Edward S. Lyon in California. Courtesy of the Lyons Redstone Museum, Lyons, Colorado.

The Origins of Lyons, Colorado

Rah for Lyons! We're not rich, nor proud but our citizens are as good as any town's citizens and some are a little bit better.
_____ *Unknown, 1891.*

The origins of the little town known as the Double Gateway to the Rockies could not be told without an introduction to the men who were responsible for its development.

Edward S. Lyon
September 2, 1843–January 4, 1931

Edward S. Lyon was born in Connecticut the youngest child of Thomson Lon Lyons and Elizabeth "Eliza" Savina Weeks Lyons. His mother was a cousin of Secretary of War, John Wingate Weeks. His siblings included Nathan, Susan, Esther, and Ellen Lyon.

On September 12, 1861, at the beginning of the Civil War, Edward enlisted as a private in Company K, 7th Regiment, Connecticut Volunteers. He was eighteen years old. During his years of service, he quickly reached the rank of Corporal. At Goldsboro, North Carolina on July 20, 1865, he received a medical discharge for a gunshot wound to the right forearm, a wound that would plague him the rest of his life. His military pension was $4.00 per month in 1871, which increased to $25 a month by 1913.

Edward S. Lyon was married four times. Wife #1 was Caroline Evangeline Barrett. They had four children: Lillie Eliza, Leonard Cutler, Eva, and Frank all born in Connecticut. Caroline died in 1873.

Wife #2 was Adeline Sherman. Their one son, Ernest died shortly after birth in Connecticut. Edward and Adeline moved to Colorado in 1881. In 1882, E. S. Lyon built their home at 404 4th Avenue at the corner of Evans. It became known as the Lyons House. Adeline died there in 1889, a distressing time for Mr. Lyon.

The following is from the Boulder County Estate Files in the Colorado State Archives, 1313 Sherman Street, Denver.

File 659—LYON, Adeline A. died Lyons March 12, 1889. The will was dated 9 April 1881 in Connecticut. The executor was her husband: Edward S. Lyon. All would go to her husband. and then to children, if he did not survive her. The property list included the house, lots, and store building in Lyons, 35 head cattle, horses and the household furniture. The witness to the will was Samuel H. Seward, Putnam County, CT, age 54, lawyer, Nellie G. Watson, residence unknown, age 34 and Eliza A. Snow, Providence RI. There is ongoing litigation involving the Evans Townsite and Quarry Co. The company wants to change streets and blocks for easier access to the Lyon's store.

Wife #3 was Carrie Boyd, whom he married on September 2, 1890 at Denver, Colorado. Their only child died shortly after his birth. A news article tells the sad tale of the little boy about, two years of age, being left alone in the kitchen. While playing, he set fire to his clothing and was burned to death. Mrs. Lyon was in the barn milking the cow at the time of the tragedy. Soon after the death, Edward divorced her.

Wife #4 was Dora Griffith, whom he married in March of 1900 at California. Dora had worked for Edward in the Lyons Post Office. She was the sister of Leonard H. Dieterich. She remained with E. S. until his death in 1931.

E. S. Lyon's accomplishments in this area were many. He was involved in establishing and constructing the town's first school. The stone building grew from a one-room schoolhouse in 1881 to the two-story expanded structure that is now the home of the Lyons Redstone Museum. Edward was appointed as the first Postmaster for Lyons.

His ambitions and ideas were expansive, however, his business problems were greater than his successes. E. S. began construction of the Lyons Hotel, but failed in this endeavor. Mr. Gilbert purchased the building, finished it, and was able to turn it into a thriving business. Mr. Lyon's large stone yard in Denver was sold to Mr. Kimball. After three lawsuits and Governor Waite's election on the Free Silver platform, which caused a bank failure in Denver, Edward at the age of 53 was broke. He gave up his dreams, left Colorado, and moved to California.

For an in depth history of the Lyon family see, *That Beautiful Valley* written by Frank Weaver, a Lyons historian, published in 1978 by *The New Lyons Recorder* in Lyons, Colorado.

THE LYONS HOUSE
404 Fourth Street
Fourth and Evans Streets

In 1882 E. S. Lyon built the family home and lived there until the late 1890s when he moved to California. The house became a 14-room boarding house for railroad and quarry workers. An 1899 newspaper credited Mrs. D. D. McAlpine, the wife of the Burlington agent as keeping a good hotel. She would greet the morning train, serve an excellent dinner, and happily answer any and all questions. Mrs. Halliday, wife of "Doc" Halliday a local engineer, managed the hotel in 1900. W. F. Cantwell leased the building in the early 1890s.

In 1906 U.S. Gilger bought the house for the family home and made many improvements, yet keeping the integrity of the outside of the structure. By 1920 it became the home of the Michael Scanlon family after the Golden Rule Store and their living quarters were destroyed by fire.

In the 1940s, Mr. And Mrs. L. A. Linch owned and lived in the home. In the 1950s, Daisy Moffitt opened her nursing home in the building. She later moved to 317 Evans Street, naming the place The Moffitt Guest Home.

By 1960 the Lyons House became an apartment house run by Mrs. Scott Pease. Dick and Ann McDowell purchased the mansion in 1963 and began extensive restoration of the old landmark. They sold the home to John Knudson in the summer of 1974. Unfortunately, a fire consumed the beautiful old mansion on January 12, 1975.

Lyon House was once located at 404 Fourth Street, Lyons. Courtesy of the Lyons Redstone Museum, Lyons, Colorado.

GRIFFITH J. EVANS
May 02 1832–September 1894

Griffith J. Evans was born May 2, 1832 (1830) in Wales. He died on July 5, 1900 and was buried in the Jamestown cemetery.

Griffith Evans came to American about 1854 with his parents, one brother, and several sisters. They settled in Wisconsin. He married Jane Owens in 1855 at Dodge County Wisconsin. She had immigrated to the U. S. in 1845 with her parents and siblings also settling in Wisconsin. She was born September 20, 1837 in Wales. Jane died in 1921 at Boulder, Colorado. She is buried next to her husband in the mountain town of Jamestown. Her brother, Will started the Denver Dry Goods Company in Denver, Colorado.

By 1858 Griff had moved to Golden, Colorado. In 1867, he and Jane moved up to Estes Park, purchasing property formerly owned by Joel Estes, who held title to the land from 1859 to 1867. Evans built a sod covered log house for he and his family. He was employed by the English Company for several years purchasing shares in the company. When he sold his shares for $1,000.00, Evans used the money to start a cattle and Dude Ranch in Estes Park. The land eventually became part of the Earl of Dunraven Empire.

July 24, 1874, Griff had some problems with one of his neighbors, the famed "Rocky Mountain Jim", James Nugent. Several versions of the encounter can be found in books and oral histories. His daughter, Nell explained that Jim had threatened "to take away" little Jennie, another daughter who would have been 15 at the time, and a fight ensued. Then there is the story of old Jim riding his white mule by the Evan's cabin. Griff fired his shotgun hit an old stagecoach, the bullets ricochet and struck Nugent at the base of the brain. Enos A. Mills writes that, "Evans was drunk when he shot Jim."

A trial held at Fort Collins exonerated Evans as Jim was intoxicated at the time and the shooting death of Nugent was considered self-defense. Jim had written "a very vile paper" regarding his hatred for Evans and it had been printed in the *Fort Collins Standard*.

James Nugent died in September 1874. Some claim that it was English gold that killed him. "Did Dunraven entice Griff to do the job the Englishman would not do himself?" Neither man was known for being able to let go of a grudge. All figured that one or the other man was bound to die.

There was a news article reporting that while working his Leadville mine, Griff was badly injured by a landslide of rock and earth falling on him. Trouble seemed to follow the man.

E. S. Lyon reported that at one time Griff Evans was "keeping a roadhouse up the river", the Miller Road House built by William "Bill" Sites. It was located at the west edge of town on the North St. Vrain Highway. The Evans homestead, west of Lyons, was built in 1870 and functioned as an inn and stage stop between Denver and Estes Park. In 1884 Evans added a butcher shop and a blacksmith shop built of local Lyons sandstone. The 20 acre ranch remained a stage stop until 1934 when the highway department purchased the rights to the road. The access road to the property is the original road used by early pioneers on their way up the St. Vrain Canyon.

Due to faulty electrical wiring, the homestead burned to the ground in February 1988. The fire ignited a hardwood counter in the kitchen and the fire spread quickly throughout the rest of the home. The property is now owned by Craig Ferguson, Planet Blue Grass. His son is named after Griff.

Properties owned by Evans in Boulder County include: Jamestown Lot 30 B7 purchased 11/27/1883; the Emma Abbott Lode registered 3/22/1884; the Bachelor Button Lode 08/08/189; the Buck Eye Lode Etal. 4/28/1898. Griffith J. Evans was the original tract owner of 160-acres with Date of Proof 19 May 1879 in Section 18, T3N R70W, now Lyons, Colorado. Another Land Patent was for Section 18, T3N R70W dated 7/20/1881 Doc. #16. 167 acres, Lot 1 NWNW 1/4; Lot 2 SWNW 1/4. The old stone house on the property was built sometime prior to 1878 and was used as a roadhouse.

When Lyon formed a townsite company from the south half of his ranch, the 80-acres was named the Evans Townsite Company with E. S. Lyon, President; H. F. Sawyer, Secretary; and Griff Evans, Treasurer.

Obituary notice: DEATH OF "GRIFF" EVANS
Griffith Evans died at Jamestown Friday morning at 7 o'clock. His death was not unlooked for, as his physician, Dr. Orfilo Allen, had said the end was near. Evans, who was known all over the state as "Griff"

Evans, was about 70 years old. He had lived in the vicinity of Jamestown some twenty years, and before that lived at Estes Park. He leaves a wife and several children, the youngest about 30 years of age. He was buried in Jamestown.

The death of "Griff" Evans recalls the killing of "Rocky Mountain Jim", James Nugent, about 1873 in Estes Park. At that time it created great excitement. The jury that tried the case fully exonerated Evans, as "Rocky Mountain Jim," who was under the influence of liquor, came to Evans in such a manner that Evans killed him in self-defense. The affair occupies an important part in some of the histories of the state."

His wife, Jane remained in Jamestown living with their son, John for about 21 years. After the marriage of her son, she moved to Boulder to live with her daughter Nell until her death in 1921.

William O. Griffith
About 1832—1900

William O. and Harriet F. Griffith came to Lyons in 1880 with E. S. Lyon. In 1884 they homesteaded on property west of Lyons, which is presently owned by Robert Bohn. In 1885 William was registered with the census bureau as a stonecutter. Mr. and Mrs. Griffith were charter members of the Old Stone Congregational Church having spent many hours in the original construction and organization. William died in 1900. Harriet died February 28, 1907 with burial in Longomt. She was 71.

They had two daughters, Dora and Mrs. Clarence Griffith Lippert and one son, William

William H. Houck
(Dates Unknown)

Land Patent Document #6, Issue Date July 20, 1881, E*SE Sec. 18 T3N, R70W, 80-acres. Section 18, SE 1/4 & NE 1/4 3N R70, 160-acres, 28 January 1879 was Quit Claimed by E. S. Lyons.

The Story Of Lyons
The Very Spot That Looked
Good To Me

In the early spring of 1880, Edward S. Lyon came from Connecticut to Colorado on the advice of his doctor. Mr. Lyon was in poor health and the high altitude was thought to be a cure. He brought Buchanan, Phillips, and William O. Griffith with him. Lyon wrote that he soon discovered that he was the only man in the group with any money. He felt an obligation to support these men and decided to find a viable occupation for all of them.

One day while out riding E. S. came into the St. Vrain Valley over Red Hill and thought, "This will be the place to be." He rode down to the South Fork of the river and met George Billings. During their conversation, he learned that Hiram F. Sawyer had a ranch for sale on the North Fork. The next day Edward purchased the 160-acres, plus all the stock, horses, cows, faming tools, and wagons. He enlarged his livestock herd by purchasing 115 head from William Sites, who was farming in the area.

The group of men that had traveled west with Lyon decided to try their hand at mining. They knew they could strike it big and do it quickly up in Fairplay. However, it took only a short time for them to come back to the ranch and the counsel of Mr. Lyon. Mining was not the quick rich scheme of dime novels and newspaper stories.

While exploring his property, Edward discovered that he had 40 acres of lime rock and 40 acres of red sandstone. He traveled into Denver to see if he could interest the railroad in the sandstone; however, without an easy way to ship the stone, no one was interested. A railroad spur was needed to make the stone business profitable. Lyon decided that working this particular property would not be profitable, so he purchased a half interest in the 40 acres on the bluff owned by Deckster Smith, son-in-law of Griff Evans, figuring this would be more profitable. Lyon traded several horses and 25 head of cattle with a promise to give Smith work in the quarry. Deck and his wife, Jennie declined the offer and decided to try their luck further north with a move to Canada.

Edward found men to quarry his sandstone from early spring until late in the fall. The English Company bought a half interest in the quarry, but did not succeed in the stone business. They sold their holdings to Hugh Murphy of Omaha, Nebraska in the early 1880s. E. S. decided to return to Connecticut and sold his shares in his limestone quarry to Rev. John Parker, whom he had brought to town "to replenish the souls and spiritual health of the community."

Once again Mr. Lyon returned to Colorado, this time with his four children. His wife, Adeline remained in the East to settle their affairs making the trip to Colorado at a later date. Edward concentrated his efforts on establishing the Evans Townsite with himself as President; H. F. Sawyer, Secretary; and Griff Evans as Treasurer. The three entrepreneurs then created a subsidiary, the Lyon Rock and Lime Quarry Company, which was capitalized with $50,000 of funds received by selling shares in the stone quarries. In the spring of 1881, a number of the shareholders came to Colorado to take a personal interest in their investment.

Hiram F. Sawyer held Land Patent Document #3019, Issue Date June 30, 1880, 160-acres, W*NE, SENE, NENW, NENE of Sec. 18, T3N, R70W and Document #3414, Issue Date May 10, 1882 160-acres W*NW, NWSW of Sec. 17, T3N, R70W. To the North and NE of this property the Lyon property, Hiram F. Sawyer purchased within Section 17 160 acres on 28 Dec 1891.

June 1882, the town of tents, homes, and businesses was laid out and called Lyons. Stories differ as to the origin of the name, some claim it to be named after Edward, others remember E. S. wanting it to be a memorial to his beloved wife, Adeline. The addition of the "s" was accepted by the townspeople, the local government, and the Lyon family. By July 25th the site was platted by the Lyons Rock and Lime Quarry Company.

Birth of a Quarry Town

The post office was established at the mouth of St. Vrain Canyon. Edward S. Lyon becames the first postmaster of the new town, Lyons, Colorado.

E. S. Lyon declared the town dry in 1884, when 'neither rum nor tobacco' could be sold. This unpopular and short-lived law of barely a year was doomed to failure in an active and growing quarry town. On payday, most of the hard working men had no interest in going elsewhere to spend their money. They wanted to relax with a good beer and a little gambling in the town where they lived.

On September 26, 1889, a reporter for the *Boulder News* made a trip to Lyons describing life in the busy quarry town.

> "One thing that immediately attracts the attention of a stranger is the large number of people and the small number of houses; the village will properly house not over 100 or 300, yet there are probably 1500 or 2000 in and about the town. The writer considered himself fortunate when he secured a place to sleep with five other men in a room about 10 feet square."

The reporter further described the available housing as tents pitched all over town, along the banks of the St. Vrain, and even dotting the hillsides. Since the townsite was in litigation, houses were not being built. "No one cares to buy ground and build a house without a clear title." Lack of a convenient water source created another serious problem. Water had to be hauled or carried from the creek to homes, tents, quarries, and businesses.

After the lawsuits were settled, the citizens of the area voted for incorporation. The election was held in Scanlon & Brice's old mercantile store. The registration books indicate that 214 persons were entitled to vote. On April 2, 1891, 167 persons cast their ballot; 128 had voted for incorporation; 39 voted against. The papers were pleased to say that there had been no fights or drunkenness during the election. Of course, all the saloons were kept closed until 7 O'clock, at which time the polls were closed. April 2, 1891,the Town of Lyons, Colorado was officially incorporated as a municipality of the State of Colorado.

During the height of the sandstone boom, the population of the Lyons section ranged in the thousands, although the census records do not show this. Many of these men lived at the quarry sites up in the hills, on Steamboat Mountain, Beech Hill, and Noland and were not counted in the surveys.

Population changes within the town borders of Lyons:
1890–574; 1900–547; 1910–632; 1920–570;
1930–567; 1940–654; 1950–689; 1960–706;
1970–958; 1980–1127; 1990–1227; 2000–1585.

—*See Appendix III, p. 264 for a list of the first property owners in the new town.*
—*See Appendix IV, p. 301 for the Municipal Organization of Lyons, Colorado 1891—1899.*

Lucy David. Courtesy of the Lyons Redstone Museum, Lyons, Colorado.

1890 Map
Town of Lyons

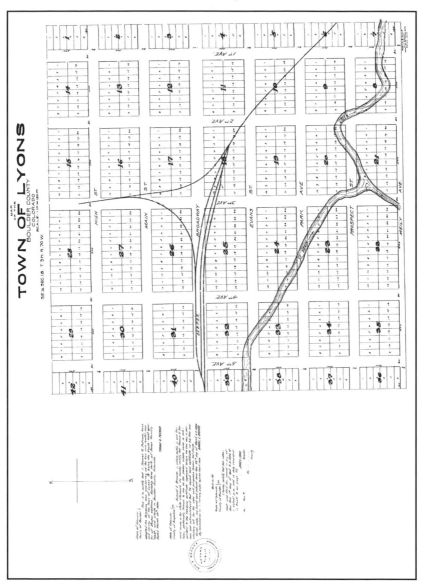

Map of the Town of Lyons, Boulder County, Colorado. Thomas G. Putnam March 29, 1890. From the Boulder County Clerk and Recorders Office, Boulder, Colorado, Book 2, Page 77.

Lyons Pioneers

Henry Franklin Ballinger
October 16, 1849–April 4, 1910

Henry Franklin Ballinger came to Lyons in 1887. He set up a boot and shoe shop at the corner of Main and 4th Street. For twenty years he made and repaired footwear for Lyons and Noland.

Axel Bergquist
September 7, 1866–August 31, 1934

Axel Bergquist was born in Sweden. He spent his early years with an uncle in Lapland before coming to the United States in 1882 at the age of 16. His interest in quarrying began in South Dakota. When he came to Lyons he met Dan Bergman. Never marrying, he remained with the family of Dan and Lena Bergman for 40 years.

The Blair Brothers

The Blair Brothers, Jack and Matt were prominent cattlemen with large real estate holdings. They held title to a ranch up the South St. Vrain, homesteaded in 1872 by John Smith. John's nephew

Nicolas Frank of Frank Brothers Meat Market in Lyons inherited the ranch. Frank later sold the property to the Blair brothers.

One of the tollgates up the South St. Vrain was located on the Blair place near what is now the Golden Andesite Rock Company. The charge for a four horse freighting outfit was $1.75 round trip. The ranch also held irrigation rights through the old Smith-Mack Ditch.

Mathew M. Blair was born October 22, 1865 in Ohio to Jane and B. Blair both from Pennsylvania. He married Sarah Anna Fletcher. She became an active member of the Old Stone Church in 1898. The heirs of Srah Blair held Patent Number 193069, 3 North, 71 West, Hall Ranch.

A small note in the Lyons Redstone Museum mentions that Jack Blair was born June 29, 1872 in Maringo, Iowa. He was the youngest of 6 children. Jack's obituary states that the Blair Brothers were cowmen of the old school, highly respected, quiet, and unassuming, "yet backing every progressive move made for the area."

Samuel H. Blair was a Lyons resident for 32 Years. He joined the Odd Fellows in March of 1904. On September 5, 1907 while descending from a climb to the top of Long's Peak, he broke his ankle and was confined to home for a short while.

Benjamin J. Blair held a Land Patent for 40 acres in the SWSW of Section 25, T3N R71W, dated February 24, 1919.

Jacob Blubaugh
June 29, 1854–October 23, 1949

Jacob Blubaugh was born in Vandalia, Illinois. Jake was a direct descendant of Daniel Boone. The family later moved to Melrose, Iowa. Jake then moved to Dodge City, Kansas becoming one of the town's teenage "pranksters." He was known for hiding the horses that belonged to Jesse and Frank James. Never one to stay still, he moved on to Nebraska to try his hand at farming, but soon returned to Kansas.

In 1887 he married Katie David at Logan, Kansas. Jacob, his wife, her mother, Lucy David, and the Charles Engert family traveled from Logan, Kansas by covered wagon. They arrived in Lyons about 1889 settling about one and a quarter mile northwest of Lyons. After their daughter, Lucy was born, November 16, 1889, they moved into a house near the railroad depot in Lyons. George was born at home in 1900 and grew up in Lyons. There was also a daughter, Barbara.

Lucy David purchased a house on 5th Street, also near the depot and operated a boarding house for the railroad workers.

Jake made a living ranching, cutting and hauling timber, and hauling sandstone for Sites and Buell Quarries.

Katie had been stricken with polio at the age of three, which left her paralyzed from the waist down. With the help of her parents, she adapted to her disability. Kate rode horseback to school. Later, she taught school in Logan, Kansas.

Francis (Frank) M. Brackett
4 Jun 1886–16 Mar 1971

Frank's father, Levi Brackett settled in what was called Brackett Gulch about 1876. Frank was born June 14, 1886 NW of Lyons at Lone Pine to Levi and Parmelia Brackett. He married Corda Floss Hirschfeld May 23, 1910 in Boulder. Their first home was at what is now part of the Ralph Price Reservoir. Mr. Brackett farmed, ranched, ran a dairy, and worked in the quarries.

One of their sons, William Levi Brackett married Frances Brodie, granddaughter of John C. Brodie. Mrs. Brackett is the president of the Lyons Cemetery association.

Frank, or 'Pop', was a member of I.O.O.F. Lodge No. 102 in Lyons and the Rebekah Lodge No. 30, also of Lyons.

He died at his home on 217 High Street at the age of 85. The Bracketts had lived in the home for twenty years. Burial was in the Hygiene Cemetery.

— See appendix I Genealogical Data Pages 195–196 for the Bracket Genealogy.

On the left is Frank Brackett. Courtesy of the Lyons Redstone Museum, Lyons, Colorado.

Alfred Bennet Brown
June 21, 1837–October 21, 1907

Alfred Bennet Brown was born in New York. After his move to Ohio, he served in the 19th Regiment, Ohio Volunteers of the Civil War, receiving a pension of $12.00 per month beginning April 24, 1897.

He relocated to Colorado, spending a year in Allenspark. In 1891 he moved to Lyons. Brown was a carpenter by trade. He built many of the early houses in the area. His own home on Stickney Avenue was built in 1899 and is still standing. In 1894, he helped with the building of the Old Stone Church, expertly creating many of the interior furnishings.

Alfred died at home after a four-year illness resulting from a broken hip. Sometime after his death Linda, his wife moved to Hollywood, California to live with her sister.

James W. Collett
July 1843–05 January 1903

James W. Collett served in the Civil War in Company H, 130th Regiment, Indiana Volunteers. The Colletts moved west by covered wagon from their home in Indiana. They remained in Nebraska until 1896 when they moved to Lyons.

James was active in the Campfire G. A. R. organization and was a member of the Old Stone Congregational Church.

John died of pneumonia at home in Lyons. Tabitha, his wife died 36 years later at the home of her daughter, Esther Twist.

Leonard Henry Dieterich
October 26, 1858—August 13, 1933

L. H. Dieterich was born in Springfield, Ohio. He came to Colorado in 1885. He arrived in the one-street town of Longmont. He worked for the railroad and later the sugar company in that town. He discovered a talent and interest in surveying keeping an office on the second floor of the Thorne General Store in Lyons.

He met and married Genetta Thomas who had come to Lyons to visit her sister, Dora Thomas Griffith, who married Edward S. Lyon in San Diego, California.

In 1900 he was fire chief, as well as clerk and recorder for the Town of Lyons. He later was elected to the Board of Trustees for the town.

On the 16th of October 1907 Leonard registered his Land Patent for 160 acres in the NE Sec. 20 of T3N, R72W. He had two sons L. H. and Howell Dieterich.

Ben Durr
November 4, 1851–March 23, 1891

Ben Durr was born in Lohr, Bavaria. He came to America in 1860, settling in Ripon, Wisconsin. Later he moved to Fulton, Missouri where he had a Portrait Photography studio. After 10 years of journalism in Missouri, his doctor advised him to move to Denver for his health. Ben was another victim of consumption. After hearing about the sanatarium facilities located north of that City, he traveled to the resort village of Lyons.

In order to keep himself busy, he began a local newspaper, *The Long's Peak Rustler*. The offices were on the second floor of the Golden Rule Store located at the west end of Main Street. He was a fearless editor living by his motto to build up and not to tear down. He died at the young age of 40. The newspaper continued until 1894.

—See Appendix V, p. 306— *History of The Lyons Recorder*

Josiah Flynn
July 22, 1852—September 5, 1936

Josian Flynn was born in Cass County, Illinois. He married Martha S. Leonard on December 11, 1876 at Indianola, Iowa. As a railroad man, Joshia moved with the trains. He came to Colorado about 1885 and to Lyons around 1891.

Charles Fullerton Gordon
September 22, 1863—January 25, 1933

Charles and Barbra Summer Gordon moved to Colorado and farmed the old Columbus Weese farm east of Lyons. After a year, they bought their own 80 acre farm next to his uncle's place southeast of Lyons. Charles was also ditch superintendent for the South Ledge Ditch Company until 1900. He was road supervisor of the Lyons district until 1907. During this time he supervised the building of three highway bridges across the St. Vrain River and several across ditches throughout the area.

The Gordons moved to Lyons in 1911. He had built a home on 2nd Street at the foot of Hogsback Mountain. Charles was marshal of Lyons from 1915 to 1917 and caretaker of the Longmont Dam until 1924. Picnickers and fishermen would call him the "Dam Man" because of his practical jokes and great sense of humor.

The family raised berries, corn, and vegetables which they sold at a roadside stand along with the wooden dolls he carved. His cherries became famous with tourists and soon he was shipping fruit to various parts of the country with Barbra's jams and jellies.

Chalres passed away at home following a stroke in 1933. Barbra died in 1948 in Longmont. Both lie at rest in the Mountain View Cemetery, Longmont, Colorado.

J. C. R. Gordon
1843–1914

Mr. Gordon served in Company K, 126th Pennsylvania Volunteers during the Civil War. Reportedly, he kept a diary giving details of events during the Spring of 1865: the surrender of Robert E. Lee, the assassination of Abraham Lincoln, and the assassination of John Wilkes Booth. Mr. Gordon was honorably discharged on May 8, 1865. On July 3, 1865 he had the privilege of meeting General Meade and General Howard at Gettysburg. He also saw the corner stone laid at the National Cemetery at Gettysburg.

In 1886, J. C. and his nephew, C. F. Gordon came to Colorado and settled on a farm near Chapman Switch. Lizzie Baughman kept house for J. C., as well as helping with the chores and farm work. For his trips to town, Gordon would either hitch up his wagon or take the train from the Switch. He served on the Board of County Commissioners from 1901–1904, holding as chairmanship in his last year.

Gordon died in 1914 from a heart failure while getting his mail from the Lyons Post Office.

John Bigland Hall
June 20, 1846–April 14, 1934

John Bigland Hall was born June 20, 1846 at Delting on the Shetland Islands, Scotland to John Hall and Christine Bigland Hall, also of Scotland. The family barely made a living, using the sea below their home for their food source. When John was 12 years old, his father disappeared. It was thought that he fell off the cliff and was swept away by the rough waves along the coast. Two years later, when he was 14 years old, John left home and went to sea in an attempt to provide for his mother and siblings. He sailed the seven seas for twenty years circumnavigating the globe twice. During the Civil War he made trips between Liverpool and New York avoiding the Union Army and their habit of shanghaiing sailors while in the Port of New York. Later, he moved to the Chicago, Illinois area and became Captain of a ship sailing the Great Lakes. He married Hannah Roberts March 28, 1878.

John, Hannah, and little Charles Byron traveled west arriving in Lyons in 1882. Hannah had not relished the life of a sea captain's wife. March 1883, they homesteaded up the North St. Vrain, building their home at the present intersection of the north end of Old Apple Valley Road and U.S. Highway 36. In 1885, while the family attended church in Lyons, the house was destroyed by fire. This forced a move two miles further up the canyon, where they built a much larger and majestic home, the present location of the Inn at Rock 'n' River.

They began ranching, however, John discovered that this was not as easy as he thought it would be. To supplement their income, John turned to lumbering, making poles and ties for the railroad. Their home, like others, became a vacation place for travelers, as well as, relief for sufferers of tuberculosis.

Members and friends of the Old Stone Church in Lyons were always welcome to hold picnics and other meetings at the ranch. Friends and guests would arrive by horseback and wagon over the rough road that ended just above the property. John was always remembered for his elegant white mustache giving him a dashing appearance.

Land Patents held by John B. Hall:

Document # 251, Homestead Entry May 20, 1862, registered June 4, 1890 160 acres from Sec. 11 N NE and Sec 12 N NW of T3N, R71W. Doc # not given, Homestead entry May 20, 1862, registered March 19, 1923 158.49 acres: SENE of Sec. 11 and Lot 7 of Sec. 1, Lot 8 of Sec. 1, and Lot 1 of Sec 12 T3N R71W.

John B. Hall circa 1915. Courtesy of the Lyons Redstone Museum, Lyons, Colorado.

John Bradley Holcomb
November 27, 1845–January 4, 1922

John served in the Civil War with the Indiana Infantry Volunteers, Company G., 130th Regiment of the Union Army. He and his wife, Eliza had farmed in Indiana. They moved to Lyons, Colorado around 1885 homesteading on 160 acres one and one-half miles west of Lyons on the South St. Vrain River. In addition to farming, John worked in the rock quarries until he was forced to quit having contracted lung consumption caused by the quarry dust, a similar disease to Black Lung contracted by coal miners.

James Henry Hutchinson
March 14, 1858—July 22, 1943

James Henry Hutchinson came to Lyons in 1889. He and his wife, Nancy Jane had five children: Glenn, William, Lena, Martha, and Minnie. James helped with the construction of the Congregational Church and remained an active member until his death. He is buried in the Mountain View Cemetery in Longmont.

Elisa Cook and John B. Holcomb. Courtesy of the Lyons Redstone Museum, Lyons, Colorado.

Thomas Lavridson
1837—Unknown

In 1890 Thomas Lavridson ran a Mercantile Store in Lyons. He built and owned a two-story stone building on the north side of Main Street known as the Lavridson Building, from which the Lavridson Brothers, Thomas and Hans, kept a meat market in 1900. A local newspaper reported that Tom managed the Lyons Opera House from 1897 to 1909. Little information still exists about the Opera House, its location, or its playbill. During this time, this very active man operated a small stone quarry presumably in the Noland/Beech Hill area. In 1906 he was manager of the Copper Ocean Mining and Milling Company.

Laycook Family

John S. and Zillah W. Laycook first settled in Hygiene in 1873.

Francis M. Laycook was a resident of the Lyons district for fifty years. He was affectionately known as "Dad" Laycook. Early in his life he lived in the mountains of Tennessee. He was drafted into the Confederate Army at the out break of the Civil War. His sympathies laid with the north. He deserted the southern army leaving the camp in Alabama to make his way north to enlist in the Union Army. His wife, Nancy died at 79 years on December 12, 1927. They had one son and two daughters.

Henry E. and Tamny Laycook filed on the Hall Ranch 3 North, 71 West on December 27, 1909, Patent Number 99116. They later homesteaded in Antelope Park. He filed June 4, 1902 for W 1/2 SW1/4 of Section 14 and N1/2 NW 1/4 of Section 23, Township 3N, Range 71. He died August 18, 1921 in Lyons at the age of 80 years.

W. E. Laycook ran for Trustee of Lyons on the Citizens' Ticket Party March 1908.

W. H. H. Lewis
(Dates Unknown)

Mrs. and Mrs. Lewis arrived in Lyons in 1897. He operated a barbershop in town from 1898–1903. He was Police Magistrate for the Town of Lyons in 1898, 1899, 1902, 1904, 1905, and 1907. He served as Justice of the Peace off and on for seven years from 1901–1915.

Mrs. Lewis ran the Lewis Restaurant and Boarding House located on Main Street near the Lyons Golden Rule Store from 1901–1915. When the building was sold to Mrs. Weir, the Lewis' moved to Washington.

The Lewis' had three sons, Orange A., Clarence, and Charles. Orange A. died of miner's consumption in Boulder on October 31, 1905. He had a wife and eight children. Clarence was editor of the *Ft. Morgan Times*. Charles lived in the State of Washington.

Thomas Lowe
March 7, 1867—June 4, 1911

Thomas was born in Staffordshire, England. He came to America in 1885. In 1890 he married Ella Sedman in the Dakota Territory. The couple moved to Lyons in 1891. At the time of his death he was the owner and operator of a resort south of town.

James Manning
June 21, 1858–May 27, 1924

James Manning and his wife Delia came to Lyons in 1888. Jim was employed by the Hugh Murphy Quarry and later worked for the John C. Brodie Quarries. The Mannings were members of the Lyons Methodist Church and he was a member of the Woodman Lodge. He was active in town politics, influencing many decisions made by the town board.

Jacob Clifford Moomaw
June 18, 1892–January 10, 1975

Jack, Jacob C. Moomaw was born in Mirage Flats, Nebraska to Charlie and Bertha Moomaw. His early years were spent in a soddy house battered by blizzards, droughts, grasshoppers, plagues, and an exhausted soil.

Charlie Moomaw traveled to Arizona, New Mexico, Texas, and finally to Colorado looking for a better home for his family. In April of 1893 the family packed a covered wagon, loaded it with their belongings, and hitched up "Jin, Joe, & Frank" for their trip to Colorado. Within ten days they arrived outside of Fort Collins. They continued their journey to Hygiene to live in the community of the Dunkard faith. When Bertha was diagnosed with tuberculosis, the doctor suggested that they move further into the mountains. They relocated between Lyons and Allen's Park, where Charlie applied for a government timber lease and opened his own sawmill. Young Jack Moomaw became a muleskinner for the mill.

The hard discipline of the Dunkard Faith gave Jack good reason to run away from home when only thirteen years old. He became a cowboy working from Mexico to Wyoming until his fascination with the sea led him to the docks of San Francisco, where he became a stevedore. When reaching the age of enlistment, he joined the Navy and had the opportunity to join in a real fight. Jack tended to find fist fights a necessary way of life. He mustered out in 1914 and returned to Colorado.

At the age of twenty, Jack decided to finish high school. Classmates Harold Dunning and Bertha Ramey remember the magnificent stories he wrote for class assignments. During these school years, he renewed his friendship with Lila Weese. Love soon blossomed between the couple. Lila's father, Columbus Weese, tried to discourage the union, so Jack left for Wyoming. Lila would have none of this, following her true love north. They were married June 5, 1915 at Douglas, Wyoming.

Lila was the recipient of several inheritances of money and land. She purchased the Land Patents on 1200 acres in Sections 10 & 11 in Township 3N, Range 70W on March 16, 1920. The Moomaws tried homesteading and farming. Lila enjoyed the outdoor work and her home, but Jack preferred a different type of outdoor life. Their homestead on Rabbit Mountain provided the amateur archeologist with many sites to explore. Much more to his liking was the lure of the high mountains. Climbing in Estes Park and collecting Indian artifacts brought him pleasure.

Jack was offered the position of guide in Estes Park taking visitors up to the summit of Long's Peak on an at need basis. He became a trail foreman in 1922 and later that year he accepted the steady job of Rocky Mountain Park Ranger.

Jack C. Moomaw had many talents. He was an accomplished painter, as well as a well renowned published author. However, his personal life was not as idyllic as Lila hoped. The couple spent much time apart. Jack would offend many of her friends by calling her, "that woman," rarely using her name. Lila died in 1961.

In June of 1945, Jack had a heart attack and had to leave the service. He sold the Weese homestead by McCall Lake and moved into Lyons. With his friend Ruby Miller, Jack wanted to open an educational museum in which to display his collections and life among the Indians. The Town of Lyons refused to approve a variance for the museum.

Jack offered the 1200 acres on Rabbit Mountain as a wildlife reserve in an effort to preserve any remaining archeological evidence. In 1985 the land became Boulder County Open Space thanks to the efforts of his granddaughter, Helen Lila.

Minnie Schwilke
September 28, 1863–March 7, 1926

Minnie Schwilke was born in Felbach, Wurtenburg, Germany. She worked as a nursemaid in Zurich, Switzerland before coming to the United States in 1884. While living with her brothers, John and Jacob she met and married Gotlieb Fredrick Aldinger.

The couple moved to Fort Collins after many crop failures in Nebraska. When Noland was in full swing, they moved to Lyons and opened a butcher shop in town. Another shop was opened in Noland. In 1899 the couple decided to return to farming and purchased part of the Wilcox farm located two miles east of Lyons. They raised fruits and vegetables and had several milk cows. Most of their produce was shipped to Estes Park.

Sam Service
1860–April 26, 1937

Sam Service was born in Ireland and came to Lyons to work in the quarries. Tiring of stonework, he hired on with H. N. Morey in the Lyons grocery store remaining several years after the business changed ownership.

In 1902 Sam moved to Estes Park where he became a well-known and respected citizen. Sam married, had three sons, and five daughters. He died in Longmont and was buried at the Fairmount Mausoleum at Denver, Colorado. Oral history interviews with Sam Service and written histories documenting his activities in both Lyons and Estes Park can be found at the Estes Park Library and Museum.

Charles A. Spaulding
December 21, 1843—June 22, 1905

Charles was born in Hillsdale, Michigan. He was a Civil War Veteran. He and his family came to Lyons in October 1885. In 1900 he was treasurer of the Lyons Campfire, a G.A.R. organization. In 1901 he was Noble Grand of the Lyons Odd Fellows. In 1904 Charles sat on the Lyons Town Board. Mr. Spaulding was also one of the founders of the Allenspark Town Company.

Four children were born to them: two sons, Frank and Harry; and two daughters, Mrs. Jennie Logan and Mrs. Nettie McFadden. Nettie was the Lyons Postmaster from 1899–1909.

John P. Swenson
August 22, 1834–November 22, 1908

John P. and Stina K. Swenson with daughter Amanda emigrated from Hjortsberga, Smaland, Sweden in 1889. When they arrived in Denver, Colorado, they joined their children, Swan Magni and Emma Johnson, who had emigrated about 1882. In 1890, the family moved to Lyons. Brother Charles, who was in the Royal Guard of the Swedish Army, joined his family in Lyons after his discharge in 1891.

John worked in the sandstone quarries of Beach Hill and later for the Burlington Railroad as a section hand. In 1896, Amanda moved to Denver to live with Mrs. John Peterson while she worked in a Swedish boardinghouse. Amanda returned to Lyons a year later. She and her cousin Clara Swanson owned and operated the Lyons Peak Cafe. Amanda married John A. Sealander on June 27, 1902.

William Tilton
April 11, 1866–February 22, 1914

William Tilton and his wife, Cora arrived in Colorado in the 1880s. They operated a general store and saw mill at Bellevue, seven miles west of Fort Collins. In 1898 the Tiltons and Benjamin Flowers, Cora's brother, moved to Lyons. They opened a sawmill at Park and 2nd Street called The Lyons Lumber Company. In 1902 the Tiltons, Flowers, and Grounds moved the business to Main and 4th Streets, renaming it the Lyons Mercantile and Lumber Company. In 1903 Tilton and Flowers went into partnership in the St. Vrain Lumber Company located at Main and 3rd. The business was sold to R. W. Shaffer in 1904. Their son, Jasper and his wife, Denise lived in Lyons many years.

Jeremiah C. Wamsley
1849–1901

Jeremiah and his wife Dica came to Lyons in November of 1890. He was town marshal for three years, 1892–1894. The following two years he was road overseer for the Lyons district. The family home was on Evans Street at 2nd Avenue. When J. C. died in 1901, Dica moved to Estes Park and became manager of a local boarding house. In 1905 she became the manager of the Lafayette Telephone Office.

Charles P. Wilcox
July 31, 1848–1921

Charles P. Wilcox was a soldier and an Indian Fighter. He often spoke of his friendship with Buffalo Bill.

Charles and his wife, Cynthia M. Wilcox arrived in Denver in 1878. They came to the North St. Vrain to ranch, settling about one mile west of Lyons. Two of Charles' brothers lived in and around Lyons, L. A. and John E. Wilcox. In 1890 Charles opened the Wilcox Grocery Store in Lyons. Competition was heavy with the Lyons Golden Rule Store and others. In 1906 they sold the store to Gaddis and Robson.

From Nebraska
to
Colorado

M any families were drawn to Colorado. It was a midway
point between the east and west coasts. Tired from the
long and dangerous journey they would pull their wagons from
the wagon train heading further west looking for farmland or
work. Quite a few of these pioneers headed for Lyons to take
advantage of the opportunities offered for a variety of jobs and
occupations needed to support the large quarry operations. One
such family was the Schwilkes. I received the following letter
from Jim Middleton, grandson of Louise Schwilke along with
his grandmothers letter describing their trip from Nebraska to
Colorado.

"Here is the note my grandmother wrote about a trip
she took with her family when she was 6 or 7. Since she
was born on 15 September 1884, she was 6 on 15 September 1890 and 7 on 15 September 1891. From that I would
guess the trip was in 1891 or 1892. I lived with her and
my grandfather for most of my early life.
She would have been traveling with her father and
mother Jacob Schwilke b. 8 November 1851 and
Gottlobine Dorothea Mohl b. 2 June 1850. In addition,
her siblings William (1873), Pauling (1876), Katherine
(1879), James (1882), Carolina (1887) and Herman (1888)."

—Letter from Jim Middleton, dated 05 September 2000.

The following is a direct transcription of grandmother's letter, including spelling, grammar, and sentence structure:

My Trip From Naponee, Nebraska to Colorado 1891 or 1892

Just as we were getting ready to leave a nice collie dog came and would not leave even when Dad tried to send him home so he just came along. We had two horses to drive to our covered wagon also brought a cow so we would have milk, she was a large read and white spotted cow, nice and gentle, named, Spot,

At the back of the wagon we had a crate with frying chicken's so when we wanted chicken we would stop early enough to dress the chicken before dark, as we only had a lantern for light at night.

One day as we were driving along we saw quite a few long horned cattle so we stopped, and Dad put the dog in the wagon, he said for me to hold on to his collar so he would not jump down the cattle might chase him and if the dog (we called the dog Shep) would go under the wagon the cattle might chase him and upset the wagon. The cattle soon went away. [??] I suppose we followed the river so as to have water.

I don't know where we were when one of our horses got sick and died. were not near anyone because when we wanted to go on our way, Dad hitched the cow beside the horse he gave Mother the lines while he walked along beside the cow until she knew what she was expected to do. When we got to where we could Dad traded the cow and horse for a Mule team then continued on our way to Lyons, Colo. When we got to Lyons we set up our tent beside the wagon until such a time as Dad had a job then we would find a place near by, and as I had heard that money was floating around I would look in all the low places and ditches to see if I could find some of that money floating, Mother ask me what I was looking for I didn't tell her until a long while later when I told her she had a good laugh.

Dad got work in the quarries at Noland a couple of miles from Lyons, we moved up there it was a small town between two hills I think there were about 200 people. I started to school there My first teacher was a man his [name] was Orr one day I was so interested in my lesson and wanted to know something about it and I was so lost in my thoughts that I ask the teacher in german the school all laughed the teacher came right down and sat beside me and said don't pay any attention to them they don't know any better He understood how tearable I felt; believe me that never happened again, and I don't think I ever realy got over it.

Mother would often send me up to the quarry with a hot dinner for Dad we lived on one hill side and Dad worked up on the other hill. And I would try and get there while the dinner was still hot. And of course it was rough walking bare foot

One day Dad was the only man up there as the rest all had gone down to their homes they were young and didn't need the extra rest. And they had left a rock with the derrick fastened to it. (As I remember it was about 6 feet square) One would turn a handle and it would pull the rock up to where Dad got it up he said for me to hold the handle so he could move the rock around where he wanted it. Also said now don't let go of it or it will come down on me. I still remember how tight I held on.

On Christmas there was a tree for everyone some intertainment, Mother, Aunt Minnie (Dad's sister), Dad's Brother John & Dad sang [—german] song [?] they clapped so hard [???] I remember When I was about 9 years old. We moved down near [Hygiene] Jim and I started out with our cows. I think we had 3 cows and they started on [the] run we tried to keep up with them, Jim knew where we were going I didn't so I was afraid not to keep up. When we got there we were realy hot. Mrs. Perkins had me lay down. Gave me a little drink when I wanted a big drink she said it might make me sick to drink to much she put [a] wet cloth on my head and face that was new to have some one I didn't know make such a fuss over me Mother was worried when they didn't catch up with us.

What a story—

65

Gotlieb Fredrick Aldinger, his wife Minnie Schwilke, and daughter Louise. Courtesy of the Lyons Redstone Museum, Lyons, Colorado.

The Alfred Brown Family about 1897. Back row from left to right: Harry Earl Jack Brown, Gypsy Brown Higgins, Cloyd Brown, and Maud Brown Evans. Middle from left to right: Louise Brown Newcomb, Alfred Brown, Linda Cloyd Brown, and Frank Brown. In front: Vivian Brown Hadley. Courtesy of the Lyons Redstone Museum, Lyons, Colorado.

Nortonville
Townsite North of Lyons

E.S. Lyon, in a rebuttal to a *Lyons Recorder* account of the beginnings of the little quarry town, included this account of the origins of Nortonville.

> "Then on top of all this comes a man from Boulder (I think his name was Stephens), said he wanted a quiet house, as he was going into the heavy stock and had leased all grazing land on the Red Hills. He said he couldn't get the railroad to build up here, as the Burlington had purchased the Foutz road [Superintendent of the railroad] and headquarters would be changed to Boulder. Like a big goose I took in all he said; swallowed hook, line, and sinker, I suppose this man turned this property over to a shrewd lawyer named Putnam [Thomas G. Putnam], and I had a three year's lawsuit on my hands.
>
> This man Putnam tried to change the boundaries and move the whole 80 acres so as to overlap the Lyons Rock and Lime Co. – 80 acres that we had laid out as the Norton townsite. We called this Nortonville. We had a town that was beating Lyons. As this man Putnam was wolf in sheep's clothing, we built this nice little village; all the very best people flocked to Nortonville."

—*The Lyons Recorder*, January 1922, "The Settling of Lyons, According to E. S. Lyon."

1890 Map of Nortonville
Lyons Rock & Lime Quarry Co's 1st Addition

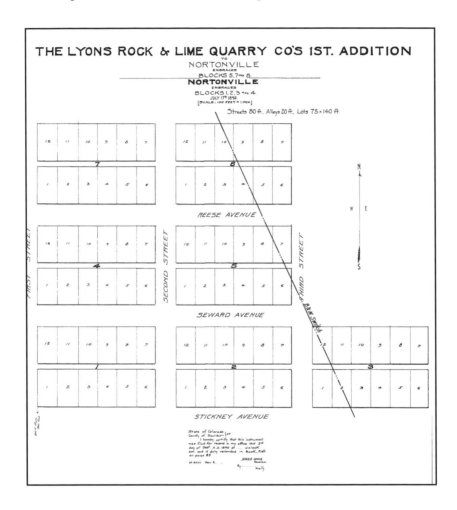

The Lyons Rock & Lime Quarry Co's 1st Addition to Nortonville added blocks 5, 7, and 8 July 17, 1890. Blocks 1, 2, 3, and 4 are on the 1885 original plat map. See Appendix III page 266, First Property Owners, Nortonville for plat map and list of home owners. From the Boulder County Clerk and Recorders Office Plat Map Books p. 85, Boulder, Colorado.

Official Description:

"The Lyons Rock and Lime Quarry Company Corporation organized under the laws of the State of Colorado S 1/2 of the NE 1/4 of Section 18 in T3N R70W in the County of Boulder and State of Colorado. Platted as a townsite, Nortonville, November 27, 1885, by Henry E. Norton, President of said company. [Henry E. Norton was a Lyons banker.]

—signed by John N. Wells, Notary Public November 25, 1885.

Location:

N-S E of 1st, 2nd, 3rd, W of 4th E-W: S of Reese Ave., Seward, N of Stickney Avenue. Block I, 1st, Seward, Second, Stickney; Block II, 2nd Seward, Third, Stickney; Block III, third, Seward 4th, Stickney; Block IV, 1st Reese, 2nd, Seward.

Includes Lots 1-12 in each block. Each Lot is 75 x 140 ft. Each street is 80 ft. Each alley is 20 ft. SW corner of Lot #1 in Block #1 begins 201 feet from East side of St. Vrain Creek and 80 feet due North of the South line of the NE 1/4 of Sec. 18 T3N R70W. Note: The lots in Lyons are 50 feet wide.

—Plat Book #2 p63 with original map and tracing cloth by Agnes O'Day. A copy made September 1913.

—Plat Book #2 p85: The Lyons Rock & Lime Quarry Company's 1st Addition to Nortonville Blocks 5, 7, & 8. July 17, 1890. With the same dimensions as the original plat with streets 80 ft; alleys 20 ft; Lots 75 x 140 feet. Added Block 7 & 8 – E of 1st, South; W of 3rd, includes 2nd; N of Reese. Block 5 – E of 2nd C of Reese, W of 3rd, N of Seward.

I was unable to find a recorded date of annexation of the township of Nortonville to the town of Lyons. It is assumed that it became an official part of the town when the second plat map was completed.

—*See Appendix III, p. 266—First Property Owners, Nortonville.*

LIFE IN A
QUARRY TOWN

1890 Hardware and Grocery store. Courtesy of the Lyons Redsteone Museum, Lyons, Colorado.

Who's on 1ST, What's on 2ND

P lat maps show that throughout the years each surveyor for the town of Lyons would put his unique twist on street and avenue names. Confusing to some, just a way of life for others.

Thomas G. Putnam surveyed and certified the layout of the township of Lyons on March 29, 1890. Road 2nd, 3rd, 4th, and 5th were oriented in a north-south directions. He designated them as avenues. East-west pathways in town were High, Main, Evans, and Prospect. All were called streets. Broadway was simply labeled as Broadway. Park and Meily, south of Main were called avenues.

By January 29, 1929, Leonard H. Dieterich resurveyed the town and renamed some of the streets and avenues, including the section known as Nortonville. North of the railroad tracks Reese was an avenue where Seward, Stickney and High were called streets. The east-west facing roads of 1st, 2nd, 3rd, and 4th were all called streets. South of Main Street the north-south residential area was renamed Avenues from Putnam's street. No, this is not all, Dietrich continued: 1st Street became 5th Avenue; 2nd Street became 4th Avenue; 3rd Street was 3rd Avenue; and 2nd Avenue had no north extension. East-west roads were Evans, Park and Prospect all named as streets with Meily remaining as an avenue. East Main Street was on a diagonal passing through 3rd Street/Avenue from Main Street past Prospect.

Today the road names are simplified. All north-south oriented roads are called avenues. Streets are east-west, Reese, Seward, Stickney, High, Evans, Park, Prospect and Meily.

Main Street, USA

E very small town in the United States began with a Main
Street. The thoroughfare defined the character of these municipalities. Churches, mercantile stores, saloons, and other shops
were centrally located for the busy pioneers in town and in the
surrounding areas.

Street Improvement

January 1891, J. C. Thompson began excavation on his property,
planning a two-story building to be known as the Western House.
He discovered that the hill on the eastern edge of Main Street
was of a high quality lime that would be a profitable quarry.
Lyons supported Thompson's proposal. Removal of the hill
would create more of a "city thoroughfare" for town. At the same
time, the Burlington Railroad authorities were negotiating for
the purchase of the Meadow Park property with the adjoining
quarter section on Main Street. The hodgepodge tent city now
in the Park would be removed and the grounds converted into
an entertainment area for railroad passengers and other travelers.

450 Main Street
McAllister Saloon

The corner land on Main Street was part of Hiram F. Sawyer's
original holdings: SE 1/4 of Section 18, Block 30 Lot 10. William
H. Houck (Hauck) purchased the patent for the west one-half of
Lot 10 in Block 30 on 20 July 1881.

A one-story sandstone building with basement was constructed on the property in 1881. It was the McAllister Saloon. Sawyer lost interest in maintaining business in Lyons and left town. In 1886 the building and lot was sold to Thomas G. Putnam for $4.50 in back taxes.

Nicholas Frank purchased the building in 1890. A *Long's Peak Rustler* advertisement announced that Lyons finally had a meat market, "N. Frank & Bros. Dressed Meat of all Kinds." The meats were guaranteed fresh as the animals were slaughtered on the Nicolas Frank homestead at the site of the present Hall Ranch Open Space. Nicolas Frank also owned and operated the Lyons Club Room specializing in wines, liquor and cigars, presumably located on Main Street.

Frank Brothers Meat Market. Picture taken 1906. Courtesy of the Lyons Redstone Museum, Lyons, Colorado.

By September 3, 1891 Charles Bradford purchased the site except for 10 feet off the road reserved for an alley. The February 19, 1897 *Lyons Topics* reported that Lyons was once again without a meat market. The building stood empty until Charlie sold the building and lot to Charles and William Frank in May of 1901. A series of legal battles over ownership of the land and building began between Elisha S. Johns, F. D. Sandy, J. H. Gilfillan, A. C. Van Deren, and Nicholas Frank. Eight years later on June 19, 1909, William and Charles Frank had made Quit Claim to the lot and claimed full and clear rights to it.

In 1927 the building became a pool hall with several different owners. By the 1960s the building was renovated for use as a restaurant and has remained so, through changing ownerships: Robert E. House, Bertha Bleeker, Cris Angelos, Don David, Tia Bennies, and in 2002 Ciltrano Mary's Mexican Restaurant.

The building was one of fifteen historic sites designated as part of the Lyons Historic District April 1980.

455 Main Street
The Golden Rule Store

Within a year of opening a store in a large tent staked out on the south side of main, Scanlon and his partner Jim Brice purchased property on the north side of Main from "Daddy" Lewis. The Lyons Golden Rule Store was built in 1889 where Kokopelli's Coffee Shop resided in those delightful old railroad cars. Michael John Scanlon and Jim Brice opened their "Mammoth Emporium" offering a potpourri of goods, plus friendly conversation. The large two-story merchandise mart was 80 feet by 100 feet with the name "Scanlon and Brice" painted in large letters across the front. The apartments upstairs were soon leased to *The Long's Peak Rustler* and to the Bloom Sisters Dress Making Shop. The partnership of Scanlon and Brice terminated in 1891.

Fred Aldinger butchered meat for the store at a slaughterhouse located about one half mile up the old north road. In the winter, he cut blocks of ice from the river and lakes surrounding town. Sawdust helped preserve the blocks to be sold in the store during the hot summer months.

Acetylene gas torches were used to light the interior. Heat was generated from stoves located throughout the building. Attempts to fireproof the store with asbestos covered by a siding of sheet iron was to no avail. In 1905, an acetylene gas explosion in the basement of the store killed Leonard Lyon, son of Edward S. Lyon.

On January 6, 1920 the Golden Rule Store was once again destroyed by fire. Arson was suspected. The Lyons Golden Rule Store out lasted the two major competitors, The Lyons Mercantile and Lumber Company owned by Flowers, Tilton and Grounds advertised as "The Big Store on the Korner" and the C. P. Wilcox Grocery located on High Street in the Old Stage House.

The Golden Rule Store owned by M. J. Scanlon. Courtesy of the Lyons Redstone Museum, Lyons, Colorado.

Longs Peak Drug Store

About 1890 on the south side of Main Street in the middle of the 400 block, Dr. E. S. Crona constructed a two-story stone building. On the street level he established the Long's Peak Drug Store with one section secured for his medical practice. On the upper floor were the doctor's living quarters.

The building was sold to E. J. Carver of Boulder in 1914. It burned to the ground in 1967.

419 Main Street
The Arcade Saloon

*The Arcade Saloon. Note the reflection in the windows. They show
the hills across the street from the bar. Courtesy of the Lyons Redstone
Museum, Lyons, Colorado.*

In the fall of 1890, Elmer Beckwith saw potential in the new
quarry town west of Longmont. The hard working quarry men
of Lyons were known to be hard spending drinkers and gamblers.

Elliott West explains that most of the men arrived in the
West without their families. The poorest laborers too often would
'drink their meal, "thus starved their bodies and weakened their
resistance to disease. Unlike all other foods, alcohol contains no
vitamins or minerals, its energy cannot be stored."

Elmer left his Longmont saloon, bought property on Main Street, and contracted with A. J. Hanson to build a saloon. In the front was the usual bar with tables and chairs and pot bellied stove. The back room, however, sported a faro table, a roulette wheel, a crap table, and several poker tables. Every night the tables would be crowded. Business was so good that Beckwith hired a manager for the Arcade and returned to Longmont.

Soon after incorporation, the people of Lyons had become tired of having the town run by saloon keepers and gamblers. Many of the quarry men had bought homes and had families, but choose to gamble away their pay. On October 18, 1892 Elmer Beckwith was charged with keeping a gambling house. Papers were filed with the District Attorney's office in Boulder County. He was called before Judge Downer on October 19, 1892 in the "People vs. Elmer Beckwith for Keeping a Gambling House." Beckwith pleaded guilty and paid a fine of $50, plus court costs of $29.03. His licenses in Longmont and Lyons were revoked.

"A substantial citizen of Lyons not talking for publication, recently recounted how he had entered the place [the Arcade Saloon] with a couple of army Colt persuaders one time to collect a bill the proprietor had owed him for some time. He cut loose on the roulette layout, shot out the windows and perforated the walls" Judge Downey of Boulder was quoted during the trail as asking, "Well, what sort of Sunday School are you trying to run up there Charles?" [Charlie Bradford a well-known and respected Lyons Saloon owner and businessman.]

—*The Old Lyons Recorder,* undated photocopy from The files at Carnegie Library, Boulder.

There was little publicity involved in closing the gambling rooms of the saloons and all concerned went on with their daily routines until 1898. Elmer Beckwith decided to run for Secretary of State under the Fusion Ticket. The *Denver Times* quickly uncovered his colorful past in Longmont and Lyons. The election was news and so was Elmer. Beckwith's business of selling beer over the bar, wrestling with drunks, and dutifully paying his liquor license was not news worthy. In fact, the City Marshall's

Office in Longmont reported that he did not have any more trouble than did any other saloon keeper. It was his gambling rooms in back of the saloons that had become fodder for the opposition. The Fusion Party backed their candidate claiming that he had reformed and would make a good Secretary of State. After all, the incident had happened six years ago. Election Day came, the votes were counted, and not one of the Fusion Party candidates had won. It was not Elmer that caused the entire problem, but the political platform of his Party, which did not coincide with the new Law and Order platforms desired by the people of the State of Colorado.

In the 1900s the *Old Lyons Recorder* bought the building for their offices. During renovation, the workmen removing the old plaster from the east side of the former saloon found bullets imbedded in the walls. Other walls were laced with bullet holes. Stories were told by old-timers in and around Lyons that bullets flew often in the old Arcade. Evidently, the Colt revolver was the way to settle an argument, a drunken encounter, or a gambling dispute.

In April 1903, the Town of Lyons held an election. The Citizen's Ticket promised that all the saloons would be closed on Sundays. *The Lyons Recorder* supported the cause with this editorial.

> "The officials of the B & M are not the men we think they are if they don't sanction the efforts of the citizens of this place to change the conditions so that instead of this place being a resort for the hoodlums and toughs of Denver to visit each Sunday, their patrons will be a better class."

419 Main Street is one of the oldest buildings in town. It was constructed of heavy native lumber instead of local sandstone as used by so many others. It is a wonder that it was never a victim of a fire, which was the fate of so many wooden buildings built in the early years of boomtowns. Today, there is office space on the street level of the building with leased apartments on the second floor.

415 Main Street
General Store

415 is one of fifteen historic sites designated as part of the Lyons Historic District in April 1980. The two-story stone building is topped with a flat roof. The building was first used as a general store. At one time, George Stickney used it as a bank. Next, it became a department store. E. P. Lass opened the Kandy Kitches. The James McCain family converted the building into a barbershop. Otto and Clara Brown used the store as a leather shop. When the Lyon's Drug Store burned in the fire of 1967, Glen and Mabel Jernigan reopened at the 415 site. Dragonwood Antiques and the Rocky Mountain Stoveworks also occupied the lower quarters in following years. The upstairs remained apartments.

THE MEN
OF
MAIN STREET

Thomas A'Hearn
November 1864—December 17, 1901

Thomas A'Hearn came to Lyons from Pennsylvania around 1886. He owned a saloon in town and was the town treasurer at the same time. He was also Chief of the Fire Department and took a prominent part in all Lyons activities.

He was known as the big Irish saloon keeper, a man whose hand was always out to help the sick, needy, and friendless.

The Frank Brothers

The Frank Brothers, William, Charles, and Nicholas came to Lyons from Luxembourg Germany in the late 1880s. They remained in the area until the 1920s when the three brothers and their families moved to California.

Nicholas (1860 Germany–1911 Lyons) homesteaded in the South St. Vrain Canyon about 3 miles west of Lyons, the Hall Ranch Open Space. He filed for a Land Patent on Section 25 Township. 3N, R71W, January 18, 1890 for E1/2 SW, SWNE, & SENW, 160 acres; Doc. #566. In 1890, he was the major investor in N. Frank & Bros. Meat Market in Lyons and supplied cured meat to his brothers from the homestead. By 1897 they had moved the market into Longmont. In 1901 an advertisement in a local newspaper declares Nicholas Frank operator of the Lyons Club Room, "Wines, Liquor, and Cigars." By 1906 he moved on to Mead where he also owned a saloon. He married Ella Goodwin in 1907.

Several of the Franks moved to Ward. William Frank married Neva Holcomb in 1894. He was manager of the Palisades Exchange Parlors. William's son Carl had severe reactions to the higher altitude, so the families returned to Lyons buying the City Meat Market from Tom Lavridson. William's oldest son died of diphtheria in February of 1901; Carl grew up and co-owned a garage in Longmont.

Charles Frank married his fiance from Luxembourg May 10, 1895 having sent for her to come share his grand adventure in America. They were married in a double wedding with Sherman & Philopena Swift Bohn. Charles went into the meat business with his brother William.

Michael John Scanlon
1866–1941

Michael John Scanlon came to Lyons in 1888 from New Britain, Connecticut. His parents, John and Margaret had emigrated from Ireland. After the death of his mother Margaret, at the age of 14 Michael went to work in a New Britain factory. He planned to become a priest and was saving money for divinity school.

Another sufferer of the dreaded disease tuberculosis Mike's brother, William died from consumption in 1888. In order to avoid the same fate, M. J. came to Colorado when he was 21 years old.

While looking for work in Denver, he met James L. Brice. They decided to open a traveling market, Scanlon-Brice Mercantile Co. In Longmont they rented a team of horses and a wagon to service the outlying landowners from Denver to Ft.

Collins. The venture was not profitable, as many of the farming families and other immigrants could not afford to buy from them. During one of his trips to Longmont, he heard about the new quarry industry developing in Lyons. He decided to dissolve his partnership with Brice and move to the new boom own.

Originally Michael lived with U. S. Gilger and his family in their stone house by the river. M.J. met Leona Capson, niece of Billy Welch of the Welch Resort. She and her mother, Jane had come to Lyons in 1889 fromSt. Johns, New Brunswick of Irish descent. The two immediately had a lot in common. They married and produced seven children four daughters, Leona, Marguerite, Dorthea and Helen; and three sons, Jack, Donald and Robert.

Leona and Michael J. Scanlon in Rocky Mountain National Park just beofre Mr. Scanlon's death in 1941. Courtesy of the Lyons Redstone Museum, Lyons, Colorado.

Mike Scanlon, a trusted friend of the quarryman was reported to have run Joe Cooney out of town one day. Evidently, Mr. Cooney cheated the hardworking men of Lyons and Noland using various racketeering schemes. One day, Michael cornered Joe in a Lyons Saloon. With revolver in hand he ordered the saloon to be cleared, except for Cooney. Scanlon being a highly skilled boxer convinced Cooney to leave town on the text train.

Both of the Scanlons were very community minded. They supported the school and the Congregational Church. Mr. Scanlon served as town treasurer in 1891 and again in 1896. In 1899 he served one term as mayor of Lyons followed by several terms on the town board and school boards. He also held the position of postmaster prior to 1920.

M. J. Scanlon was able to return the favor of the Gilger's when he discovered them living in a tent in Meadow Park. Mrs. Gilger was seriously ill. They were invited to live with the Scanlon family until times changed for the couple. After the fire of 1920, Mr. And Mrs. Gilger returned the favor and opened their home to the Scanlons.

With the death of her husband in 1941, Leona Scanlon remained in the family home at 314 Main Street until October 1945. She moved to Milford, Connecticut with her daughter Helen Evert and then with Leona Dunbar in 1956.

The ashes of Leona and Micheal, those of their two eldest sons, plus several other family members were scattered under a favorite pine tree at a look out point on nearby Steamboat Mountain. This was the senior Scanlon's favorite spot. Each day he would hike to the summit. Whenever he was needed at the store, Mrs. Scanlon would step outside and wave a white dishtowel to summon him home from his reveries.

Cal Durbin's Billiard Hall & Saloon–Lemps St. Louis Beer. Courtesy of the Lyons Redstone Museum, Lyons, Colorado.

T. J. Thorne's General Merchandise store. East is a Blacksmith & Wagon Shop. Courtesy of the Lyons Redstone Museum, Lyons, Colorado.

High Street
Just North of Main

340 HIGH STREET
1881 School Building

In 1881 Edward S. Lyons began construction of a 30 foot by 40 foot stone school building. The one-story building would be the town's one-room schoolhouse during the week and their church on Sundays. Pride in the Lyons sandstone ensured that the building would be built from locally quarried stone. To allow the children the most comfort of the times, Mr. Lyon sent to Chicago for school seats. The man continued with his grand visions for his lovely little town nestled in the foothills.

When school opened in the fall of 1882 there were forty children enrolled, however, attendance varied greatly with the seasons. Work on the farms, in the orchards, and in the quarries took precedence over book learning. A degree was not needed to teach reading, writing, and arithmetic, just a firm hand and a willing nature, so T. J. Thorne accepted the position as the first teacher at the new school.

Lyons population grew and so did the need for a second teacher. By 1891 113 children were squeezed together in seats built for two students. The citizens came to the aid of their town and a second story was built in 1895 using volunteer labor and materials. The wooden upper story proved to be unsafe. Even side supports could not steady the constant swaying of the top floor. School would be dismissed during the constant high winds experienced during the fall and spring.

Lyons School after renovations. Courtesy of the Lyons Redstone Museum, Lyons, Colorado.

By 1903, the two-room schoolhouse had once again became crowded, further testimony to the growing town. The school board decided that a new four-room building was essential. Charles Bradford, Joshia Flinn, and A. B. Brown initiated construction with the stipulation that the original two-story building be incorporated into the new structure. The four-room schoolhouse began with the elementary grades on October 16, 1902. Principal S. W. Shenefield governed 173 students and three teachers. Each room had a pot-bellied stove and a water pail. The privies were located to the north of the building. It was much later that the building was updated with water pipes, rest rooms, clothes closets, a fire escape, and a steam heating system. Children wishing to continue on to high school would attend school in Longmont, Boulder, or Denver. It was not until 1924 that Lyons had its own high school. 340 High Street remained a schoolhouse for 96 years.

The building is one of fifteen historic sites designated as the Lyons Historic District in April 1980.

—*See Appendix V, p. 315 for the 1881–1900 Boulder County Annual Superintend Reports: Lyons School District #47 and Noland School District #53.*

426 High Street
The Stone House

The Stone House located at 426 High Street, Lyons, Colorado includes both Block 30, Lot 5 and Block 29, Lot 12 in the SE quarter of Section 18 in Township 3 North, Range 70 West. Sawyer and Houck held the original titles in 1879. Thomas G. Putnam of the Evans Townsite & Quarry Company owned the land until 1890. Presently, the building is the site of Ralston Brothers Antiques owned by Steve and Christine Ralston.

Edward S. Lyon constructed the stone house in 1884 and Thomas J. Thorne opened his general store soon after construction was completed. During the early years of town, the post office was located in the store. It was easy for people to retrieve their mail, catch up on past activities, and gossip all at the same time as picking up a few groceries. On the second floor of the building Leonard H. Dieterich, a local surveyor kept his office. Business was brisk, the town was growing, and buildings were few. In the 1800s the Stone House also served as the Lyons Stage Stop.

Due to financial problems, beginning in the early 1890s, Edward S. Lyon failed to pay taxes on Block 29, Lot 12 in both 1893 and 1897. In 1898 the Boulder County Treasurer sold the property for back taxes to J. H. Gilfflin.

Charles P. Wilcox purchased the Stone House on April 3, 1903 adding on to the west side of the building. Wilcox continued in the grocery business changing the name to C. P. Wilcox Groceries and Notions. Charles installed a Howe Wagon Scale in front of the store to weight the coal and seed he sold. For a fee farmers could weigh their products before taking them to market. By July 1, 1907, C. P. deeded lots 5 & 12 to A. B. Gaddis. October 12, 1908 the deed was transferred to Cynthia M. Wilcox.

By 1930 lots 5 & 12 were quit claimed to J. A. Lee through the administrator of the estate of Mrs. Wilcox. In 1938 the building changed hands once again from Lee to James Fitts. By 1946 Joel A. and Carrie W. Nicholson held title to 426 High Street. Ten years later in August of 1964 Karl R. & Genevieve Schwarz purchased the building and land. By November of 1974, they sold the building to Ralston Brothers, Inc.

Fortunately for all of us, each of the owners maintained the historical integrity of the building. The Ralston's cared enough to apply for National Landmark Status for the Stone House. Thanks to their efforts the original stone building built in 1884 by Edward S. Lyon is available for all of us to enjoy.

This building is one of fifteen historic sites that was designated as part of the Lyons Historic District in April 1980.

The Old Stone Church
Fourth Avenue & High Street

On March 8, 1889 a small group of local people gathered together to organize a congregation under the direction of Reverend H. F. Thayer of Longmont. Within a year the church had seventeen members. Rev. Thayer served the church from 1889 to 1894 traveling between Longmont and Lyons.

The town's founding father, Edward S. Lyon was deeply concerned for the youth of his town. He felt that they needed the stability and guidance of a permanent pastor, "because the town has many saloons and the kids have to have some spiritual upbringing." He encouraged the Reverend Henry Harris of Michigan to move to Lyons and become a vital member of the community. Young Rev. Harris arrived filled with ideas and a desire to work hard to establish a house of God in Lyons.

As the Reverend ministered to his new flock, he was convinced that Lyons needed and could sustain a permanent church building. In 1894 construction began under his guidance. The membership freely contributed their time, money, materials, and labor in this endeavor. Mr. H. F. Currier of Greeley donated the bell to be hung in the church tower. The corner stone was laid by the end of April 1894. And a very short time later, the church was dedicated on September 23, 1895 with the Rev. C. H. Pettibone of Denver officiating.

Rev. Thayer's finance committee consisted of E. E. Norton, C. Bradford, Mrs. D. D. McAlpine, and L. H. Dieterich. The three members of the building committee were R. B. Ground, Alex Chisholm, and Mrs. R. B. Ground. Construction was completed at a cost of only $3,147 much to the pleasure of the congregation.

The sandstone church was a one and a half story building measuring 40 ft x 60 ft. The walls were twenty inches thick of solid sandstone laid on a stone foundation. Each block was hand cut and laid in irregular, non-continuous courses creating a mosaic pattern on the outside of the church. Mortar used to bind the hand-chiseled stone was a mixture of lime and sandstone powder, undoubtedly made in one of the local limestone kilns. The parsonage stood on the southeast corner of Fourth and Main until the early 1920s. E. S. Lyon was content to know that the children of Lyons both present and future would have what he considered proper guidance.

In continuation of the pride and respect for the labors of this quarry town, the Lyons Historical Society ensured that the Old Stone Congregational Church and the original congregation would not be forgotten. The church was listed in National Register of Historic Places as of December 12, 1976.

The Dynamite Storage Building
427 High Street

A small sandstone block building stands behind the Kokopelli train cars on High Street. M. J. Scanlon, owner of the Lyons Golden Rule Store once used the building to store dynamite for the quarries. As the town grew so did concern surrounding the potential danger of storing volatile material within the town limits. The Town Council insisted that the dynamite be stored at the quarries, a safe distance from town.

The dynamite building is one of fifteen historic sites that was designated as part of the Lyons Historic District in April 1980.

Above: The Old Stone Congregational Church, Fourth and High Streets.

To the Right:
Rev. Henry Harris Minister of the Old Stone Church from 1893—1895. Both courtesy of the Lyons Redstone Museum, Lyons, Colorado.

Seward Street

The following homes are part of the Lyons Historical District, designated on April 29, 1980.

409 Seward

409 Seward is a one-story home built in the 1890s. John Montgomery family once lived there. O. J. and Bertha Ramey owned the building as a rental for many years. In the 1980s, Tim and Lynda Kelling of Lyons and Jerry and Kathy Soukup of Longmont owned the property as a rental. Several others have owned the property including a recent sale in 2002.

413 Seward

413 Seward is a small two-story home that old-timers remember as the Jensen Home. It was also built in the 1890s. It was owned by Martha Weese as a rental property in 1980.

425 Seward
Chisholm Home

425 Seward is the Chisholm Home. Blacksmith Alexander Chisholm purchased the land for $125 in 1889. The large sandstone home was part blacksmith shop and part residence. The outside walls are eighteen inches thick constructed of two stonewalls separated by as air space for insulation. The house has changed ownership over the years: Sherman Swift, Charles Gibson, James Day, Cora Tilton, Josephine Vale, the State Bank of Lyons, John Middlemist, and Vivian Trueblood.

Lyons Cemetery

According to local historian Frank Weaver, now deceased, the cemetery was founded in 1880. The earliest recorded burial was found in the records of the Howe Mortuary in Longmont. All that was listed was that a miner by the name of Hoag died on 28 June 1888. There was no marker. Local oral history suggests that many of the quarrymen, who died of lung congestion contracted from the heavy clouds of quarry dust, were placed in unmarked graves during the early boom years. Most of the Swedes, Finns, Italians, and Irish immigrants working the quarries were without families or savings to see to their burial, thus ending up in unmarked graves in Potter's Field. In 1978, Bob Scanlon, vice president of the Lyons Cemetery Association told a *Denver Post* reporter that he was positive that one of the Lyons' Madams, who died in poverty was buried in "Potter's Field" located on the northeast side of the present cemetery. He refused to give her name, claiming that it would not be the thing to do. Children who died during the diphtheria and influenza epidemics of the 1890s and 1900s also lie without markers or any written record of their burial. The oldest remaining readable tombstone is engraved October 21, 1890, 'Son of Ella and D. Hartline.'

Association records show that John E. Lall called a meeting to be held June 17, 1931, for the purpose of organizing the cemetery as a nonprofit entity. R. E. Ground then of La Mesa, California signed a quit claim deed to the St. Vrain Lodge #1002, I. O. O. F. His land was to be used for the cemetery. The Lyons Odd Fellows Lodge in turn agreed to deed the property to the Lyons Cemetery Association. The first officers of the association were: John E. Lall, president; Phil Bohn, Vice President; Mrs. Eva Stevens, Secretary; Mrs. Sarah Walker, Treasurer; and directors Mrs. Eliza Depue and C. B. Rundell.

On October 8, 1931, another meeting of the association was held. They agreed to have 500 membership cards printed to be sold throughout the year at $1.00 each. They hoped to raise desperately needed funds for the upkeep of the cemetery. By May of 1932 the treasurer's report showed only $46.88 had been received from the sale. Labor costs for the site were recorded for that year: B. F. Fleming, 6 days, $16.00; B. S. W. Swift, 1 day labor, $3.00. Cemetery lots were selling for only $10.00, hardly enough to cover basic maintenance needs.

The first officially recorded sale of plots was Deed #1 purchased by Amanda Sealander August 19, 1932. During the fall of 1932, the Town of Lyons made a Quit Claim Deed for the east side of the present cemetery property, land that had once been owned by Frank L. Reese. Records show that Mr. Berger completed a preliminary survey, however, his map and notes have been lost.

By March 2, 1933, the association adopted the bylaws of the Hygiene Cemetery. Attorney Secor approved them for use in Lyons. A full lot, 8ft x 14ft, cost $25.00 and a half lot sold for $15.00. Because of the number of rocks in the Murphy Addition there would be an additional charge of $2.00 over the normal cost for opening and closing a gravesite. During this time of organization it was decided that the Brodie family would not have to pay for a deed within the area called the Brodie Section. The association, however, held the right to control and fix prices for opening and closing gravesites in all sections.

At the May 1933 meeting, unanimous approval was given to purchase forty Chinese Elm trees from W. E. Hervey for $10. each. He agreed to add some evergreens to fill in where needed to improve the appearance of the cemetery.

Complete association records of interments began in 1940 when Gene Smith, the local sextant was hired to run the cemetery. There is no record of which church employed him. Later, Mary Colard volunteered to keep the records, adding a card filing system that simplified referencing family plots and burials. Frances Brodie Brackett continued maintaining complete burial records, when Mary moved to Canon City.

In 1942, surveyor L. H. Dietreich with O. J. Ramey, C. B. Johnson, and R. M. Owen reworked the tract and verified titles for the cemetery. Payment included $10.00 to Mr. Dieterich and $9.00 to the rod man, A. M. McDougal. The St. Vrain Lodge paid $5.75 for the survey stakes. Officers of the Cemetery Association at the time were Bob Owens, President; Charley Johnson, Vice President; Claude Stevens, Secretary; and Floyd Smith, Treasurer with Harry Brown and Fred Engle-Niner Directors.

In 1979 Mary and Clair Colard donated $597.27 dollars for the purchase and installation of a new chain fence. In 1987 a sprinkling system was installed as a gift from Frank Weaver.

The DAR took over responsibility for placing white stones on each of the Civil War Veterans' plots. This task was later turned over to the Lyons American Legion. All American Veterans are entitled to a free headstone furnished by the United States Department of Defense. The Lyons Cemetery Association ensures that an American flag flies over each of these veteran's graves on national holidays.

Past officers of the Lyons Cemetery Association include: R. M. Owen, C. B. Johnson, Claud Stevens, Floyd Smith, William Brackett, Bob Scanlon, Dorothy Stevens, Roberta Swift, Clair Colard, Mary Colard, Darlene Thompson, Bill Martin, Peter Harkalis, and Frances Brodie Brackett.

The cemetery map being used today was compiled from information given to Larry Webster in June 1971 by Vaughn Kinsey.

Location and Legal Description

GNIS of Lyons as recorded in 1999: 40 13 29N 105 16 15W. It lies in Township 3N; Range 70W; 1/4 of Center of NE W 1/4 of Section 18; Sixth p. m., Lyons, County Boulder, State of Colorado.

The abandoned railroad grade and lines have been removed to make room for cemetery lots.

Directions to Cemetery

To reach the cemetery from Longmont, drive west on Ute Highway (CO 66), which becomes US 36 through Lyons; from Boulder drive north on the Foothills Highway (US 36) turning left at the stoplight.

Entering town on Highway 36 look to the right for the large yellow sign indicating the cemetery, turnNorth on 3rd Avenue. The terminus of 3rd is the entrance to the cemetery.

Description of Cemetery Lots

Each lot contains four plots. Cemetery lots are 4 ft x 8ft. They have been extended recently to accommodate the inclusion of burial vaults. Streets run north and south and are 8 feet wide, except in Blocks 5 and 8, where they are 4 feet wide. Alleys run east and west and are 4 feet wide. Driveways are 16 feet wide.

By 1932 a full lot of four spaces cost $10.00. In 2001 the price was $1,200.00.

Entrance to the Lyons Cemetery. From the collection of Diane Goode Benedict.

Shootout
at
Charlie's Bar

William C. Watt Held For Killing
John Kearney

It was a chilly December night five days before the Christmas holidays. John Kearney and Thomas Walen left the Hugh Murphy Quarries in Noland with their pay in their pocket for a night of drinking and gambling down in Lyons. Sometime in the early morning hours of the twenty-first, they left the Bucherdee place and headed for Charley Bradford's saloon. John was looking for his partner William Baxtor and a game of poker. As he went through the doors, he saw Baxtor, Fred Billings (who was the only man not drunk), W. M. Ryan, Doc John Smith and Edward Baker. John joined the group and took up his hand. William C. Watt came in about 4 a.m. from Bucherdee's saloon. Poker was the game and drinking was the stay. Watt ordered drinks for the crowd. Some say they were drinking a fermented extract of rye, a concoction of malt and barley; others said they were downing hot whiskies quickly followed by divers or beer every few minutes throughout the early hours of Wednesday morning. Kearney was reported to have had seven hot whiskies in less than twenty minutes. Both men were so drunk that they had to get another man to deal the cards. Thomas, who was just watching and drinking finally fell asleep in a chair behind the large stove.

A jackpot was on the table and Watt opened for $1.75. Everyone dropped out of the round, but Kearney. He drew three cards and Watt one. Watt suggested they divide the pot and Kearney agreed. Watt held two pairs, kings and fours, while Kearney laid down a pair of sevens.

Twenty minutes later another jackpot came up. Kearney opened for $2. Once again the two longtime friends were alone for the round. Watt drew one card; Kearney stood pat. Watt again suggested that they divide the pot, but Kearney refused and put $5 on the table. Watt passed and Kearney took the pot. Baxtor, drunk and tired from playing poker all night, went to sleep on the nearby pool table despite the cold in the room.

By this time William, who had been drinking heavily had had enough. He insisted that John play poker for every cent he had. Kearney pulled out a little money sack and placed a roll of bills on the table. "There it is. I'll play you poker for it." Watt responded in anger and when John took the bills off the table to put back in his pocket, Bill jumped up, walked around Billings, pulled a pistol from his hip pocket and pointed it at Kearney. The .38 Smith & Wesson went off just as John raised his hand knocking the revolver to the side.

Ryan yelled, "For God's sake, Bill. Don't kill the man."

"I will, I will," replied Watt, leaping at Kearney, forcing him backward and firing again. The bartender, Elias Johns, who had not been drinking, rushed forward and grabbed the pistol just as the second shot went off. This time Kearney dropped to the floor pleading, "For God's sake, Bill, don't kill me."

Around 8 o'clock in the morning, from his office across the street, Dr. George W. Gammon saw Kearney drag himself to a chair. He rushed over to the saloon to see if he could be of help. John was carried to the doctor's office complaining of pains in his leg. Gammon proceeded to probe for the bullet, which had entered the victim's left groin. No one considered it serious and all went home. On December 28, 1892, John Kearney, a small man two-thirds the size of Watt and weighting only 135 pounds died of peritonitis. The "situation" had changed from just another incident to murder.

Constable Bill Thorne was the one who told Watt that John had died. Bill was remanded into the care of Deputy Sheriff Hank Green and placed in jail until the coroner's jury could convene. On Tuesday, December 29, 1892 the hearing was held with Deputy District Attorney Campbell, Coroner J. G. Trezise, both of Boulder, and clerk Captain Sipple. Jurors Leonard Henry Dietrich, Thomas A. Hearn, Nicholas Frank, William Sites, E. R. Meeker, and W. C. Dyer quickly brought in a verdict,

Coroner's Inquest:
"State of Colorado County of Boulder

"An inquisition holden at Lyons in Boulder County State of Colorado on the 26th & 27th day of Dec A D 1892 before J. G. Trezise Coroner of Said County upon the body of John Kearney. There lying dead by the Jurors whose names are hereto subscribed the said jurors upon there (sic) oaths do say that the said John Kearney came to his death at 10:40 O'clock A. M. on the 26th day of Dec A D 1892 as the result of a gun shot wound the said gun being a revolver loaded with powder and ball and fired by Wm. Watt on the 21st day of December 1892 in Charles Bradford's Saloon at said Lyons in Boulder Co, Colo. at about 8:30 O'clock A M we further find that the said shooting of said John Kearney by said Wm. Watt was felonious.

In testimony whereof the said jurors have here unto set there hands the day and year aforesaid L[eonard] H Dieterich, Thos A. Hearn, M. [Nicholas?] Frank, William Sites, E. B. Meeker, W. C. Dyer. Attest J. G. Trezise, Coroner of Boulder County."

Watt was moved to Boulder, where William Ryan filed as the major complaining witness. The judge denied bail and he was placed in jail. The preliminary hearing was held January 7 and 8, 1893. On the first day, Judge Adams called William Ryan, Dr. Gammon, and Ferdinand (Fred) Billings to testify. The event was heavily attended by Lyons residents, half took the side of the deceased, the other half witnessed for the defense. The case was the ongoing topic of conversation in Boulder. This was the most important criminal case that anyone could remember being tried in the county.

Reporters for several local newspapers were interested in life in a Lyons saloon, reporting that many of the witnesses had said that they spent all of their time drinking, both day and night, in the town's saloons. When they got tired and too drunk to function, they would simply sleep on the floor. The prosecuting attorneys tried to determine, when Lyons' residents considered a fellow intoxicated. One witness testified that shooting hot whiskies with chasers continuously of a day and night could "make a man tolerably drunk." Interest in the case, which was much like a soap opera to the citizens of Boulder County, was so intense that one item on the front page reported that Bill Thorne of Lyons drove into Boulder on the thirteenth of January to visit Bill in his cell.

The William C. Watt case was called to District Court on Monday, May 1, 1893. Judge Downer was on the bench. District Attorney Garrigues and Assistant District Attorney Charles M. Campbell led the prosecution. The Honorable Lafe Pence, H. M. Minor of Longmont and Thomas E. Davison of Denver were counsel for the defense. With his wife by his side, Bill was cool, but serious as he watched the jury selection. Forty challenges were made during that day. It became difficult to find a full jury of his peers. One news article stated, "Frequently it is said, men are so bitter in their hostility toward saloons and drinking and games of chance that they permit these prejudices to overcome the evidence." By 3 o'clock the next afternoon Clerk Wilder swore in Foreman Timothy O'Connor and jurors Edward Berryman, Elias Eby, G. W. Blaine, Henry Meyring, Z. Bradfield, C. L. Wood, W. M. Findlay, W. H. Barber, R. A. Duncan, J. F. Hedman, and W. B. Rea.

During the trial, Bill's attorneys attempted to prove that his drunkenness was habitual and led to blackouts; therefore, he was not responsible for what he did. They equated his condition to insanity. Witnesses called for the defense were Major Small, Fred Bucherdee, Charles A. Bradford, Lee Battles, and banker E. E. Norton all of Lyons. Also called to the stand were C.

F. Miller of Longmont, W. A. Welch, the defendant's partner from Lafayette John R. Durbin, as well as other unnamed residents of Lyons. The men attested to Bill's good and honest character.

For the prosecution, Mrs. Roberts stated that Watt had a reputation for being bad and that he had, "a quarrelsome disposition." Dr. Stradley of Longmont testified that he had told Watt that he must stop drinking or he would soon experience delirium tremors. He further warned that unless he quit drinking, "he would commit suicide, kill his wife or a friend or do some desperate act." The prosecution countered with the charge of practicing medicine without a license brought against Dr. D. N. Stradley by E. L. Graham earlier in December. The defense countered that just before Christmas, Judge Robinson had discharged the case, declaring that since the good doctor was a graduate of the Curtis Physio-Medical Institute at Marion, Indiana and held a diploma and that it "was a piece of spite work by a Longmont man." Next, the prosecution placed into evidence an earlier indictment against William Watt and Charles Bradford for malicious mischief in breaking a window and shooting out the lights in May's saloon. They further presented evidence that the defendant was frequently drunk and would remain drunk on most occasions. In fact, if he had a few dollars in his pocket, he would set up drinks for everyone in the bar, thus his large contingency of friends in the courtroom.

Thirty-eight year old Bill Watt turned out to be his own worse enemy. He claimed that he had been cut up and on the wrong end of fights enough times that he wasn't taking any chances with his old friend John Kearney. "I've been cut and slashed enough in this town." Frank Wilson had stabbed him under the ribs after being asked to pay a saloon bill. Supposedly the other fellow stabbed him just out of sheer meanness. Bill had carried the Smith & Wesson since, "he had gone into the gambling business at Lafayette and bought [the] revolver to protect his money." He further testified that he was in Lyons Tuesday because it was payday and the 'boys' would have money.

Closing statements by both sides were reported as "quite eloquent and thorough." The verdict was reached quickly. Foreman Timothy O'Connor, "We the jury, find the defendant, William C. Watt, guilty of voluntary manslaughter." Sentencing would be from one to eight years at the discretion of the court. The judge set the sentence of eight years in prison to be served in the State Prison at Canon City.

Scattered evidence indicates that Watt died of insanity at the State Prison in Canon City. His wife continued to live in Lyons. She died on Thanksgiving morning 1904 and was buried in the Lyons Cemetery. The obituary declared that, "Mrs. Emma Watt was one of the old-time and respected residents of Lyons, died at her home on South Fifth Avenue" She is buried in the Lyons Cemetery in an unrecorded lot.

"Wants Settlement of Old Claim"

"In 1895 Mrs. W. C. Watt, now deceased broke her hip by falling in front of the Laycook Store on Main Street and was awarded $600 by the court. The judgment has now been affirmed on appeal, and William Grant, her son and heir, asked the town board at their last meeting, through his attorneys, for an offer in settlement. Interest has increased the original claim to about $1100. The matter was referred to the town board's judiciary committee."

—*The Old Lyons Recorder, July 17, 1913.*

Soiled Doves

Most of the mining towns of the west had their "Ladies of the Night." The body houses of Denver were known throughout the country. The larger houses ranged in size from small residential homes to large, elegant pleasure palaces. The Row, Larimer Street in Denver, was known for its House of Mirrors, a three-story business with several drawing rooms, a ballroom, fine kitchens, bedrooms upstairs, servants, and a permanently employed piano player. Cribs were single frame buildings with a bedroom, a door and one window on the street side, often a kitchen-living room was located in the rear of the building. In "the outback" was the necessary room. Independent young girls and women, who built up their own clientele, operated the different houses. Books about the brothels in Aspen, Central City, George Town, and Telluride can be found in any bookstore.

Denver madams were not shrinking violets, but well-known entrepreneurs: Jennie Rogers, Mattie Silks, Rosa Lee, Eva Lewis, Miss Minnie Hall, and Lizzie Preston. In the summer months, Mattie would leave her lovely home in Denver, take a large tent, and several of her girls up to Jimtown [Jamestown]. This was a common business practice for many of the summer-run mining and quarrying camps.

Smaller communities were often inclined to hide the fact that there was a brothel or a local room housed by a Half-Life Lady. Lyons was one such town wishing to maintain the charm of its fine village, often mentioning in the local newspaper how weeks had gone by when there were no unfortunate incidences in town nor in the quarries. However, Lyons was a quarry town and it is difficult for me to believe that this particular business did not exist. There are newspaper reports of men who took the train to Denver for a weekend of gambling and a stop over at one or another of the Row establishments. But I am sure that not every quarry man took the long train ride nor could he afford to do so each week.

An 1891 article in the *Long's Peak Rustler*, Lyons, Colorado tells the story of a fire, "in the large house across the creek." The blaze began in the kitchen and in a short time there was nothing left of the structure. The *Rustler* claimed not to know the ownership of the house only that there was no fire insurance.

"It was occupied by a lot of women from Denver. A few things only were saved. Loss about $3000."

Hmmm, one tends to think that these ladies from Denver were definitely here on business.

Bob Scanlon, son of Michael Scanlon, Lyons pioneer and grocery store owner, was quoted in *The Denver Post*, 1978.

"I am positive that one of the Lyons' whorehouse madams is buried in the cemetery I'd rather you wouldn't print her name. As a boy, I delivered groceries to her. After her girls left, she became a derelict. I liked her."

There is no tombstone, obituary, nor funeral home recording the life and death of the Lyons' Madam. As a pauper, this Soiled Dove would have been buried without ceremony in Potter's Field, located in the Northeast section of the Lyons Cemetery. Few of these plots have markers, those that do exist are simple rocks buried in the ground without inscription

George Murphy, a Lyons Tai Chi teacher recently told me the story of the ghost of one of the town's Daughters of Joy upstairs of what is now the South St. Vrain Anglers'. The young woman was petite and shrouded in a floating blue dress. She was said to be a friendly spirit roaming the hallways, drifting from room to room. One evening at a session of the Healing Arts Group, which met upstairs, the participants noticed that the spirit was gone. George said he missed her gentle wanderings and easy presence. There remained only a feeling of emptiness. A feeling I am sure experienced by many of the Soiled Doves who worked the camps, the mines, and the quarries of the West.

Doctors and Undertakers

Dr. O. M. Burhans
August 1845–September 7, 1910

D r. Burhans was born in New York. He married Emma Daniels in 1871. By 1890 they moved to Lyons so that he could practice medicine in the new quarry town. His office was located in the south room of the Western House at the east end of Main Street, according to a February 19, 1897 news advertisement. Dr. Burhans was the health officer for the Town of Lyons for several years. During the years of 1906–1907 he spent time at the Cook Medical Institute in Denver. He was a member of the Star of Jupiter Lodge. Dr. Burhans is buried in the Lyons Cemetery.

Dr. E. S. Crona
December 28, 1838–March 2, 1919

Dr. E. S. Crona was born in Smoland, Sweden. He attended medical school in Stockholm, Sweden and Belvean, New York. His training was in both medicine and pharmacy. He came to America in 1884 and arrived in Lyons in 1888.

Dr. Crona married Eva R. Graham in Denver on June 25, 1901. She became her husband's assistance in running the Long's Peak Drug Store as well as his medical-pharmacy practice.

The back entrance to the Crona Drug Store building. Eva R. Graham Crona and Dr. E. S. Crona. Courtesy of the Lyons Redstone Museum, Lyons, Colorado.

Dr. Crona owned an interest in the Mercurious Copper Mine two miles up the St. Vrain River. In 1907, one of his miners, John Atkinson died from the bad air that was trapped in the mine. Soon after, he sold his shares. Like many other residents of Lyons, the doctor spent a good portion of his time searching for gold, copper, and other methods for a quick dollar. After he sold his drug store, Dr. Crona bought a controlling interest in Crona Heights, south of Meadow Park, where he attempted quarrying. He also owned a ranch at Antelope Park.

The good doctor was described, "as a man deep in mind, quiet in disposition, and always ready to help a friend." He passed away in March of 1919. His funeral was at the Congregational Church in Lyons. Burial was in the Longmont Cemetery.

Dr. W. D. Matthews
(Dates Unknown)

According to the Colorado Business Directories for 1891 and 1892, Dr. W. D. Matthews was listed as a Lyons physician. He, his wife Sadie, and their son Rhodie joined the First Congregational Church in 1892. In the late 1880s, Dr. Matthews built the Mountain View Hotel on 4th and Seward Street in Lyons as a sanitarium. Mrs. Matthews taught at the Lyons school.

Dr. George W. Gammon
April 22, 1844–February 13, 1908

According to a newspaper report, Dr. Gammon practiced in Lyons during 1881.

"Drs. Mathews, Crona, and Gammon were gathered together to help fight, "The Grippe" —February, 1881.

He operated a drug store in town as well as his medical practice. In 1900 he was appointed health officer for Lyons. His wife, Addie ran a millinery store from 1892–1904. Though Dr. Gammon was one of eight, he and his wife did not have any children.

Robert Benjamin Ground
1843–1920

The Grounds had a son, R. E. and a daughter, Mrs. E. E. Norton. R. B. served on the Lyons Board of Trustees from 1892 to 1894. He was the town treasurer from 1897 to 1900.

Along with their undertaking business, father and son were involved in a variety of other enterprises. R. B. Ground and Son Feed, Flour and Undertaking Business was located on Main

Street. At the same location, they also operated the Lyons Mercantile and Lumber Company from 1893–1897. R. E. Ground, the son, continued in the undertaking business for many years.

Albert Edward Howe
1868–1944

Albert Edward Howe was born in St. John Province, New Brunswick the youngest of eight children. His father died when he was a year old, followed by his mother when A. E. was only seven years old. He moved to Boston, Massachusetts to find employment in his uncle's furniture business, but when twenty-one years old he came to Colorado and became a rancher.

The Howe Ranch was located on the North St. Vrain River. The vegetables he raised were brought to town by horse and buggy. During the winter he cut large blocks of ice from the surrounding rivers and lakes to sell in the summer. It is assumed that he stored the ice blocks in the same way most of the other entrepreneurs did, with sawdust. He married Lura Dean McFadden on March 3, 1897 at the Old Stone Church in Lyons. Five of their eight children were born in Lyons.

In addition to his ranch, a short distance outside of Lyons in the shadow of Steamboat Mountain, Howe owned a group of cottages available as summer rentals. The St. Vrain Cabins were a popular summer retreat.

Albert Howe's political career began in Lyons. He was a member of the local school board, served several terms on the Lyons Town Council, and in 1904 and 1906 became the deputy county assessor for two consecutive terms as a Republican.

The Department of the Interior, U. S. Land Office at Denver on February 4, 1910 published the following notice of Howe's homestead filing.

> "Albert E. Howe of Boulder, Colorado on March 19, 1903 made homestead entry No. 21,469 for the East one half of the East one half Section 9, Township 3N, Range 71W. Filed a notice of intention to make a five-year proof to establish claim to the land"
>
> Claimant witnesses: J. B. Hall, Wm. A. Welch, B. J. Blair, C. B. Hall, all of Lyons, Colorado."

Sanitariums
Lyons Second Major
Business

"Do not delay coming to this great winter resort of con-
sumptives. If the Hotels and Sanitariums are full, the citizens will provide you with snug tents and good beds.
Warm houses here are a superfluity. Delay is death. Come
to this earthly paradise where blizzards are unknown,
where lungs grow out on pine stumps, and old pipe stems
turn into bronchial tubes."

—*The Old Lyons Recorder.*

As Edward S. Lyon had done, many others came to the mountains and foothills of Colorado on the advise of their doctors.
The clean, cool air of the high plains and foothills, sunlight, good
rich food, rest, and high altitude was thought to provide a cure
for most respiratory diseases, especially pulmonary tuberculosis (TB).

Hygiene, Colorado derives its name from the Hygiene
Home. It was a large and well-appointed sanitarium laid out in
the valley southeast of Lyons by Jacob S. Flory. Business was
very successful, however, the numbers of "seekers of the cure"
coming from the east exceeded the capacity of the house.

The people of Lyons began to open their homes to individual travelers seeking the healthful environment for their respiratory problems. Home care was not adequate to help combat this dreaded disease. Short obituaries running in the Lyons newspapers give testimony to some of these poor souls, who were then buried in the Lyons Cemetery:

"Ben Durr came to Lyons in early December of 1890 as so many others to get relief from the dreaded tuberculosis. To help the time pass and with the help of 20 businessmen from town, he raised $200 to start *The Long's Peak Rustler* newspaper for Lyons. The office was on the second floor of the Scanlon and Brice Mercantile Store. He died of consumption in 1894.

Mrs. Esther Emelia Lahti was a daughter of Mr. and Mrs. Fred Carlson and was born at Harney, Minnesota. She contracted tuberculosis and came here for her health. Three years ago she was married to Mr. Emil Lahti.

Thos. Y. McMorris came to Lyons about 8 weeks ago seeking relief from that terrible disease tuberculosis. But from the time he stepped from the cars he had steadily grown weaker and weaker. The deceased was 33 years

S. B. Moe died at his home in Lyons, aged nearly 48 years, of tuberculosis.

Virgil Wier, aged 28 years, died at the residence of J. B. Howard in Chimney Hollow. Death was caused by tuberculosis. Deceased came here eighteen months ago, but was unable to make recovery from the disease. Most of his time was spent with J. B. Howard and family.

Adolph Torchiana came to Lyons to recover from the dreaded disease. While part of the community Adolph shared his musical training learned in his homeland of Germany. He gave private lessons on the piano and organ, as well as providing the music for church and school programs. His particular favorites were Beethoven and Mendelssohn. Never recovering from consumption, he died at the home of Mr. And Mrs. Christopher Columbus Weese June 1905 at the age of 28 years."

By 1894 it was thought that consumption was conquered. A Cincinnati scientist had created what medical journals and physicians called the only cure available. Dr. Amick's treatment, unfortunately was not all it was thought to be. Patients continued their journey to the cool, clean mountain air, quiet, and good food offered by the sanitariums and resorts of Colorado.

Mountain View Hotel
The First TB Sanitarium

Soon it was realized that better accommodations and care should be provided for these travelers. Colorado had gained a reputation as the cure for any and all respiratory diseases. In the late 1800s the two-story Mountain View Hotel was built on the northeast corner of 4th and Seward, known as Nortonville in 1890s. Several newspapers claim that the hospital/hotel was located "up on the hill north of the Lyons cemetery". Whether this is the same structure or two different institutions remains unclear. The Mountain View was built of wood in the vernacular style, originally sided with clapboard, but later covered with aluminum siding. The roof was a flat lean-to. In the front of the building, ornamental wooden brackets were used to support the roof overhand. These were removed when the front porch was enclosed to expand interior footage.

The hotel served as a TB Sanitarium, as well as extra classrooms for children in grades one through four whenever there was overcrowding in the local schoolhouse. This seems a strange combination for those of us who are now aware that tuberculosis is one of the most feared communicable disease. In 1901, Charles W. Bird, a carpenter and plasterer, remodeled a room in the hotel to better accommodate these extra rooms for the school children.

In 1903 "Doc" J. W. Halliday, an engineer for the railroad, cut the building in two and moved the structure to its present site on 349 Main Street, changing the name to the Burlington Hotel.

A 1903 newspaper describes the move and renovation,

"It was cut in two and he used a horse powered winch and cable. Later that year, he installed a new heating plant, which would surely draw in tenants. The plasterers were at work refurbishing the interior of the 1/2 structure and the carpenters were put to work building a porch for future guests."

In the early 1900s the hospital became the office of Dr. Kincaid, a local family doctor, then a boarding house for the Burlington Railroad workers. Other owners have been Mr. And Mrs. Hines in 1945, O. L .& Dorothy Paxton for 25 years with Ichihinda Bloomfield as manager. The building is presently the Lyon's Den Bed & Breakfast owned by Jim and Nancy Doughtery.

Thorncroft

In the 1890s, Three miles northwest of Lyons on the old Apple Valley Road stood the Thorncroft Sanitarium. T. J. Thorne, a Lyons teacher and lawyer, along with his wife, Lillie Lyon Thorne managed the complex. The buildings were isolated and hidden from the old highway by a grove of cottonwoods allowing the patients much needed privacy. Porches were located on two-sides of the main structure having room for thirty-five guests to enjoy the healing, fresh air around the clock. After Mr. Thorne died in 1904, Lillie continued to operate the sanitarium.

In 1917 after Lillie married Austin Smith, a camp worker, the name was changed to Bella Vista. The emphasis of their business changed from sanitarium to a "cottage camp" for tourists.

Unfortunately, after years of serving the many ill patients at Thorncroft, Lillie Thorne Smith succumbed to the dreaded disease.

Thomas J. Thorne. Courtesy of the Lyons Redstone Museum, Lyons, Colorado.

Lillie Lyon Thorne. Courtesy of the Lyons Redstone Museum, Lyons, Colorado.

T. J. Thorne
May 13, 1857– March 11, 1904

Thomas J. Thorne came to Colorado in 1882 when he was 25 years old another victim of tuberculosis. While teaching the children of Lyons, he met Lillie Lyon and fell in love with the16-year-old student. He and Lillie were married after she graduated in 1884. They had two sons. Their granddaughters, Karen Hakonson and Luella Linquest live in Longmont, Colorado.

Although Thomas' occupation was that of teacher, his avocation was the law. In 1903 he received his law degree, was accepted to the Bar, and "hung up his shingle" in Lyons. Teaching, however, proved to be a much more secure income and he accepted a position in the Fort Collins school system.

The entrepreneurial bug was part of the life of Thomas similar to that of his father-in-law, Edward S. Lyon. At one time he ran a general store under his own name; he built a two-story building on the north side of Main Street, which later was purchased by Lavridson; and he founded Thorncroft for those persons suffering from TB and other respiratory diseases.

Welch Resort

President Benjamin Harrison signed the original deed for the 1889 homestead of Jabez P. Billings. On part of his land, Jabez founded the famous Camp Billings across the road from where the Welch Resort would be built. Men from all over the country were drawn to the rustic camp, its seclusion, excellent hunting and fishing, and the companionship of an unspoiled land. He had holdings in Sections 11 recorded June 25, 1889; Sec.14 recorded June 25, 1889; Sec. 10 August 24, 1892; and Sec. 15 recorded August 24, 1892 in township 3 North, Range 71 between Lyons and Pinewood Springs.

In 1893 the Welch Resort was built as a group of cottages to house the many TB patients being sent from Denver to Lyons by Dr. Sherman D. Bonney. To manage the increasing need for more rooms, the resort was expanded in 1896 and 1897. The Welch's private quarters, which burned down in 1946, were located in the main lodge which contained a large kitchen, the dining room, a lovely fireplace, and several rooms. Other buildings on the property included an icehouse, a coach house large enough for three coaches, a three-story barn for milk cows and the horses with hay storage on the top level. Surrounding these buildings were the cabins, many with screened-in porches so the patients could enjoy the healthy mountain air both day and night. "Uncle Tom's Cottage," the only remaining guest house, has a unique log architecture with seven interior rooms and seven doors leading into the dining room. It is assumed that the other cottages were built in a similar style.

In 1901 an octagonal building was erected on the property to be used as a casino with billiards, poolrooms, and a large dancing pavilion. The public was often welcome to share in the many dances that were held there. A few of the wealthier clients held private parties in the facilities. At this time there were thirty-six boarders, the largest number since the resort had opened.

The Kelso Lodge was built in 1906 for the wealthy Dietz Family of St. Louis. The two-story log structure had an overextended porch. The interior contained a central living room with a 20-foot ceiling and large fireplace with seven bedrooms each having its own washbasin and an outside entrance, a special treat for those in the money. A Dietz son had tuberculosis. Welch installed a shower imported from Switzerland with 3-heads and a temperature control unit which surrounded the child with a 'healing' steam. Although each of the living quarters on the property was tastefully decorated, this building was the most elaborate and well appointed.

Extensive landscaping was added to enhance the already beautiful surroundings. A large orchard contained a fully stocked trout pond. Fishing was allowed in the pond, as well as in the St. Vrain River. Billy irrigated his orchard and lawns using a water system of his own invention. He also had his own sawmill run by a steam engine he improved, allowing him to construct all the buildings on the property with native lumber.

The lodge west of Shelly's Cottages, was once owned by Don and Marilyn Kauffman. In 2000, Ed Kumpf and Denise Berg opened the Kumpfenberg Manor in the 100+ year old home as a short of long term guest house. There brochure reads:

"Teddy Roosevelt and Al Capone loved it. Your family will too."

William "Billy" A. Welch
1861–1938

William A. Welch was born in 1861 to Aristides and Henrietta Welch in Pennsylvania. Aristides owned the Erdenheim Stock Farm, which he established in the early 1860s. His horses were internationally renowned having won at Ascot, the Kentucky Derby, the Prekness, and the Belmont Stakes. In 1890, Louis Kittson purchased the country estate. "In December 2001, the Whitemarsh Township Residents Association signed an historic Agreement that sets in place the legal and organizational structures that will make possible the preservation of a large portion of Erdenheim Farm."

Billy is listed in the 1880 National Census as living with his father, Aristides and brother, Robert. He was 18 and a Pennsylvania Law Student. When he moved to Lyons from Denver, he used his $500 monthly allowance to buy property up the North St. Vrain. By the time he was finished he owned approximately 2000 acres with the resort and additional property near Big Elk Meadows.

The obituary for William A. Welch appeared in the *Boulder Daily Camera*, May 28, 1938 stating that he had died May 27, 1938 at a hospital in Denver. He was 77 years old, "having lived 50 of his years in Lyons." It was reported that Sarah E., his wife had died two years previously.

I telephoned the Olinger Crown Hill Cemetery in Denver. Their records show that Sarah Elizabeth Welch was buried on July 28, 1936; and William A. Welch was buried on May 31, 1938.

Carvell Summer Resort

In 1894 Lewis Albert Carvell and his eldest son, Arthur traveled to Lyons, Colorado where they found employment as a carpenters at the Welch Resort. April of that year Lewis applied for citizenship papers in order to be able to take advantage of the Homestead Act. He purchased land one-half mile downstream from the Welch Resort to build his own sanitarium/resort. After completion of the main building, the resort had twenty rooms ready for patients. Emma, his wife and her children ran the sanitarium, while Lewis continued as a carpenter in Lyons and later for F. O. Stanley in Estes Park. The resort was in continuous operation until 1920.

Lewis Albert Carvell
August 6, 1864–September 10, 1953

Lewis Albert Carvell was born in Ireland. He moved to St. Johns, New Brunswick, where he met and married Emma Capson, daughter of the widow, Jane Capson. One of their sons, Donald married Mildred Kincaid.

When Emma died in 1924, Lewis gave up his job at the power plant in Estes Park. He sold his Lyons property, The Carvell Summer Resort and married Katherine Urban Epley.

TB is contracted from an infected person. It is air borne only from a sneeze or cough. However, the disease in spittle from a carrier or infected person can last up to several hours on a street or sidewalk. Because of this, in early Colorado History, spitting was considered a jailable offense and quarantine laws were enacted.

With the introduction of antibiotics and early detection there was a decline in pulmonary tuberculosis by 1940. A new outbreak occurred in 1992 among AIDS patients and with the large influx of Third World Immigrants. Doctors discovered that the once dormant strains had become more resistant to accepted treatments. Recent pressure has been put on the State Legislature to tighten Colorado quarantine laws for the 21st Century and chemical companies are working on upgrading antibiotics.

Too Much Water
The Floods of 1894
and The Early 1900s

Sudden torrential rains, a nonporous soil, and heavy snow melt flows were a constant danger to the towns in the foothills and mountains. Earthen dams built to protect the villages below could not withstand the full force of Mother Nature.

On a Wednesday morning heavy rains from the east fell on Longmont. The storm traveled west over Lyons and settled at the headwaters of the St. Vrain River. By afternoon the entire valley from the railroad tracks over a mile to the south was under several feet of water cutting off telegraph communication. Boulder was flooded from the rush of water roaring down Boulder Canyon. To the north, Loveland suffered great losses from the rage of the swollen Big Thompson.

As he rode out on horseback to inspect the aftermath of the fury of the St. Vrain River, Sheriff Dyer reported the details of the flood of May 31, 1894 and its aftermath in Lyons. "It was water, water everywhere," he lamented. Overlooking the St. Vrain Valley the Sheriff saw a lake three miles wide formed from the floodwaters flowing into Longmont. The lower part of Lyons was washed away. Twenty houses laid in ruin. The Estes Park toll road and Sheriff Dyer's privately owned toll road were both destroyed. Not one road had survived within the district.

Reported losses from the flood were extensive: W. H. Hubbell, livery barn, granary, and feed $3,500; J. S. John's, residence and furniture, $1,000; F. P. Kerr, residence and furniture, $1,000; and the E. E. Dubrise house, $600. A number of other homes and buildings were destroyed or damaged from the water. Expansion bridges were lost and the damage to the new fire system required thousands of dollars to repair. Days after the flood, several residences could be seen teetering on the bank of the river soon to disappear as so many had before them.

After the storm, many of the Lyons residents moved to the north side of town. Several men with a team of horses pulling a wagon load of goods tried to cross the St. Vrain at Meadow Park. The three men on board were saved; however the horses, wagon and household materials were lost. The current was so intense in the Park that people were being pulled across the water with ropes.

During the time of clean up, a large population of rats plagued the town and the health of the residents.

By the end of June the B & M railroad repair work crews were still trying to salvage the line from Longmont to Lyons. The flood had washed away one and one-half miles of track affecting Montgomery, the Coal Creek Bridge, and the switch at Standard Mills. Over eighty men were hired to work on the tracks. A few did benefit from the catastrophe, Fred Delfer of Longmont held the contract for 100 pounds of fresh meat to be sent to the rail camp each day.

Seven years later on September 11, 1901, another cloudburst, this time over Allenspark, caused a four-foot rise in the North St. Vrain. The Lyons' and Longmont's Water Systems were unusable. There were mudslides in the South Fork and Big Thompson Canyons. Several bridges were damaged. The Fourth Avenue Bridge in Lyons was washed away by debris swept along by the tremendous currents of the St. Vrain River. The bridges at Thorncroft Sanitarium, the private bridge at the Welch Resort, and the Morrisey Gulch Bridge were washed away. Reports were that the Sites and Buell Bridge cost $600 to repair.

On the William Billings ranch located on the North St. Vrain the destruction was the most severe. Water roared through the ranch house moving the building approximately sixteen inches off its foundation. The family furnishings were swept out of doors and windows. One entire side of the house was destroyed. When a rescue team arrived at the ranch, Mrs. Billings and her two children were found dazed from shock and exposure

Only two years later, in 1903 another flood ravaged the area. Bridges, riverbanks, and homes were again damaged or destroyed. The only good thing that came out of this particular disaster was the discovery of a "sizable" gold nugget found by the crew repairing the South Fork Bridge.

Frequent heavy rains upon a nonporous soil continues to plaque the foothills and valleys of Boulder County. Even with construction of modern damns, flooding remains a common occurrence throughout the area.

St Vrain Lodge No. 102 Independent Order of Odd Fellows

A t least one lodge of the Independent Order of Odd Fellows could be found across the nation in every town and city, no matter how small or large. Men gathered together in their secret societies for fellowship and to perform "good works" for their neighborhoods, towns, and cities.

The St. Vrain Lodge No. 102 I. O. O. F. in Lyons was instituted October 14, 1892. There were five charter members: Leonard H. Dieterich, W. O. Dyer, Jeremiah C. Wamsley, Daniel W. Slaughter, and C. W. Thomas. On the same day, nineteen new members were initiated into the group: Gottlob (Gotlieb) Frederick Aldinger, J. B. Anderson, Fred B. Buchardee, J. D. Cenduots, Dr. E. S. Crona, Thomas Dorman, James R. Dutso, E. H. Erikson, Nicolas Frank, John Haldine, William Hubbell, Edward S. Lyon, L. Y. McHomes, Charles A. McLaren, E. R. Meeker, Svur Mor (Sverre Moe?), Jacob Sahnell, John S. Smith, and H. W. Worey.

The membership grew quickly. A few recognizable names included: George Billings, Jabez P. Billings, Matthew Blair, Jacob Blubaugh, Frank M. Brackett, Harry Brown, George Cheney, John Cheney, J. R. Cunningham, U. G. Gilger, John B. Hall, James Lowe, Leonard C. Lyon, Ed McCall, Frank R. Montgomery, Robert B. Montgomery, Arthur Ohline, Volney H. Rowley, Charles Rundell, and Samuel Service.

The sister Rebekah Lodge, Excelsior Rebekah Lodge No. 30 was also consititued in October of 1892. Unfortunately, I do not have a list of charter members, but assume that the membership was comprised of the wives of the men of Lodge 102.

121

Birth of a Quarry Town

After the turn of the Century the Lyons Odd Fellows purchased a corner building on 4th and Main Street. The group met
on the ground floor until 1907 when a second floor was added.
Years later, as membership expanded, the Lodge purchased the
building next door adding a clubroom, kitchen, and diningroom.
November 6, 1967, a fire started in the durg store directily
to the west of the lodge hall. Traveling across the roof, the fire
consumed the Odd Fellows Hall completely destroying the building and everything inside. A new hall was dedicated on December 10, 1972.

—From an unpublished paper written by Charles E. Ramey.
—*See Appendix V, page 317, "Societies in Town."*

OF ROADS
AND RAILS

Lyons to Estes Park Stage Coach on the North St. Vrain Road. From the collection of the Estes Park Museum, Estes Park, Colorado.

Stage Coach Travel

During the 1800s stage coach travel was a busy industry in and around Lyons. An excellent account of early transportation from Lyons into Estes Park can be found in a paper written by Lucille "Perry" James. In 1878 Gilbert and Hubbell operated a Concord stage pulled by four horses out of Longmont. The run up the canyon was about 40 miles with a mid-way point at mile twenty-three. Along the way passengers were be unloaded to help heave and push the coach out of deep holes in the road, or over sharp jutting rocks, or through mud and ruts left by heavy rains. Passengers would once again get off the stage half way up the canyon for a change of horses, a welcome occurrence after hours of bouncing in a wagon. The exchange would often take longer than necessary since the horses were usually off grazing, not waiting at the stage stop as Hollywood portrays. In 1883, a new road was built from Lyons to Estes Park over Rowell Hill, by the Little Thompson, and through Moose Park. The shortened route benefited the many passengers who would debark the train at the Lyons Depot and transfer to the stage for their day long trip up the canyon.

In 1888 William N. Hubbell and his family settled in Lyons. During this time he also bought out Mr. Gilbert's interests and formed the Longmont-Estes Park Stage Line. Hubbell had traveled by covered wagon from Minnesota to Colorado in the 1870s.

Two stage lines ran daily, The Hubbell line, which went as far as the Elkhorn Lodge in Estes Park and the Richards & Edwards mail stage, formerly known as the Sprague Line. Abner Sprague lived in Hidden Valley and Estes Park. Sprague owned sawmills, a hotel, and a ranch. In 1907 he was the surveyor for the new Lyons Road.

Another stage line owned by Mr. Cantwell advanced his business by using an 8-horse team and a better coach. Pictures at the Estes Park Museum show that open horse-drawn carriages were used in the summer months to transport passengers. Harry Tallman, who ran a livery business in Lyons, also operated stage lines up the St. Vrain Canyon to Estes Park. Franklin Hornbaker was one of the stage coach drivers between Lyons and Estes Park. He lived at the foot of Mt. Meeker.

One traveler from Denver to Estes Park described his journey in Anne Morrison Arnold's book. *Steads Ranch and Hotel: Echoes Within the Moraines, p3.* After riding the Burlington train from Denver, the travelers were transferred to the spur that took them to Lyons.

> "Arriving at dusk, they rested overnight at the Burlington 11-room Hotel, eagerly awaiting the stage to Estes Park. The 'stage' was a farm wagon with seats, and the canvas covering came down so low it blocked the views." The disgruntled tourist said after many hours they finally arrive in Estes.

The route over the toll road followed the St. Vrain River past the Griff Evans Stage Stop west to the Little Thompson Creek. From there they traveled up Muggins Gulch and through Estes Park, crossing northwest of Moraine Park and into North Park. The stage passed by old Rocky Mountain Jim's cabin, the lord and master of Muggins Gulch. This did not please old Jim Nugent, who would frequently shout at the passengers, "in a manner not fit for women to hear and often would brandish about his rifle in exasperation at the intrusion of civilization."

James Archie, who drove the stage to Estes Park from the Lyons railroad station, swore that going down the Arbuckle, he had to tie his passengers down with a rope. That was when the road to Estes Park followed the road up through Antelope Park, then continued north and down the Arbuckle to the Creek, "which it crossed at Willie Billings silo a mile or so above Welch's." According to Mr. Billings, it was not even a road, just a trail up to the 940 acre Arbuckle Resort. The Arbuckle was a popular resort owned by Frank P. Arbuckle's widow located on what is now the Longmont Dam Road. She held 940 acres of

Lilliam and William N. Hubbell, owners and operators of the Lyons Estes Park Stage Line. Courtesy of the Lyons Redstone Museum, Lyons, Colorado.

Hubbell Stage Coach. Courtesy of the Lyons Redstone Museum, Lyons, Colorado.

land giving the eastern tourist a taste of the old west. The white frame house sat where the road met the St. Vrain River a mile or two before the dam.

The Estes Park trail, also known as Blue Mountain Road, lead off Highway 36 to the North and into the Little Thompson area. Archie's description of the location of the stage road is much more picturesque,

> "...after that, a road leading up a Gulch to the north, opposite a house on the south side of the St. Vrain which, at the present time (1954) sit half furnished, and has all summer, at least. There is a farmhouse of sorts at the beginning of the Gulch, but practically no visible road up the Gulch can be discerned. It was this road which included the famous Rowell Hill."

Rowell Hill was also known as Roll Over Hill. There was a 2,200 foot gain in slightly more than two miles stressing both horses and men. The treacherous road claimed one life as late as 1903, when once again the stage turned over.

James Archie hauling flooring for the Stanley Hotel in Estes Park, circra 1908. Courtesy of the Lyons Redstone Museum, Lyons, Colorado.

The Railroad

In 1882 the Denver, Utah and Pacific Railroad was first built to service the Mitchell coal banks twenty-three miles from Denver. By 1884 the line was extended to Longmont, Colorado to handle agricultural crops. Within the year, nine more miles of track was laid heading up from Longmont to the quarry town of Lyons. This track sounded the death knell for the little community of Pella, which was cut off from the main rail line.

A railroad station was erected in 1884 east of the junction of Highway 7 on Section 18 SE 1/2, Township 3N, Range 70W to service the new stop. On August 28, 1885, Superintendent Foutz and Edward S. Lyon of Lyons brought together a group of newspaper editors from around the state for a ride in the Superintendent's special car. The full-day trip included a visit to the Lyons quarries and a dinner "fit for a king" prepared by Mrs. Lyon and her daughter. The party consisted of D. P. Kingsley, editor of the *Grand Junction News*; Robert Gauss, assistant editor of the *Denver Tribune-Republican*; R. J. Valkenburg of the *Erie-Canfield Independent*, A. M. Hubert, of the *Longmont Press*, and H. L. Hayward, editor of the *Longmont Ledger*. On September 26, 1885 the extension of the Denver, Utah and Pacific Railroad from Longmont to Lyons was completed. The newspapermen wrote glowing accounts, "We congratulate the Lyons Town Company on their excellent prospects"

According to the original Land Patent Records the UP RR Co. purchased property from 1883–1897 in Sections 1, 3, 5, 7, 9, 11, 13, 15, 17, 21, 25, 27, 31, 33, Ranges 69 & 70, Townships 1S, 3N, 1N, & 2N. The Denver, Utah and Pacific Railroad merged with the Chicago, Burlington & Quincy, then the Colorado & Southern, and finally the Burlington Northern.

129

From town, three branch lines were built to carry sandstone from the quarries to the main line: the Lyons Tower Stone, the Stone Mountain, and the Noland Land and Transfer railroads. Sometime around 1890, the entire line including the branch lines were converted from narrow gauge to standard gauge track. About this same time the Noland Land and Transfer Company with offices in Longmont purchased the spur from Lyons to Noland. They extended the rail north, west, and back again to the south into the large quarries across the rails west of Tower [Noland]. The line was renamed the Stone Mountain Railroad. Later, two additional spurs were added to pick up loads from the Noland and the Beech Hill quarries. The trains would make the turn around at Beech Hill for the trip back down the mountain.

The privately owned Stone Mountain Railroad was unique with its switchback on the southern half of the line between Lyons and Noland. The Z-shaped zigzag was built on the west-facing hill to accommodate the climb. The first engines were low-powered rod-driven steam engines and needed an acceptable grade in which to run. Michael Rowe describes the trip, "The train would run off the end of the tail track on the lower level, where it was stopped. A switch would be closed behind the train, and the train would back up into the connecting link of track, climbing out of the valley. When the train got to the end of this connecting link, the train would be stopped, another switch would be thrown, and the train would start off again"

In December of 1890, Stone Mountain Railroad ordered one of the new Shay-type geared locomotives under patent in June 1881 by a Michigan logger Ephraim Shay. It was developed to handle the rough and uneven tracks of the logging beds, as well as the steep grades and sharp curves found in the wooded areas of Michigan. The Shay's top speed when carrying heavy loads up a 14% grade was 8-10 m.p.h.. The boiler was offset to one side of the frame and attached to the frame were three vertical cylinders that in turn rotated a crankshaft mounted just above the wheels. The crankshaft turned the horizontal driveline connecting the bevel gears mounted on each axle. In 1905, a second and larger locomotive was purchased. It had 32" drive wheels and 11" x 12" cylinders with a steam pressure up to 200 p.s.i.

In January of 1891 the railroad company finally gave in to the powers of Lyons and constructed a crossing at the intersection of Second Avenue and Evans Street. The trains would sit at the intersection for hours while being weighed or hooking cars for the trip to the quarries stopping all pedestrian and wagon traffic. *Further information can be found in "Noland, Quarry Town to Ghost Town, p. 153."*

About this same time the Burlington people negotiated the purchase of the Meadow Park property, as well as the quarter section surrounding the land. The park was intended to be used by tourists and rail travelers for a quiet rest and picnics. This was the end of a community of tent dwellers that had lived in the park since the beginning of the quarry boom. Meadow Park is still used as a quiet resting stop and picnic area by travelers on their way to Estes Park.

A passenger train pulled by the Shay Engine at the Lyons Depot, late 1890s. Dad Fuller, second from left and Joe Flynn, third from left. The names of the other men are unknown. Courtesy of the Lyons Redstone Museum, Lyons, Colorado.

Time Table for May 22, 1901

<u>Arrives Daily, Except Sunday</u>

No. 181,	Passenger	11:20 a.m.
No. 183,	Passenger	7:20 p.m.
No. 185,	Freight with passengers	9:05 a.m.

<u>Departs Daily, Except Sunday</u>

No. 181,	Passenger	7:15 a.m.
No. 184,	Passenger	12:50 a.m.
No. 186,	Freight with passengers	10:15 a.m.

A June 25, 1899, newspaper account reported, "The morning train fromDenver arrives at Lyons just before noon, the stages for Estes Park leaving after one has had an excellent dinner at the Lyons House, a well-kept hotel, conducted by Mrs. D. D. McAlpine, wife of the genial agent of the Burlington, who is never too busy to give any information the stranger may desire to render him assistance."

In early spring 2001, while having coffee at the Kokopelli CafÈ in Lyons, John W. Ramey reminisced about the early days of the railroad in town. John fondly remembered watching the train go up past the Lyons Cemetery, located at the north end of 3rd Street, on its run up to the quarries. He said that the train would start in reverse from Meadow Park and go as fast as it could up past the cemetery. There was a slight grade there that would catch the train, if it got stuck, it could not get up the grade. Many times the engineer would have to return to the park and make another run up the hill. In the winter the railcars would slip on the icy or snow covered tracks making the trip not only dangerous, but costly to the quarry owners.

John told me that backing up the train into the quarries would keep the water stored for the steam engine away from the "dry pip" and into the front of the boiler. He told me that crown sheeting was put over the firebox in order to ensure that the box stayed dry. But even that was not a simple solution. If the firebox became too dry, the lead [saw] plug would melt. The fireman kept constant watch in order to keep the fire at the proper level to generate steam, yet not overheating the engine. "It was a hard, hot job," said John.

The last load of sandstone was brought out of the Brodie Quarry on December 19, 1941, announcing the end of railroading in Lyons. Later in 1942 during the final clean up by the railroad, John was delighted that the workmen let him make the last train trip up to the quarry. They picked up three empty cars that had been left and returned them to the depot to wait for their final destination. John W. Ramey rode the rails experiencing the end of an era of the sweet-sounding train whistles, the whooshing of the steam engines, and the chugging of the pistons as they drove the engine forward. The horse and wagon made way for the Shay Engine. Now the railway gave way to the flat-bed trucks, shifting gears as they made the steep grade up to the quarries

RUN AWAY TRAINS AND ACCIDENTS

All was not the sweet sounds of locomotives. With progress, power, and speed also came death and destruction. William Gecke, a railroad car repairman was killed August 22, 1890 in runaway train down the grade at Towers near Lyons. He was 26 years old and married

Fatal Accident
A Stone Train Dashes Wildly Down the Mountain, Killing Three Men and Maiming Others

"A terrible accident happened at Towers, near Lyons, in this county [Boulder], Friday by which three men were killed and three others badly injured. The grade to the quarry is very steep and in coming down, in some way, a stone train got beyond the control of the engineer and brakemen and dashed wildly to destruction. The crew consisted of Jas. [James] Considene, conductor; C. E. Norton, engineer; Jas. [James] Miller, fireman; Frank Paulding, brakeman; J. R. Strayer, switchman; Wm.

Gerke and Tho. [Thomas] Torgurson, car repairers. There were seven cars and one engine in the train, the cars in front going down. When the train got beyond control most of the men jumped landing on the rocks below. Norton, Torguson and Gerke were almost instantly killed. Considene, Miller and Strayer were badly cut and bruised but will recover. Paulding's clothing was caught between the stones so that he could not jump, and he escaped without a scratch. When the train reached what is known as the 'dump' six of the cars left the track and were completely wrecked, the engine and one car remaining on the track uninjured. Some of the men lived at Lyons, others at Denver, all being married, and it was a sad scene when the dead and managled bodies were brought home."

—*Boulder News*, Thursday, August 28, 1890 #44, Boulder, Colorado.

Brakeman Dies

"October 20, 1899, Harry Ritter, a Burlington brakeman, was killed when crushed between two railroad [freight] cars while switching cars near Lyons. He was about age 30 and unmarried. Coroner Trezise said an inquest was unnecessary."

—*Herald Weekly*, 25 Oct 1899:2, Boulder, Colorado
—*Boulder News*, 26 Oct 1899:8, Boulder, Colorado

Aged Lady Injured

"On Sunday, Dr. Bancroft, chief surgeon of the Gulf system, went to Lyons to visit Mrs. Bloomquist the lady injured by the north going passenger train Friday morning.

From Sheriff Dyer, the *Camera* learns that the lady is 75 years of age and lives with her daughter at Lyons.

She started out for chicken feed and walked to a farm south of NiWot, a distance of 15 miles from home."

—*The Boulder Camera* 12 Feb 1894, Boulder, Colorado.

Loose RR Cars Careen Through Town

"A sand car was used to collect dust and sand left from the rock cutting operating in the quarries. The sand was dumped on the railroad bed between the tracks. The water car was used to haul water to the quarries for drinking and domestic use in the boarding houses. These two cars came loose in the Murphy-Brodie Quarries north of Lyons (north of 5th Ave.) and careened through the town ending in Meadow Park. The cars amazingly negotiated a few tough turns managing to remain on the tracks to the end of the line."

—Interview with John W. Ramey January 9, 2001.

Death, Diphtheria, and the Railroad

Dr. Burhans was inundated with calls from parents and adults. Throat infections, fevers, and loose bowels were plaguing the townspeople. He suspected that it was something in the drinking and cooking water drawn from the St. Vrain River.

It was discovered that an employee of the B. & M. R. R., while constructing a dam for the round house, had dumped a load of manure behind the red stone rubble. Water began seeping through the dam polluting the stream. After a month or two of drinking the water, the deadly bacteria and microbes attacked the town's people, especially affecting the newborn and the elderly.

The railroad responded immediately to the emergency tearing down the dam. There were no chemical methods available for cleaning the spill in the 1890s. The citizens along the river would have to wait for the natural flowing of water to cleanse itself of the pollution.

–*The Long's Peak Rustler.* December 19, 1890, Vol. 1, No. 2, p2, Lyons, Colorado.

Telegraph Office at the Lyons Depot - Colorado Day, August 1, 1897.
Courtesy of the Lyons Redstone Museum, Lyons, Colorado.

Lyons Railroad Depot
1884–Present

Mark Boyd, a Longmont contractor is credited with building the Lyons Railroad Depot in the summer of 1885. The Colorado Historical Society lists the depot as having been erected in 1884, East of Junction at Highway 7 on Section 18, SE 1/2 Township 3N, Range 70W. It occupies lots 9, 10, 11, and 12 in Block 31 of the City of Lyons.

During these years thousands of tons of sandstone were shipped from the nearby quarries. Almost four million dollars worth of gold from both the Smuggler and Golden Age mines was also shipped from the Lyons Depot. Passenger travel supplemented this freight traffic as the Burlington and Missouri Railroad scheduled excursion trains from Denver to Lyons continuing up the South St. Vrain to Estes Park.

Several men served as station masters in Lyons: D. D. McAlpine, the first station master served from 1892 to 1900 and E. P. Sweeney continued from 1900 to 1938. Caroline Sweeney Lass, in a 1980s newspaper interview remembered growing up in Lyons and the many hours she had spent watching the trains while her father was at work. By the 1930s the rail business declined and the depot remained unoccupied for many years. In the late 1950s, James D. Kelley of Lyons purchased the depot from the Chicago-Burlington & Quincy Railroad. In 1951, the railroad once again functional, hired C. M. Ketler as station master until December 1960 when the Lyons Railroad Depot was officially closed.

In 1971, Ralph B. Arnold of Boulder entered into a contract to purchase the building and grounds. He was to pay the Jacobsen-Lyons Stone Company $2,500. Arnold found evidence that the land did not belong to the firm, but to the railroad company. The parties agreed to a price of $1,000. During the busy days of mining and quarrying, common practice was for the "company" to own the land and mineral rights with the surface being leased for building construction by second parties. The deal for the depot was completed in May 1971, however a bill of sale transfer was never filed.

Although Arnold intended to open the depot as a railroad museum, it remained empty until 1974 when a group of Lyons citizens decided to save the structure from demolition. Burlington-Northern wanted the building removed or demolished. The Town of Lyons offered Arnold $4,000 for the building in March of 1974, planning to make renovations to the building for a library. Jacobsen-Lyons Stone Company informed Arnold that he still owed the company $1,500 of their original agreement and refused to deed the property. Arnold refused all offers and the town filed for ownership in District Court October 1974. The three and one-half year dispute over legal ownership of the land was settled by an agreement drawn up by the Lyons town attorney George Pomainville. Arnold owned part of the depot tract with the other section belonging to the Burlington-Northern Railroad as part of the right-of-way along the tracks. The town of Lyons agreed to pay Jacobsen-Lyons Stone Company an additional $1,125 for the land and Arnold an additional $375 for the building.

By 1973 the Lyons Historical Society had been formed to save the depot. After several fund raisers, the group approached the town board for financial support. Mayor Vaughn Carter and Dorothy Paxton, president of the society agreed that the town would contribute a levy of 1 mil toward saving the depot. Grants were applied for and received from El Pomar Foundation of Colorado Springs. Restoration was under the direction of James and Alice Emerson.

In December of 1974, after many hours of work by volunteers, the National Park Service listed the Lyons Railroad Depot in the National Register of Historic Places. Grants were then obtained from several Colorado business foundations for the building to be converted into the Lyons Depot Library. The renovated facility was dedicated in November of 1977.

The former baggage room became a small washroom using old railroad fixtures. A stonewall still shows initials of train crew-men from the 1800s. The ticket agent's window was also retained. The exterior was enhanced with an early horse-watering trough hewn from a single block of local Colorado pink sandstone. The trough stood at the head of Main Street for many years. The original rough planking was replaced by Herb McConnell during the initial renovation.

Today the Lyons Depot Library is a busy place filled with books, periodicals, and audiovisual materials. It is owned and supported by the Town of Lyons. The library is the smallest member library of the Central Colorado Library Systems, thus giving Lyons Depot Library cardholders access to all the public libraries within the central system, including the interlibrary loan system.

Construction on the North St. Vrain Road. Courtesy of the Lyons Redstone Museum, Lyons, Colorado.

The Lyons Road

C ap Brown tells the story of when he helped move the Griff Evan's family from Lyons to Estes Park in the fall of 1871.

> "I think I mentioned the condition of the furniture as none too good at the start, but after being rescued from three turnovers and finally deposited in the little log shack that comprised the only house in Estes (the Jacob's House) it was worse."

From 1871 to 1874 there was only one road from Lyons to Estes Park. It wound up the Old Apple Valley Road next to the North St. Vrain past the John B. Hall Ranch then north up and over the famed Rowell Hill, past the Miner place, and to the Little Thompson. Following the Little Thompson, the road of sticky mud, rocks that seemed more like boulders, and potholes, sometimes was so narrow that the wagon wheels would be on the edge of a drop off. The road continued past Rocky Mountain Jim's cabin in Muggins Gulch.

Rowell Hill, partially visible from Highway 36 at the present Rock 'N River Resort north of Lyons, sent fear through most early travelers. Entire sections would wash out after a heavy rain or snowmelt. Within a short space, the vertical rise in elevation left the area nearly impassible to negotiate.

Not satisfied with the only route from the terminus of the railroad at Lyons up to his hotel in Estes Park, F. O. Stanley raised money from hotel owners in Estes Park, businessmen in Lyons and Denver, as well as officials of the Chicago, Burlington and Quincy Railroad. He hired Abner Sprague of Estes Park to do the initial survey work. John B. Hall of Lyons and his son, Charles Byron Hall were hired to supervise the construction. Five crews were hired to install new bridges as well as upgrade the old wagon road. Hall charged Stanley $16 for his services, plus the hire of a horse, wagon and driver.

The road began at the entrance to the foothills above Lyons with new sections created including one through the Welch Resort avoiding Roll Over Hill [Rowell Hill] and continued to the existing road at what is now known as Pinewood Springs. From there the road to Estes Park drops and rises through Rattlesnake Gulch graded to accommodate the new automobiles that Stanley would use to bring guests to his hotel. The finished road was completed on time, widened to eighteen feet, hopefully ensuring plenty of room for breakdowns and making it possible to pass another wagon or stage.

F. O. Stanley was not make the first automobile trip from Lyons to Estes Park. T. A. Brady in a Chicago Motor Vehicle, probably a Chicago Twelve Passenger Brake or Hotel Bus in May 1903 has been certified by the Colorado Automobile Company as being the first. The Stanley Steamer and F. O. Stanley made the second trip establishing a regular motoring route up the North St. Vrain.

Turnovers of heavily loaded horse-drawn wagons and Stanley Steamers are tragedies to be filed away with the past. Today, the road is even wider sporting colorful line markers guiding modern motorists. The well-maintained highway is intended to prevent accidents, however, icy roads, low-land travelers, tourists, and inexperienced newcomers continue the storyline of rollovers, lost possessions, and injuries. These incidents are much fewer and further apart than in the pioneer days and delightfully the once six-hour trip to Estes Park can now be made from town to town in thirty minutes or less.

Lyons and Estes Park Toll Roads

In the early days there were several stage lines going up both the North and South St. Vrain canyons. The hue and cry of the day was, "Want to use the road, then you have to pay a toll." Private individuals built tollgates along the trail to collect money for maintenance of the road and for personal income. The first gates were simple poles reaching across the road, easily moved aside when the fee was collected.

In the beginning, the roads were used mainly to haul produce between Denver, Central City, Black Hawk, and towns further north. This prompted the pay-for-use tolls throughout the Colorado Mountain road system. Fees were fixed by the legislature from a dollar per wagon and team to ten cents for loose animals. The law further stipulated that a distance of ten miles between tollgates "would be acceptable".

> "From the number of Franchises issued in Boulder County in the seventies [1870s] for Toll roads they must have been a paying proposition. The Legislature sat sixty days and passed Toll road Franchises all the time. When they adjourned it was estimated that every Citizen owned about three Franchises and it was believed that unless Congress gave the Territory another degree of longitude, there would not be enough room to accommodate the Toll roads. The end of them were hanging over the boundary lines like fringe."
>
> _____A 1945 *Boulder Camera* article

One tollgate belonged to Alexander Q. MacGregor. It was up the North St. Vrain starting at Steamboat Rock just above Lyons extending north for a mile, turning northwest to the Little Thompson, and following the creek into Pinewood Springs.

By 1894 A. J. Hanson operated a tollgate on the South St. Vrain near the present Hall Ranch Open Space at the entrance of the present Golden Andesite Rock Company. The first toll keeper, Newell Sizer and his family lived on site. D. W. Spangler of Allenspark replaced Newell Sizer, followed by Norman A. and Bessie McCall Billings. In 1910, J. I. Jacobs was hired to collect tolls.

The Toll House had been built to provide accommodations for the gatekeeper and his family, as well as food, and corrals for travelers and their livestock. The toll was five cents for a bicycle and fifteen cents for a buggy. In order to avoid paying for a four-horse team, $1.75 round trip, teamsters would unhitch two of their animals and walk them over the hill and down the other side, driving only a wagon and two-hitch through the tollgate. The difference of $0.55 was worth the extra effort and time.

Traveling the northern canyons became more and more precarious as the population increased and Estes Park became a prime destination. Thomas P. McFadden was the bridge contractor for a new toll road being built up the North St. Vrain in 1895. His partner was Sheriff Dyer. Unfortunately, Thomas did not reap the rewards nor suffer the problems of tollgate ownership. On May 28 his twelve-year old son fell into the roaring St. Vrain Creek. Dad jumped in to save Howard from the high water only to be swept away and drowned. Mr. McFadden was buried in the Hygiene Cemetery, Row 15 Lot 88. Sheriff Dyer became soul owner of the gate and collected all fees.

By 1900 the citizens of Lyons had become discontented with paying a fee each day as they traveled to and from work. Mr. R. B. Ground, the local undertaker and his son wrote to Judge Boughton of Ft. Collins asking his opinion as to whether or not a toll could be lawfully collected. The local lumberjacks and sawmill owners, however, could not wait for an answer. They had had enough of what they called a penalty for "good honest work". Mr. Ground feared for his beloved Lyons, as thirteen men, reportedly unarmed, used horses, ropes, teams, and chains to tear down the Estes Park Tollgate located on the North St. Vrain. These hard working men were from Lyons making daily round trips to the sawmills further up in the hills.

The Lyons Recorder responded to the incident, "The people of Lyons have always been in sympathy with the boys at the saw mill and [with] the teamsters. Mr. Knapp, the gate keeper, is the only one who has ever showed a gun." It should be noted that Mr. Knapp was alone at the tollhouse trying to defend his job as well as the tollgate.

On July 14, 1900 Jay H. Boughton, judge of the Eighth Judicial district in Ft. Collins answered Ground's plea with an apology for his late response. His suggestion for a legal solution to the problems between the tollgate owners and the sawmill owners was to file, "an appeal bond that would cover any toll which may be collected by the company during pendency of the appeal from the patrons of the road".

By December the newspaper reported that the Lyons and Estes Park Toll Road was a thing of the past. "Let's all give thanks and praise to the boys who have brought about this condition by their pluck and stick-to-itiveness. Now that the Estes Park Road is open to everybody we look for a much greater tourist travel next summer than ever." The bottom line was that all citizens, including those not using the road were taxed in order to maintain the routes up the North and South St. Vrains.

The *Longmont Times-Call* interviewed Villa Billings Lee, her parents Norman and Bessie McCall Billings were tollgate keepers for two or three years and Nettie Rivers, whose grandparents were the first gatekeepers. They spoke of the Lyons Tollhouse as a comfortable three-room home constructed for the gatekeeper and his family. Villa remembered that she and some of the other children liked to frighten tourists. They hid in the bushes by the side of the road and howled like coyotes. Mrs. Lee said that her sister was quite an expert and tourists would be quick to tell their mom that there were coyotes near the trail.

Mrs. Rivers recalled that Frank Hale Stickney, a Longmont banker and other Longmont businessmen financed the tollgate project on the South St. Vrain. Mountain cattle, horse ranching, and the active lumber industry demanded a speedy and safe method of transporting products to market. The steep canyon walls would need to be dynamited to create a narrow road on the canyon floor. Once again the cry went out, "Let the users pay."

A 1938 *Lyons Recorder* interview of local residents stated that the toll road system had not died completely with the 1900 referendum. There was a working tollgate on the Matt Blair place [later the Hall Ranch]. The road up the canyon had been built and bills needed to be paid. The South St. Vrain toll road remained in existence until April 1910, when it was bought from the operating company for $800 and the road opened to public travel. Boulder County paid $1,000 for their right of way.

Tollgate on the North St. Vrain. Courtesy of the Lyons Redstone Museum, Lyons, Colorado.

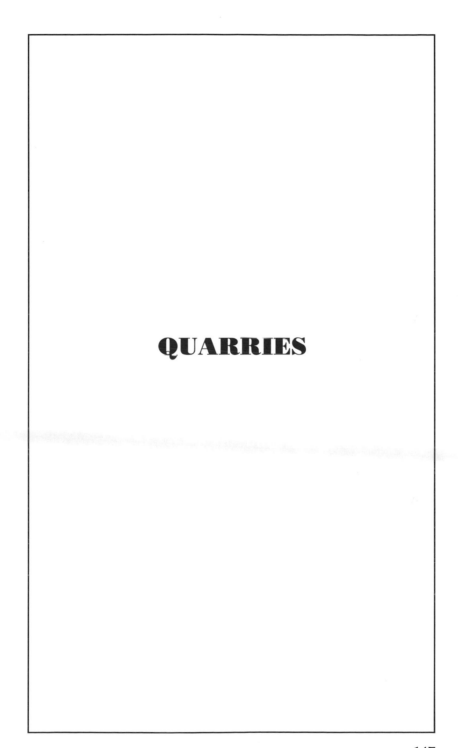

QUARRIES

The Geology of Lyons
By Robert J. Benedict

Lyons' oldest rocks formed 1,400 million years ago with the intrusion of Silver Plume granite. In comparison the oldest dated rocks in the Boulder area are nearly two billion years old. Part of the Precambrian basement complex, the Silver Plume granite is the dominant rock west of Lyons starting from the west margin of Apple Valley to the Diamond of Longs Peak.

There is a large gap in the geologic record that spans the late Precambrian to the early Pennsylvanian period that is missing atop the basement complex. This interval is marked by long periods of continental erosion with brief periods of transgressing seas. The record resumes about 300 million years ago during the Pennsylvanian period when-continents were colliding and a north-south highland rose to the west of Lyons, the "Ancestral Rockies". During this uplift vast amounts of alluvial sediments where deposited by rivers rushing out of the highlands creating what is now the Fountain formation, an arkosic conglomerate forming the steep lower slopes of Steamboat Mountain in Lyons and the Flatirons in Boulder, Colorado.

Of economic importance, the Lower Permian period brought to Lyons its namesake strata, the Lyons formation. It lies above the thinning southern extent of the Ingleside Formation that forms the steep upper cliffs of Steamboat Mountain. 250 million years ago shallow seas invaded from the east while sands swept in from Wyoming leaving giant dune deposits. Large-scale cross bedding produced by blowing sands was frozen into the well-sorted quartz sandstone. Very few fossils other than amphibian footprints and raindrop impressions exist. The quality of the Lyons sandstone, its pleasing red to buff gray color, and its tendency to fracture into flagstones of convenient size makes it an ideal and valuable building material. The Lyons formation can be found up and down the Front Range in a wedge from the Colorado-Wyoming border thickening to the south reaching about 700 feet thick near Colorado Springs. South of Lyons, the formation is steeply inclined from the uplift of the present day Rockies; but the large, moderately dipping exposures of the sandstone around Lyons make this locale ideal for quarrying. Many quarries exist in the area especially in Steamboat Valley and atop Steamboat Mountain.

Overlying the Lyons sandstone is the late Permian early Triassic Lykins formation. Composed of tidal flat and flood plane deposits the fine-grained red shale and limestone sequence is about 600 feet thick. Exposures can be found in Stone Canyon but Quaternary stream and slope deposits mostly cover the formation there. Its lime deposits are thought to have supplied the raw material for the mortar made at the old limestone kiln located east of town.

By the middle of the Jurassic period some 150 million years ago the "Ancestral Front Range" had been leveled. Warm moist conditions existed at the time. Mountains were rising far to the west in Utah and Nevada shedding sediments that traveled eastward depositing them on a large flat flood plain. The Morrison formation known for its dinosaur fossils was born. It outcrops on the slopes of the east side of Stone Canyon.

Seas later advanced and retreated time and again over the 70 million year Cretaceous period. Thousands of feet of strata were laid down consisting of near shore and marine sediments. Of note is the 500 feet thick early Cretaceous Dakota group forming a hogback that fronts the Southern Rockies for some 200 miles found just east of Lyons. During the late Cretaceous period the uplift of the present day Rockies began. For the last 70 million years uplift and erosion has dominated the evolution of the landscape - building mountains to the west while removing vast quantities of rock to expose the Lyons sandstone and other strata on which the town of Lyons is now built.

Geological Time Line for the Lyons Section

Geologic Era	Geologic Period	Milions of years ago	Lyons Area Geology
Cenozoic		65 - 0	Uplift and erosion
Mesozoic	Cretaceous	136 - 65	Laramic Formation
			Fox Hills Formation
			Pierre Formation
			Niobrara Formation
			Benton Formation
			Dakota Group
	Jurassic	190 -136	Morrison Formation
			Misc.
	Triassic	225 - 190	
			Lykins Formation
Paleozoic	Permian	280 - 225	Lyons Formation
			Ingleside Formation
			Fountain Formation
	Pennsylvanian	325 - 280	
	...	570 - 325	Erosion
Precambrian		Up to 570	Silver Plume Granite (1400 million yrs BP)

Courtesy of Robert J. Benedict, Boulder, Colorado.

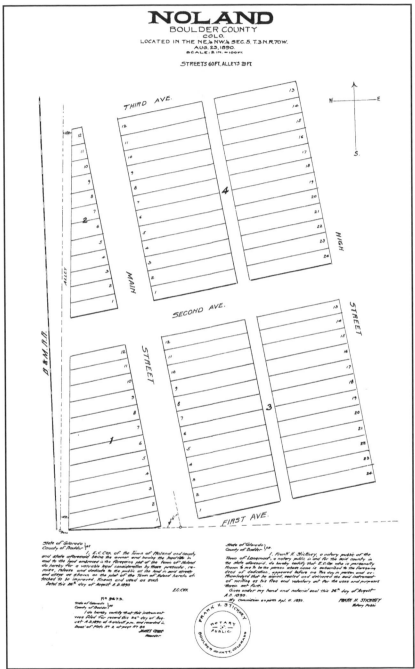

Noland Plat Map August 26, 1890, Frank H. Stickney. From Boulder County Clerk and Recorders Office Plat Book 2 P. 86.

Noland
Quarry Town to Ghost Town

The site of Noland, once called Tower, was a Native American outlook for hostiles, intruders, and later pioneer wagon trains. There are many accounts of quarrymen and their families discovering Indian burial sites and artifacts throughout the Noland and the Lyons sections. Art Ohline, a native of Colorado and a Lyons resident, often told of the Indian writings he and his friends found on the cliffs of Indian Ridge. He lamented that most of it had been chipped off and hauled away for garden and home decorations.

Noland was located four miles north of Lyons between Stone Mountain and Indian Ridge at 40° 15′ 33″ N by 105° 15′ 14″ W. Efraim C. Cox, the father of Mrs. C. K (Bessie) Hirschfeld, homesteaded the area in 1887. His venture into sandstone quarrying attracted many other developers. The town was officially platted at the Boulder County Courthouse in 1890, a year before Lyons was incorporated. Streets were named and lots surveyed. In order to keep track of his quarry and real estate interest, Cox move his family to the little quarry town.

A.A. Mathews purchased 500 acres of land adjoining the Cox property and leased it out to various quarry operations. In 1889 the Colorado and Nebraska Sandstone Company with foreman W. D. Slaughter was the main quarry employing 127 men. The Murphy Red Sandstone Quarries owned by Hugh Murphy of Omaha, John C. Brodie, manager had 112 employees in the same year.

Charles K. Hirschfeld of Lyons, son-in-law to Mr. Cox, joined him in Noland and opened a boarding house, general merchandise store, and later a post office. Postmaster Hirschfeld, who played the cornet, organized the Noland Band. On summer nights the men climbed to the top of Hogback Mountain and serenaded the town of Lyons. Bertha Lewis remembered the day the Noland Band played for the wedding of A. E. Howe, owner/operator of the St. Vrain cottages and later the Howe Mortuaries. The Noland Band performed throughout the state of Colorado to rave reviews.

Housing in Noland ranged from tents to lovely clapboard houses. Single and married men without their families relied on the boardinghouses for food and lodging. The Nebraska House could handle up to 300 men. It was once considered the "grandest" in the west. Cold rooms constructed with thick stonewalls, for vegetable and meat storage were buried partially underground near the boarding facilities. Mrs. I. S. Wright, of the Nebraska boarding house, would frequently drive into Lyons for "some trading." The cold rooms were kept well stocked. The old frame Nebraska House survived into the 1950s.

Later, Anna Neilson Ohline, the mother of Arthur Ohline, Sr. of the Little Thompson Canyon, managed the Nebraska House as well as cooked the meals. Three times a week, teenager Ed McCall would take groceries purchased from the Golden Rule Store in Lyons up to the two major boarding houses in Lyons.

"I remember how much I charged her," said Ed, "eggs sold for eight cents a dozen, potatoes for 75 cents a hundred pounds, salt six cents a pound and coffee ten cents a pound. Overalls went for 35 cents."

The Matthews Boarding House, located next to the Nebraska House, installed some of the first electric lights in the area. The Matthews soon became known for its weekly dances held in the dancehall upstairs. It was run by Grandmother Harrisson, the grandmother of Bertha Lewis.

In 1956 both boarding houses were torn down by a Lyons construction company in order to use the hand-chiseled stones for landfill. All that remains of these major structures are the foundations and one arched underground stone room showing an entrance by one of the two narrow doorways. This storeroom is where the cooks hung sides of beef for daily meals.

Charles M. Cheney was Justice of the Peace and Andy Olson was constable of Noland. The population ranged from 800 to 1,000 (some accounts say 3,000), composed primarily of men from Sweden, Finland, Ireland, and Denmark. Even with four saloons, the town was peaceful with no serious crimes committed. However, payday was the signal for professional gamblers from Longmont to board the Stone Mountain Railroad and head for the little quarry town to offer a little sport and to "share" the wealth with those hard working men. They took their places in the saloons and tents waiting for their prey.

> "Noland has 50 buildings, frame or stone, 75 tents, dugouts, 2 saloons, 1 general store and another started, 1 bakery and one watchmaker. There are 100 men at work in the quarries shipping out 7 cars of stone daily. The St. Vrain region, Lyons, Noland and Beech Hill, has 32 quarries and 859 men employed.
>
> A schoolhouse appeared later as did 3 more saloons, and a barbershop owned by Mr. Harrison. Tom Weaver owned the local blacksmith shop."
>
> —*The Longmont Times-Call, Vol. 1 #1.(year?)*

A view of Noland looking northeast. The two boardinghouses can be seen in the left to left center of the picture. Courtesy of the Lyons Redstone Museum, Lyons, Colorado.

The Noland Band. Courtesy of the Lyons Redstone Museum, Lyons, Colorado.

Stone Mountain Railroad

During the snow and melt of winter, the quarries would close as the ground became too slippery for the horse drawn Studebaker wagons. But demand for Noland sandstone was year round. In 1890, the need for more modern transportation was addressed. Stone Mountain Railway was built to service Noland and Beach Hill. Judge Secord and Charles Day of Longmont were the principal backers at a cost of approximately $30,000. The remaining 25 stockholders invested $300,000. The six-mile long stretch connected with the famous Burlington Hotel in Lyons and ran up what is now the Stone Canyon Road. The railroad was completed January 8, 1891, having taken six months and $55,000 to build. Q. Grant was general manager of the broad gauge railroad. John Wright was superintendent until three years before the railroad closed. S. P. Norton stayed on as superintendent until the end came in 1906. Orange J. "Shorty" Lewis was engineer and played violin for the Noland Band. His daughter Bertha Lewis and her friends were known for, but never caught, clinging to the front of the engine as it made its wild ride down the mountain. Up to thirty carloads of stone a day was shipped out of Noland. On the return trip, the railroad transported water from the St. Vrain for the town.

> "The new Stone mountain railway, connecting with the Burlington at Tower Hill and extending around Beek Hill [Beach/Beech Hill] for five miles, reaching over thirty of the richest sandstone quarries in the State, was finished last Thursday and is now in operation. The road has been building for over six months, and the total cost of completing it was $55,000.

The little road will soon pay for itself and it is in good hands. It was built by Longmont and New York Capital. Mr. C. E. Day, of Longmont, is president, and Mr. Thomas Butterfield, formerly of Rutter, Wyman & Atwood, of Denver, is connected with the enterprise. The [track] is broad gauge and is built entirely of steel. J. Q. Grant is general manager."

—*Boulder News.* Unreferenced photocopy. Denver Public Library, Department of Western History and Genealogy.

In 1890 there were reports of problems with construction on the Stone Mountain Railroad. Work was stopped for several weeks and railroad construction crews fought off the bitter cold in their poorly constructed temporary housing. An interview with the principle parties involved stated that Ed. Callahan had agreed that the railroad company could cross his quarry. However, after Ed returned from Denver with a contract, The Stone Mountain RR people refused to sign. Mr. Callahan told them they had to change the proposed route to a section lower down from his land. Stone Mountain claimed that the train was beneficial to the quarries and Callahan, "the obstinate Irishman", was just being obstructive. Moving the tracks would create a greater risk of wrecks and casualties because of a steeper grade at the proposed new site. Mr. Callahan responded that the present site, "would shut me off entirely from the face of my quarry" I could not find a report concerning the final disposition of the dispute; however, the railroad was completed and made daily runs from Lyons through Noland to Beach Hill and back until the closure of Noland.

Things went smoothly for the railroad until 1891, when four crewmen were killed. The little Shay Engine was equipped with handbrakes; however, on this day some of the brakes had not been set on the loaded cars as the train entered the dangerous switchbacks. Three brakemen were killed when they jumped from the out of control train. Soon after this incident a quarry worker was crushed to death by one of the freight cars. Swiftly, rumors began to spread through the town. Was the town jinxed?

Charles Kesler and Alice Belle Hirschfeld with their family at home in Noland. The waterless well can be see to the left front of the house.

A view North on main street Noland. Both photographs from the collection of Frances Brodie Brackett.

No Water Makes This a Dry Town

Lack of water was considered an inconvenience for the residents and workers of the small town. A water diviner was called in by C. K. Hirschfeld. The diviner claimed that there was water under the main street, but no one wanted a hole in the middle of the main road through town. A well was dug in Mr. Hirschfeld's front yard. After digging down 125 feet, the hole was still dry. No water was found. Never one to waste an opportunity, Charles converted the pit into an underground refrigerator for his growing family. And so the town continued using the cisterns filled by the trains for their water supply.

Superintendent McFadden assigned young Peter Jacobsen, who had immigrated to the United States from Denmark in 1890, as water boy to the railroad crews. Twice in the morning and again twice in the afternoon, Peter would fill up his two pails downhill at a spring and trudged back up the incline to supply essential drinking water to the railway workers. Sitting in the shade during rest periods, McFadden would teach the young immigrant English. When the rail construction was completed, young Jacobsen stayed on in Noland for the next two years as a stone cutter for the quarries. On Sundays he walked all the way down to Burlington to visit his Uncle Fred Jacobsen on the farm and back up for work in the morning.

The Noland schoolhouse was the pride of the town. Built with $1,600 from a fund raiser, the school housed grades one through eight. C. K. Hirschfeld's daughter, Floss attended all eight grades in the one-room building. Another fundraiser run by the children was so successful that a new organ was purchased. The building became the social center for the community, as well as offering Sunday school to those not wishing to make the long trip into Lyons.

—See Appendix V p. 310—School Administration Records 1881-1900.

Death of a Quarry Town

The Panic of 1893 caused commercial and residential build ing in the country to come to a crashing halt. The quarries in Colorado were forced to shut down. Around 1900 the stone business was revived and the camp was in full operation again. As late as 1902 there was still hope that Noland's sandstone would come back into demand and save the town from extinction. However, in 1903 cement became the building material of choice. It was less expensive and molds could be formed on the building site, thus saving delivery time. Charles K. Hirschfeld stayed until 1903, then moved on to business elsewhere.

> "In 1906, when a process for mixing cement on site and pouring it into wooden forms was perfected, builders quickly switched to this cheaper, faster method of construction."

The final death knell sounded when the post office closed in 1918. Soon after the camp was deserted, the telephone poles were removed, and the railroad took up the tracks sending them to Oak Creek, Colorado. The stock of goods owned by C. K. was hauled down to the depot in Lyons and shipped out of town by the Strauss Child Mercantile Company.

Noland died as have so many quarry and mining towns of the west. It added to the list of ghost towns once prosperous and hopeful, where men went to work at hard labor, seeking their fortunes for themselves and their families. The skeletal remains of the boarding houses are gone, torn down as easy landfill for developers. The frame buildings were long ago destroyed. Tents were folded and moved to the next "boom" town. Once again we lost a little of our past.

The Men Who Worked
The Quarries

Charles Kesler Hirschfeld
April 20, 1854–January 19, 1940

Charles Kesler and Alice Belle Hirschfeld came to Colorado by the shear determination of Alice who had always wanted to live in the State. Charles was content with their farm in Ohio. One evening she challenged her husband to a game of poker with the winner to decide where the family would live. She won the hand. The Hirschfelds with Alice's mother and father, the E. C. Coxes moved to Longmont.

Ephram Cox and his wife homesteaded in Noland and opened a small quarry. Charles and Alice followed, built a home, and opened a boarding house. Within one month their boarders increased from four to fifty men. Alice took care of the boarding house and Charles opened a general store, later becoming the Noland postmaster. They left Noland after the panic of 1893 being the last business to close. Mr. Hirschfeld moved his family to Allenspark to profit from the mining industry, where they opened a general store, but left after two years and moved back to Noland once again opening a large merchandising business.

Charles loved music and gathered together quarry workers and merchants to create one of the best bands in Northern Colorado. Daughter Floss began taking music lessons when she was eight. One of her teachers was the highly regarded, Adolph Torchiani, who died of consumption at the age of 28. Floss continued on to become a music teacher and have her own dance band. She married Frank Brackett May 23, 1910. Sister Dewey continued her music education by playing the organ at the main theater in Port Charlotte, Florida.

In 1904 Charles bought a farm east of Lyons. In 1910 he moved the family to 208 Seward Street. He was elected Justice of the Peace for the Town of Lyons 1916–1921. They moved to 256 Main Street in 1919 and then on to Boulder in 1932.

Phillip H. Bohn
1851–August 26, 1917

Phillip H. Bohn was a native of Germany. When he was four years old, his family moved to the United States, settling in Illinois. In 1886 Phillip moved his family to Fort Collins where he worked for the Union Pacific Railroad. Around 1892 they moved to Lyons and Phillip went to work for the quarries at Noland. A continuation of the history of the Bohn family will appear in the next book on Lyons covering 1900–1950.

Gilead P. Cheney
March 24, 1838–July 12, 1907

Gilead and his wife Emily moved to Lyons in 1886. They built a home in Noland where Gilead worked in the quarries. He died at home in Noland at 79. Services were held in the Lyons Methodist Church.

John George Cheney
1852–1936

John George Cheney and his wife Amanda Eveline moved to Lyons in 1889. They built their home on the road between Lyons and Noland. John George worked in the quarries and later moved his family to a home at 4th Streets and Stickney and in Lyons.

Epharim (Effraim, Efrim) C. Cox
Unknown—October 16, 1891

A deed of transfer handled by B. L. Carr and F. P. Secor, lawyers in Longmont, Colorado began, "this 16th day of August A. D. 1893 by and between Betsey Cox, Charlie Cox, and Alice Hirschfeld, sole heirs at law of Ephrim C. Cox deceased" This of was the legal transfer of ownership to his heirs Lots Nine, Ten, Eleven, and Twelve in Block Six of the First Addition to the town Noland. The document was filed on September 2, 1898 in the County of Boulder for $100. There was a five year difference between writing the document and its eventual filing.

Charles V. Engert
Augus 1, 1861—March 5, 1949

Charles Engert came to Lyons in 1891. He was a bookkeeper for one of the Lyons stone companies. He also served as deputy town marshal for Boulder County, Marshal for Lyons, and Lyons Postmaster from 1920—1936.

Alfred Jamison
December 19, 1850—January 5, 1914

Alfred Jamison came from McPherson, Kansas to operate a saw mill in Left Hand Canyon. About 1890 he moved to Lyons where he worked as a stone cutter in the quarries. They built a home on the Old Apple Valley Road. He died of stone cutters consumption.

James S. Johns
February 20, 1861—October 31, 1943

James S. Johns was born in Warren County, Iowa. He married Louisa Flynn. He, Louisa and Her brother Joshia moved to Lyons in 1893. James worked in the Noland Quarry where he received 75 cents perday. He would walk over the Hogsback to get to work in the early morning and return in the afternoon to their home at Fourth and Evans.

During one of the many floods their home was swept away. They rebuilt in the same location. Mr. Johns was a town trustee for 1900, 1906, 1907, 1908, 1915, and 1916.

Erick Johnson
April 2, 1855—December 6, 1923

Erick Johnson was born at Umea, Sweden, where he married Gustave Albertina Ostrum. Mrs. Johnson came from a family of twenty-two children.

The Johnsons came to America in 1882 first settling at Sioux Falls, South Dakota. Erick worked as a stone cutter in South Dakota, Wisconsin, and Nebraska. They moved to Leadville, Colorado in 1889. In 1890 they settled in Lyons on Park Street.

He was a stone cutter, then foreman for the Murphy and Brodie quarries. Mrs. Johnson operated the Longs Peak Cafe and Rooming House in the Thorne Building on Main Street.

Erick was mayor of Lyons in 1902 and 1905. In 1904 and 1905 he was President of the Board of Education. In 1906 he was on the Board of Stewards for the Methodist Church.

In 1909 the Johnson family moved to a ranch about nine mile southeast of Steamboat Springs at the foot of Rabbit Ears Pass. He tried quarrying stone, which he found to be of poor quality. In 1912 the family moved to a larger spread.

Charles Miller
(Dates Unknown)

Charles Miller and his bride Susan Brown Miller bought acreage along the Noland Road. Charles was not interested in the stone industry. His main interest was farming. He supplemented the family income as a ditch rider.

Dan Slaughter
1855—August 25, 1923

Dan Slaughter was born in Illinois. He came to Lyons in the early 1890s. For many years he was superintendent of the Nebraska Quarry.

About 1908 he quit the quarries and bought a ranch at Allenspark, where he raised cattle. His brother Henry ran the Crystal Springs Hotel at Allenspark.

John G. Sjogren
October 26, 1859—May 26, 1930

John G. Sjogren was born in Sweden. He came to America in 1883 and located at Dell Rapids, South Dakota. He came to Colorado about 1889. On December 11, he married Charlotte Marie Johnson in Denver. When they moved to Lyons they located in the 400 block of Park Street. John was a stone cutter for the quarries.

They were members of the Old Stone Church and the Woodmen of the World. Mr. Sjogren was on the town board of trustees in 1906.

Charles J. Hjertquist, the lovable Swede who gave his life to save others in a Nederland, Colorado mine catastrophe. Courtesy of the Lyons Redstone Museum, Lyons, Colorado.

Beach Hill Quarry. Courtesy of the Lyons Redstone Museum, Lyons, Colorado.

Beech Hill

Continuing west from Noland past the Ohline Ranch is another quarry site called Beech [Beach] Hill. No one seems to know how the name came about. Could there have been a Mr. Beech or could it be due to the large sand deposits that lay in between the red stone of the quarries giving the area the feel and look of a large beach suspended high in the deep blue skies of Colorado? Over the years, both spellings have been used in newspapers, stories, and official documents.

During the early days of quarrying at the top of the mountain, the railroad company carved out a large round about for the trains. This made for easier travel down the treacherous mountain grade from Beach Hill, through Noland, to the main railroad tracks in Lyons. Beach Hill never became a town. There was no post office, no municipal service, no grocery store, or general store. Food was shipped up from Lyons and the children living in the area had to make their way into Noland or Lyons for an education. Beach Hill was stone and only stone. The business was quarrying. Community and a social life was found elsewhere.

On Beach Hill among the trees, sands, and quarries are the remains of stone cabins used by the workmen. The floor of one stone cabin was laid with a magnificent flagstone pattern. When I visited the site, I could imagine the men as they walked to the quarries for a day of work to return to their homes at the end of their shift for the evening meal.

Still visible are the quarry pits with cabling anchored by stone and metal railroad ties forming a rectangle, high over the hole, one setup at each corner. The Deadman, as this arrangement is called, was used to hoist the handmade wooden buckets, about 4 feet x 2 feet, filled with quarried stone to the top of the open pit. Several of the original buckets are still lying near the pits. They are marvelous examples of the craftsmanship and ingenuity of the blacksmith. Made from local lumber and spanned by forged heavy made-to-order iron straps, anchored by locally forged bolts, and strung to the cables with huge iron hooks. They carried load after load of stone to the surface.

From one of the Beech Hill quarries a stone approximately four feet wide and eight feet long was taken out and sent to the Louisiana Purchase Centennial Exposition of 1904, better known as the St. Louis World's Fair. It took two railroad cars to carry the stone slowly down the steep slopes.

'Capt. Sipple and Hon. Wm. Sites have charge of arranging for exhibiting the stone of Boulder County at the World's fair. There is a move now on foot to get the quarry in this city to donate stone for a handsome column to be placed in the Colorado department at the fair. Also to have enough flagging donated to lay a walk at the grounds 75 feet long and 25 feet wide. The state will pay all expenses after loaded on the cars, and the stone will belong to the parties donating it and can be sold after the fair. Mr. Sites is very anxious that this section should make a good exhibit at the fair, and it is the best opportunity that our stone dealers will ever have to let the world know of the fine quality of stone produced.

We are confident that every quarry owner will see the importance of this matter and willingly do his part toward advertising our chief product. Mr. Sites has a draft of the column and full particulars and will gladly furnish all information. We will have more to say on this subject next week.'
—*Lyons Rustler*, undated photocopy of an article

Edwin Johnson writes that men like his father, Swan M. Johnson, lived in Lyons and walked the eight miles each day to work at Beech Hill. He worked 10-hour days, six days a week, and walked the eight miles back to his home in Lyons. Ed remembered a house on the bluff that belonged to his grandparents, John R. and Sinta K. Swenson. Edwin's grandfather John Swenson and his Uncle Charles Hjertquist worked for the Tom Lavridson Quarry in Beech Hill. Some of the other larger quarries belonged to Hugh Murphy, Larsen, and the Loukonen family. John's brother Ernest drove a team of horses that provided power to one of the derricks that moved the stone onto the transportation wagons.

Today the old Beach Hill railroad bed is used as a road for large semi trucks hauling stone and offering access to the quarry owners and workmen. As Ed Callahan and the Stone Mountain RR people in the early days of quarrying found compromise difficult, the workers and owners of Beach Hill in 1954 faced an access controversy with the homeowners on a shortcut up to the quarries. The Lyons-Beach Hill Road, an extension of Steamboat Valley Road north of Lyons was once County Road 226. By 1929 Boulder County did not feel maintaining the road was of any value and so released obligation to the site. In 1954, three local Lyons men, James Kelley, Leonard Loukonen, and Arthur Ohline with the help of attorney William E. McCarthy put down $400 earnest money and petitioned that the road once again become public property so that they could get to their worksites. The county decided that the $25,000 to rehabilitate the road and the money needed to repurchase right of way was more than the road was worth. There were few homes on the road and the remainder of the land was used for grazing. Stone Canyon Road, the old Noland Road that follows the former quarry railroad bed is still the route used by the Loukonen family, Vasquez family, Randy Perdue, and Robert Phillip to get to their holdings in Noland and Beach Hill.

Some of the larger quarries were the Hugh Murphy holdings, Tom Lavridson Quarry, Larsen Quarry and the Loukonen Quarry.

John C. Brodie and Hugh Murphy. From the Collection of Frances Brodie Brackett.

The Murphy Quarries

The primary Murphy quarry was located NW of Lyons. He held rights up on Beach Hill, however, it remained virgin ground until the 1990s. Several sources also place his holdings in and around Noland. Hugh Murphy's quarries were well kept and his workmen were respected. From all accounts it appears that Murphy should have received the "Best Places To Work" award during his time spent in the area.

He fed the men in a dining room capable of holding 500 people. The Bill of Fare changed every day throughout the week. Refrigerated cars from the Omaha Packery shipped beef and pork. Cooking for the men was done on an immense iron range. Bread, cakes, and pies were baked in a baker's oven. In the summer, an icehouse was used to create refrigeration for the groceries bought wholesale for the camp. One of his cooks was paid $100 a month. Cottages were built. Large boarding houses were constructed with rooms for the foreman, bookkeeper, and others creating a stable atmosphere and work environment.

"Wednesday was Murphey's [sic] pay day. Considerable anti-typhoid was taken on board. A few got slugged in a social way, but no one hurt as usual.

$100,000 changes hands here every pay day, 10th to 15th of each month, and $350,000 worth of red stone is sent out every thirty days."

—Undated, photocopy of a news article

An archival box at the Norlin Library at the University of Colorado contained general correspondence, legal correspondence, insurance correspondence from the Maryland Casualty Company, orders for stone, as well as purchase orders and vouchers for quarry supplies.

The following letters are two examples of many received at the office of the St. Vrain Quarries:

"Lyons House
Mr. Rich

Ther is a Man Boardr My house by the name of Frank E. Winton he is Working at Murphy he started of the 6 of Jan. Mr. Brodie told me to notify you so if he should draw his loan you could let me know am Oblidge Me.

Mrs. Halliday"

Another letter from one of his customers offered a suggestion for shipping sandstone over long distances.

"Lincoln, Neb.

From James Rivett
To Mr. H. M; Lyons, Colo.

Carload of dressed stone shipped to Crete arrived bad condition – due to way loaded. Spauled off pieces, damaging the ends.
Suggest loading them crossways in the car with something between them."

The lack of any water source on the property was a problem at all of the quarries. Vouchers for the month of November 1904 are for payment of contracts with the Noland Sand and Transfer Company of Lyons for water delivered to the St. Vrain Quarry, now on the William Boone property. Weekly deliveries totaled 750 gallons of water for the crusher, 600 gallons of water for the teams [of horses], and 1,350 gallons of water for general living needs.

A sampling of other vouchers in the box is for horses and carts Hugh rented from local stables for both the quarry and for his personal comfort.

"Louis Carvell, Lyons hire of 2 horses at 10 cents/hour for 74 hours $7.40; Charles McFadden 2 horses at 20 cents/hour; C. A. Spaulding team and surrey for 14 days $28.00. Charles McFadden 8/31/1905 carthorse Chief at St. Vrain $11.50. Chief was a favorite among the quarries. Many of the vouchers specified the horse by name. Team for Beach Hill $126.60; Louise Carvell team $25.50; A.M. Carver & Sons team & surrey $1.50; John Schwilke for use of 1 cart horse twice $20.50. Charles McFadden and C. F. Hill, the blacksmiths were paid for horseshoeing and repairing the survey."

Payroll sheets for one week in October, 1907 included the following men: "G. S. Fraser, foreman, 20 hours $13.75; M. Labrialo, cutter 28 hours, $1750; M. Labrialo, cutter 20 hours, $12.50; Jacob Frasher, tool boy 29 hours, $5.45; M. Satterwhite, team, 1 1/2 hours $0.70; M. Wendelier, blacksmith 4 3/4 hours $2.75; and C. Cormack, cutter 45 hours, $28.10. In November the same men were employed, plus E. Knorr Miller, team for 2 hours $1.00 and G. Natterman, cutter for 16 1/2 hours $8.45. Other names mentioned on payrolls were for cutters, A. Massora, Tom Esposito, Geo Natterman; laborer, P. Gallacher, W. S. Perrin, team; and paving cutters Robert Percy and R. G. Roberts."

Hugh Murphy
(Dates Unknown)

A story written in February of 1891 by Ben Durr, owner of the *Longs Peak Rustler* describes Hugh Murphy of Omaha, Nebraska, the man and the business owner.

"We went out to the quarry to see Hugh Murphy. We also got to see the quarry. Hugh Murphy, is, however, a quarry himself. You can get slabs of wit and humor out of him that are endless and a foot thick. He has a mind that can size up anything or anybody almost in a flash. Liberal and open hearted, business from head to foot, with a tremendous energy and capacity to do. Hugh Murphy stands out a unique character by himself.

"He has risen in life from printers devil to owning a business requiring 175 men to conduct in its various departments, here and abroad.

Mr. Murphy is about 5 ft, 10 1/2 inches. Weight about 225. Square built from head to foot. His forehead comes up square and his heels come down square. Round, smooth, ruddy face, a mouth that suggests firmness, and betokens humor and kindness, open countenance, large blue eyes and dark short hair. On the street he walks briskly and plants his feet down solidly. He wears good plain clothes but puts on no style. He uses first class language and is polite to everybody. Mr. Murphy makes his home in Omaha, where he has a wife and three children, and a very comfortable residence."

Although he spent many hours at his quarries attending to business, Hugh Murphy maintained business offices in Denver. Maryland Casualty Company made inspections of the boilers, insuring them on a yearly basis, as well as handling worker injury policies. American Car and Foundry Company of St. Louis supplied RR cars and The Colorado Iron Works Company of Denver supplied ore milling and smelting machinery. Guy Le Roy Stevick, a Denver attorney, was hired to secure an opinion on the right to drive over private lands in Lyons. The total bill was $10. Some things do change.

HUGH MURPHY, SAINT VRAIN QUARRIES, LYONS, COLORADO.

To *Noland Sand & Transfer Co.* DR.

ADDRESS *Lyons Colo*

DATE *Nov 30th 1904* FOR ITEMS FOLLOWING OR AS PER BILLS HERETO ATTACHED:

1904

Nov	1	{ 1 tank water set at crusher } or used at crusher			1 50	Crusher
		1/2 " " " quarry			1 50	Water
"	2	1 tank water set at cistern			3 00	Teams Feed
"	7	1 " " " quarry			3 00	Water
"	14	1 " " " "			3 00	"
"	14	1 " " " cistern			3 00	Teams Feed
"	21	1 " " " crusher			3 00	Crusher
"	23	1 " " " quarry			3 00	Water
"	26	" " " " crusher			3 00	Crusher
"	30	" " " " cistern			3 00	Water

27 00

27 00

APPROVED FOR PAYMENT:

RECEIVED *Nov 30th* 190 4, OF HUGH MURPHY,

Twenty seven 00/100 DOLLARS,

IN FULL PAYMENT OF THE ABOVE ACCOUNT.

PLEASE RECEIPT AND RETURN WITHOUT DELAY. DO NOT ALTER OR REMOVE ANY OF THE ATTACHED BILLS

The Noland Sand & Transfer Co.

J. B. Thompson Sec

Hugh Murphy, St. Vr. Qrs.

City of DENVER, State of COLORA[DO]

PAY ROLL.

FOR PERSONAL SERVICES RENDERED

On _____ District No. _____ for

THE C. F. HOECKEL, B. B. CO. DENVER. 68134

No.	NAMES OF MEN	How EMPLOYED	No. OF HOURS	RATE	AMOUNT	T.C. No.	AMO
1	G S Fraser	Foreman	13	68¾	8 95		
2	C Cormack	Cutter	20	62½	12 50		
3	M Labiola	"	20	"	12 50		
4	J Fraser	Tool Boy	21	25	5 25		
5	M Satterwhite	Team	3	50	1 50		
6	E Knorr (Wagner	"	1	"	50		
7	M Wendelin	Blacksmith	3	55	1 65		
			81		42 85		

The St. Vrain Quarries northwest of Lyons during the time when they were in full production. Owned by John C. Brodie. From the collection of Frances Brodie Brackett.

On the left, p. 176. At the top of the page is an invoice for the St. Vrain Quarries. Bottom is a sample of a Hugh Murphy St. Vrain Quarry Pay Roll. Courtesy of Norlin Library Archives, University of Colorado, Boulder, Colorado.

St. Vrain Quarries, Also known as the Brodie Quarries

In 1890 a 60-bed boarding house, cistern, blacksmith shop, and several other wooden structures were built at the quarry NW of Lyons. Housing facilities handled from 250 to 300 workers. At the peak of the stone industry, the Brodie quarry had up to 500 men working at one time. Water was not available to the quarries and had to be hauled in and stored for humans, animals, and quarrying. A 6 x 6 foot cistern still exists between the boardinghouse foundation and the remains of the blacksmith shop. The cistern and blacksmith shop were given Boulder County Historic Landmark designation in 2000.

The big red sandstone boarding house had six rooms, a large dining room, kitchen, and offices. Four huge chimneys rose above the long roof of the L-shaped building. Prior to the building being razed by fire in 1957, the old records were still in the office along with a beautiful, old wooden filing cabinet with forty-nine pigeonholes fitted with small wooden doors and individual locks. An 1893 ledger told the story of Scandinavians and Italians employed by the quarry for 20 cents an hour general labor and $1.50 an hour for quarrymen. In the kitchen a cook with a magic touch created good meals for the men. She was paid $45 a week. Mary Ryan, who also cooked, was paid $25 a week, later receiving a raise to $30. Their grocery list was extensive: 71 quarts milk from J. A. McFaland; vegetables and chicken from Matt Wenzel; pork roast, veal roast, shank, lard, beef, fish, ham, mutton leg, and pork chops from Frank Brothers; bread, plums, chocolate, peas, oranges, soap, apples, bran, etc. from M. J. Scanlon in Lyons.

The blacksmith shop had large double doors facing the quarry allowing wagons to be rolled in for repairs. It was built of local stone hewn with care. The windows and doorframes have a delicate curve, showing the care the men had for their workplace. The stone step boasts the test holes made from forged tools. Shoes were made and shod on mules and horse from the double forges, one to the north, the other to the south. In the fall and winter, as the intense cold winds roared down from the north, the two windows on the north side of the building were bricked over.

William D. Boone presently owns the Brodie Quarries. The Boone home is at the entrance to the quarry at 3 Steamboat Valley Road and both lie on private property.

John Campbell Brodie
1861–1940

John C. Brodie was born in Furness, Scotland on August 16, 1861 the son of John and Mary Campbell Brodie. His father, grandfather, and great-grandfather were in the stone business in Arberdeen, Scotland. He was proud to boast that his relatives had been important figures in the stone business for years in Scotland. He served an apprenticeship as a stonecutter in London, England.

When he came to American he worked with the stone and marble quarries first in Missouri. In 1883 he married Angelina Sibson of Del Rapids, South Dakota, where he was president of the Del Rapids Granite Co. and president of the Sioux Falls Bank.

John and Angelina moved to Colorado after eight years in South Dakota. He took the position of superintendent for the Hugh Murphy Quarries. Mr. Brodie purchased the quarries north of Lyons from Murphy in 1892 at a cost of $10,000. He changed the name to St. Vrain Quarries. The business became the largest sandstone concern in western American, employing between 450 and 500 men. Mr. Brodie is often characterized as giving complete attention to details on all of his projects, thus his success was guaranteed with each of his business ventures. The quarries were noted for the quality and size of the paving blocks and well-cut curbing stone which were part of his street paving and municipal business in the partnership of Brodie and Anderson in Denver. He was elected president of the Colorado Construction League and several other business and technical organizations.

Mr. Brodie was a 32nd Degree Life Mason and belonged to several chapters of the Masonic Order including the Consistory Number One of Denver, Colorado. As his quarry business prospered, he and Angelina moved the family into the Sayer-Brodie Mansion in Denver in 1908.

John loved games of chess, checkers, bridge and others, that demanded extreme concentration. He read biographies and history to further stimulate his active mind. Robert Burns became one of his favorite authors.

John C. Brodie died of a heart attack August 5, 1940, in San Francisco, California , while on vacation. He was buried in Olinger Crown Hill Cemetery, Denver, Colorado.

John C. Brodie. From the collection of Frances Brodie Brackett.

James Albert (JA) McConnell. Courtesy of the Lyons Redstone Museum, Lyons, Colorado.

Lyons Limestone Kiln. Courtesy of the Lyons Redstone Museum, Lyons, Colorado.

Lyons Limestone Quarry and Kiln

E dward S. Lyon originally owned 160-acres in the Lyons section. This included limestone and sandstone outcroppings. The limestone quarry was first leased to W. H. Case. He built the first kiln constructed of local sandstone and lined with firebrick. A small limestone outcropping north of town was quarried and burned in the kilns. The pink powder produced was then mixed with local sands to match the unique color of the Lyons Red Sandstone. The Buckhorn Lime was used as mortar for the sandstone.

William and James McConnell had heard about the Quarry boom in Lyons and snow shoed out from Cranberry Lake to the train station in Watertown, New York. After they arrived, the brothers bought the limestone site from E. S. Lyon in 1885. They erected a second kiln. The local outcropping was still being quarried, however, limestone was also being brought in from the Pace Ranch, east of Longmont near 3rd avenue at the sandstone cliff. The McConnell brothers sold the operation in 1892. The Lyons limestone outcropping was in Township 3N; Range 70W; SE 1/4 of SE 1/4 of SW 1/4 of SW 1/4 of Section 17. It covered less than 1-acre.

Production did not equal the financial rewards that were expected and all operations at the kilns came to a halt in 1894. Remains of the two kilns are located on private property behind the U Pump It Gas Station at 4065 Ute Highway.

In 1900 a new kiln was constructed on 5th Street near the train depot, inside the town limits of Lyons. The operation was capable of producing 150 bushels of lime per day. Problems arose when the local citizens began to object to the nauseating pollution spewing from the kiln. A better quality of lime was discovered in Missiouri. Soon after limestone quarrying in this area ceased and the kilns were left to deteriorate.

The McConnell Brothers

In 1878, James Albert McConnell, 17 and his brother William (Bill), 23 traveled to Nova Scotia to mine gold. When they heard of the mining prospects in Colorado, they returned to New York to settle their affairs. The boys and two of their sisters headed to Cripple Creek, Colorado. Bill married Emma Lghtburn in 1874 at Cripple Creek. About 1885 the McConnells moved into the Lyons area to investigate the quarry industry staying at the Sites' Boarding House, now the Fish Hook Fence Co., 4099 Ute (US 36), E. of Lyons on the North side of the road.

The boys purchased the Lyon Limestone Kiln from E. S. and built a second operation on the Sites' property, behind the present U-Pump It Gas Station. During the late 1800s they built a 2-story home just east of the Supply Ditch House.

In 1892, J A married Bertha Jane Reese, the daughter of John and Kate Reese. Their wedding trip was by train to New York to visit J A's sister Elizabeth Fanning. The couple remained in the area for the following two years. Their first child Ethel was born there. By 1894 they returned to mining at Cripple Creek.

Upon the death of her father in 1887, Bertha inherited the McConnell Farm west of Hygiene. It was not until 10 years later that she and J A moved from Cripple Creek to the farm. Orville was born there in 1896. In 1899, the McConnells moved to a farm near Eastlake, where Bernie was born in 1900. Bertha sold the McConnell farm to John Goss. In 1979, the house was torn down for a newer home.

William moved his family to a farm adjoining Albert's in Eastlake. Emma died there when their sixth child, Mary Dayton was born. The baby was raised by James Albert and Bertha. Another child, Lily was taken by the Lightburn family and raised in Denver. Bill cared for Zola, Nina, Luther, Willy and Ted.

Bertha inherited the John Reese farm, plus her brother's property. She and J A spent the rest of their days on the Site's Place. *See References and Notes p 336 for further information.*

Blacksmiths

"The most important function in the nomad's world is that of the blacksmith; his craft of creating the tools, weapons, and utensils so essential to this harsh existence is believed to be taught him directly by the gods. All those born to be leaders were first born smiths they're considered partly magi and partly gods."

—Katherine Neville, author of *The Eight* and The *Magic Circle.*

James Robert Cunningham
1865–1953

James Cunningham, a blacksmith worked in the stone quarries around Lyons, Noland, and Beach Hill. In 1896 and 1897, J. R. was on the Board of Trustees for the Town of Lyons. In 1898, he was elected to the post of Mayor.

In 1915 the family moved to Bisbee, Arizona hoping the dry, desert climate would help Mrs. Cunningham. She suffered from asthma. They returned to Lyons around 1922.

Alexander Chisholm
March 12, 1855–May 24, 1917

Alex came to Colorado in 1876, but moved on to Montana. He returned to Lyons in 1880. His talents as a blacksmith were much in demand in the quarries as well as by the citizens of Lyons.

Alex was elected to the first board of trustees of the Old Congregational Church. He was also active in community affairs. In 1893 he served on the Board of Trustees for the Town of

Lyons. At another time he served on the school board at the Mont-gomery School. Shortly after this, the Chisholms moved to a farm two miles east of town. They raised sugar beets and had dairy cows. Mary made butter and sold it to the Golden Rule Store. Alex continued his blacksmith business from the farm.

Sherman S. Swift
April 15, 1867–March 16, 1934

Sherman's family traveled to Colorado in the early 1870s home-steading near Mead. Sherman came to Lyons in 1889 to work in the stone quarries. His talents for blacksmithing were soon rec-ognized and he opened his own blacksmith shop. Sherman also ventured into hard rock coal mining in Allenspark, but as many did, he returned to Lyons. He supplemented his blacksmithing by working for Charlie Bradford and Thomas A'Hearn. At one time he served as a city councilman. In 1930 Sherman returned to mining at the Smuggler on the South St. Vrain. His wife Anna joined the Old Stone church in 1900 and remained a faithful and good worker for the next sixty-seven years, serving as the church clerk. Anna remained in the family home at Stickey and 3rd until her death in 1967.

Swan Magni Johnson
April 3, 1863–May 30, 1938

Swan preceded his parent's trip to the United States by seven years arriving in 1882. Swan's parents came to America in 1889. They traveled on to Lyons in 1890. Mr. Swenson worked in the stone quarries on Beech Hill as well as for the Burlington Rail-road. Swan worked at the Globeville Smelter in Denver from 1882–1890. Swan, his wife and two sons moved to Lyons where he became a stone mason working on the University of Colo-rado in Boulder, many of the stone homes in Lyons, as well as laying much of the stone used in the Lyons High School build-ing. He was also a blacksmith and would sharpen the tools used in the sandstone quarries

The Johnsons lived in Lyons from 1890–1931 when they moved to Denver.

Blacksmiths 1884–1899

The following blacksmiths are listed in the Colorado State Business Directory: T. J. Thorn, 1884; Wilson & Son, John, 1885; J. A. Richard, 1888; Alex Chisholm, 1889–97; Hubert Eddy, 1890; Mat Keotch, 1890–1; Peter Chrest, 1891–2; C. M. McGuire, 1891; H. Aldrich, 1892; Wm. Richardson, 1892; Walsh Bros., 1893–6; Fred J. Anderson, 1897; and Swift & Anderson, 1899.

A muck (stone) bucket made in a local blacksmith shop. The bucket is lowered into a quarry hole by way of a tripod rig called a Deadman. Each of the 20-30 ft poles is anchored with railroad ties and stone. Cabling is threaded through pullies attached to the poles to give greater leverage in brinigng the stone up to the surface. Photo taken by the author.

APPENDIX I

GENEALOGICAL DATA

GENEALOGICAL DATA

Note: Genealogical notation will be used throughout this section.
January 11, 1890 will appear as 11 Jan 1890.
> *b. birth date, d. death date, m. marriage, dau. daughter, wd. widow*

Thomas A' Hearn
<u>1900 Census Record</u>
Ahearn, Thomas Nov 1866   33   b. IN Parents IRE,
Saloon Keeper
    , Ellen Lyons Oct 1868 31 b. Eng
    , Thomas Feb 1892 8 b. CO
    , Francis Sep 1894 5 b. CO
    , William V.   Jul 1896   3   b. CO
    , Datherine M.   Jan 1898   2   b. CO
Lyons, William father-in-law Jan 1839   61 b. Ire wd., Farm Labor

<u>Record of Burials in the Lyons Cemetery:</u>
Block 4MA Lot 39
A'Hearn, Irene M., d. 06 Dec 1893

<u>Obituary:</u>
"Died in Longmont 17 December 1901 of a heart attack. Well-known
citizen of Lyons. Leaves a wife and five children. [They took the body
back to Pennsylvania and remained with his family.] Was a member of
the Red Men. Certificate of Insurance for $2000 in a Catholic Society.
Owned property in Lyons (saloon/pool hall, Allen's Park, and lots in
Noland, as well as an interest in a mining claim."

William Baker
William Baker, b. 28 December 1826 in Tennessee,
    died 06 April 1907 near Hygiene, Colorado.

<u>Marriages:</u>
William Baker married Mrs. J. P. Franklin 20 June 1868.
    He adopted her two daughters.

<u>1870 Boulder County Census:</u>
120 A – in and beyond Pella area – Burlington Post Office –
    St. Vrain District 13- 2 July 1870.
Baker, William, age 40, b. TN, Farmer;
        Real Estate $5000, Personal Property $2000
Amelia, age 40, b. TN, Keeping House.

Birth of a Quarry Town

1885 Boulder County Census Records:
Baker, William C. Farmer 38 b. MO
Sigler, Mr. S. A. Mother 61 Widow b. NY

Burial Records for the Hygiene Cemetery:
Row 12 Lot 72
William Baker, d. April 6, 1907, Aged 80y. 3m
Pricilla Baker, d. September 6, 1904, Aged 72 y, "Rest Sweet Rest"
Row 12 Lot 89
Pamelia Baker 1832–1904

Henry Franklin Ballinger
Records of Burials in the Lyons Cemetery:
Block 4MA between Lots 23 & 24
Ballanger, Mary Ann   25 April 1862–01 Jul 1928
Ballinger, Henry Franklin.   b. 16 October 1849 in Pennsylvania,
                              d. 04 April 1910 at Lyons of pneumonia.

Bergman Family
Record of Burials in the Lyons Cemetery:
Block 2 Lot 35
Bergman, Dan, b. 06 November 1860, d. 01 February 1933.
Bergman, Lena, b. 28 March 1865, d. 21 July 1936.

Axel Bergquist
Alxel Bergquist,   b. 07 September 1866 in Sweden,
                           d. 31 Aug 1934 inLyons, Colorado.

Records of Burials in the Lyons Cemetery:
Block 2 Lot 35
Bergquist, Axel   b. 07 September 1866, d. 31 august 1934
Bergquist, Osear,   b. 14 October 1863, d. 01 April 1918

Billings Family
The four brothers who came to Colorado:
George,   m. Henrietta
Ferinand,   m. Nellie Wilkins, widow (b. 1843, d. 1921) d. 1900s
Jadez P.   m. Elizabeth (19 Sep 1858–31Oct 1926) in South Dakota
Norton,   b. 1851, m. Elizabeth Browers in Davenport, Iowa,
                  d. 1918. Elizabeth died in childbirth.
                  2nd wife Theresa Gilroy (18 Oct 1861–30 May 1946)
                      on 23 November 1878 at South Dakota.

Children of George and Henrietta Billings:
George "Manny"   b. 1878, d. 1942
Frances   b. 1875, d. 1961
Susan   dates not available

Children of Jabez P. and Elizabeth Billings:
George,   d. at 6 at Camp Billings
Alice   m. Ray Woodmanzie

Children of Norton and Elizabeth Browers Billings:
Etta,   b. 1870 at Marshalltown, Iowa
Norman Arthur,   b. 1874 at Marchalltown, Iowa.

Children of Norton and Theresa Gilroy Billings:
Maude Frances   b. 1879,d. 1968
Grace Bedell   b. 1881,d. 1893
William   b. 1885,d. 1963
Herbert Thomas   b. 1887,d. 1967
Adeline Adell   b. 1889,d. 1968
Gladys Irene   b. 1893,d. 1966
Hazel Ellowee   b. 1897
Nina Imogene   b. 1899.

1880 Census:
Billings, George 34 MA MA RI Farmer Pella
        , Henrietta   35   England
        , Frances   4   CO MA Eng
        , J. P.   3   CO MA Eng
        , (George S. on 1885 Lyons Census)
        , Susan   1   CO MA Eng
Billings, William F.   34   MA MA MA Farming
        Mary C.   29   VT VT VT
        Mary Abby   11 mths CO MA VT
            (Valmont-living with Brother-in-law of William's.
            Chas. H. Cowdrey)

1885 Census:
Billings, N. H.   Farmer   MH   35   MA

        Teresa   Wife 25   MN
        Etta   Dau   11   MN
        Norman   Son   10   MN
        Maud   Dau   5   Dak

191

| Grace | Dau | 2 | Dak |
| Baby | Son | 1/12 | CO |

Billings, J. P.	Farmer	MH	28	MN
,Elizabeth	Wife		25	MN
,George	Son		5	MN

Record of Burials for the Lyons Cemetery:
Block 7 Lot 8
Bessie Billings   12 Mar 1877-08 May 1964
No Record
Nellie Billings   13 Jan 1842-24 Feb 1921
Block 9 Lot 28
Norma Bessie   19 Jan 1919-06 Apr 1958
Norman Arthur   05 Nov 1874-03 Feb 1964
Block 9 Lot 4
Patricia Billings   19 Mar 1957-28 Feb 1964

Record of Burials for the Hygiene Cemetery:
Row 10 Lot 55
Grace D. Billings   d. 29 Oct 1890
          Daughter of N. H. and Tressy Billings, Aged 8yr 4mo.

Charles W. Bird
Record of Burials in the Lyons Cemetery:
Block 9 Lot 28
Bird, Charles W.   b. 25 February 1861, d. February 1947
No Record
Bird, Eliza,   b. 21 November 1875, d. 08 January 1933.

Blair Family
Sarah Anna Blair,   b. 1830 at Ohio, d. 02 Dec 1904
                              at home in Lyons.
Marriages:
Mathew M. Blair and Sarah Anna m. 01 January 1851 at Morrow County, Ohio.

Children of Sarah Anna and M. M. Blair:
John Ashen   b. 17 March 1853 at Ohio, d. 1928 at Marengo Iowa
                    m. Myrena Calcina Rogers
James E.   b. 1855
Charles S.   b. 18 February 1857 at Iowa, d. 11 January 1941
                    at Nebrashka, m. Melissa Motzfield 1884 at Neb.

Elizabeth J.   b. 1859 at Iowa
Sarah Emma   b. 1861 at Iowa, d. 1944 at Denver, CO m. Eberle
Mathew M. Jr., b. 22 October 1865 at Iowa,
                        d. 16 October 1948 at Lyons
Samuel H.   b. 17 February 17, 1869 at Iowa, d. 30 April 1923
Benjamin J.   b. 29 June 1872 at Iowa, d. 3 January 1933 at Lyons.

1885 Boulder County Census:
Blair, Sarah A.   Oct 1830 widow OH
    , Mathew M.   Oct 1865   IA Quarryman
    , Samuel H.   Feb 1869   IA Teamster
    , Benjamin J.   Jun 1872   IA Teamster

Record of Burials for the Lyons Cemetery:
Block 3MA
Lot 42 Benjamin Jack   b. 29 June 1872, d. 03 January 1933.
Lot 58 Matthew M.   b. 22 October 1865, d. 16 October 1948
Lot 59 Matthew M.   b. 14 December 1825, d. 28 August 1899
Lot 59 Samuel H.   b. 17 February 1869, d. 30 April 1923
Lot 59 Sarah A.   b. 22 October 1830, d. 02 December 1904.

Blubaugh Family
Jack Blubaugh, b. 29 Jun 1854, m. Katie David (19 Sep 1866
                        at Bushnell, Illinois–22 Aug 1931),
                d. 23 Oct 1947 at a Longmont Hospital..
Katie David was one of fourteen children born to Isom and Lucy David.
        She was a semi invalid confined to a wheel chair.
        Bur: Green Mountain Cemetery in Boulder, Colorado.
Lucy Tate,   b. 19 Sep 1825,
                m. Isom J. David (14 Oct 1819–03 Dec 1883),
                d. 10 Feb 1913.

Children born to Jack and Katie David Blubaugh:
Lucy,   b. 16 Nov 1889, m. Peter Brodie MacDonald 30 May 1909.
        d. 15 Sep 1974.
        Children: Dorothy b 10 Feb 1913 at Lyons.
                William Grant, b. 13 Jul 1920
George Edward , b. 05 Aug 1900 at home,
                m. Katherine Keller at Estes Park.
        Child: Barbara, b. 30 Jan 1929 at Estes Park
Barbara, b. ?, m. Thomas Hanes (b. 29 Mar 1927 at Chicago) at Denver.
        Children: Mrs Ellen Craig Stites,
        Mrs. Janet Peter Kennedy, plus three other children.

Birth of a Quarry Town

<u>1900 Boulder County Census:</u>
Lyons 04 June 1900 ED 165, SH 3 L2 5th Avenue

Blubaugh, Jacob	36	July 1863,	IA PA KY Teamster
, Katty E. David	31	Sep 1868	IL KY KY
, Lucy	11	Nov 1888	CO IA IL
, George E.	9/12		CO IA IL
David, Lucy (M-in-L)	63	Aug 1836 wd	KY KY KY
, Nathan (Bro-in-L)	27	Feb 1873	IL KY KY Teamster

<u>Record of Burials in the Lyons Cemetery:</u>
Block 9 Lot 8

Blubaugh, George	05 Aug 1900	18 Dec 1986
, Kaye	05 Mar 1902	21 Oct 1990

Phillip H. Bohn

Phillip H. Bohn, b. 1851 in Germany, m. Amelia Lippoldt
(07 Dec 1854–17 Nov 1923), D. 26 Aug 1917.

<u>Children of Phillip H. and Amelia Lippoldt Bohn:</u>

Amelia L.,   b. 20 Feb 1892, d. 29 May 1897
Georgie,   b. 17 Aug 1895, d. 18 Sep 1895
Another child died in infancy
Charles,   b. Lyons, m. Della Davison 12 Nov 1903,
Frank,   b. 12 Jul 1893, m. Flora Murray 01 Sep 1924, WWI,
               d. Sep 1950.
               One child: Robert, b. 16 Jan 19 At Stamford,
                       Connecticut, m. Grace Cone (15 Jan 1932 at
                       Connectcut) 14 Mar 1953, d. Sep 1950.
               Bur: Cypress Cemetery, Saybrook Point, Old Saybrook
                       Connecticut.
Herman,   b. 1879, m. Christine Jensen (1884–1961) 25 Apr 1906,
               d. 1955.
               Children: Clarence (20 Feb 1907–08 Jul 1938).
                       Dorothy (26 Dec 1910–2001), m. J. E. Stevens
                       (02 Nov 1894) 09 Jul 1949.
                       Child: Mary Lou, b. 29 Mar 1951, m. Robert
                               Webb (20 Aug 1947). Children
                               Robert, b. 12 Sep 1967 and Richard,
                               b. 08 Nov 1968.
Henry   b. 1881, m. Mabel House (1884–1961), d. 1948.
               Son, Sherman
Wesley Bohn   b. 18 Jan 1903 at Lyons, m. Freda, d. 30 Dec 1979.
               Four children: Shirley, Richard, Rodney and Julie.

194

Edward m. Louis Mills, Longmont.
Children Edward and Ralph.
Phillip, Jr. b. 30 Sep 1896, m. Nina Billings 16 Dec 1917,
d. 20 Nov 1964 at California.
Children: Kenneth,, Marjorie, Eileen.
Raymond m. Tena Galbreath
Children: Peggy and Marion Anna, b. 21 Jul 1877, m.
Sherman Swift 10 May 1894, d. 17 Aug 1967.
Children: Eldon and Lucille
Clara no records
Dora m. Mazett.

Record of Burials in the Lyons Cemetery:
Block 6 Lot 6
Bohn, Amelia S.   b.07 Dec 1854   d.17 Nov 1923
    , Phillip H.   b. 1851   d.26 Aug 1917
Block 6 Lot 7
Bohn, Henry William   b. 20 Sep 1881   d.01 Apr 1948
    , Mabel M.   b. 12 Apr 1884   d. 26 Apr 1951
    , Sherman Wesley   b. 18 Jan 1903   d. 30 Dec 1979
BLock 6 Lot 10
Bohn, Verna
Block 7 Lot 3
Bohn, Clarence H.   b.20 Feb 1907   d. 12 Jul 1938
BLock 7 Lot 4
Bohn, Christine m.   b. 07 Oct 1884   d. 27 Apr 1970
    , Herman W.   b. 07 Oct 1879   d. 25 Apr 1955
Block 10 Lot 22
Bohn, Amelia l   b. 20 Feb 1892   d. 29 May 1897
    , Georgie   b. 17 Aug 1895   d. 18 Sep 1895

Levi Brackett Family
Levi Brackett, b. abt. 1821 in Tennessee, m. the widow
Permelia Sophie Howard.
d. 07 October 1898 in Lyons, CO. bur: Hygiene.
Parmelia Sophie Howard,
b. 06 April 1850 in Springfield, Miss.
d. 02 August 1931 at Longmont, Colorado,
Bur: Hygiene Cemetery.
m. James Samuel Weese at Springfield, MO.
Later married Levi Brackett, an uncle to James Samuel Weese.

Children of Levi and Permela Weese Brackett:
Francis (Frank) Marion Brackett,
    b. 14 Jun 1886 at Lone Pine, NW of Lyons
    d. 16 Mar 1972 at home in Lyons, bur: Hygiene, CO
    m. Corda Floss Hirschfeld 23 May 1910 at Boulder.
Mary L. Brackett   m. Wright Slaven - a registered nurse.
Melissa M. Brackett   m. Norm Johns who died; m#2. Roberts.

Children of Francis (Frank) Marion and Corda Floss Hirschfeld Brackett:
Frances Maxine
Merle Lucille   m. McGeorge at Denver, Colorado
Shirley Madeline   m. Arnold Eliase Sanford at Lyons.
                         Children: Keith, Frank, and Michael.
William Levi   b. 17 September 1916, m. Frances Brodie,
                         d. 04 September 2001.
                         Two children: Janet and Jack;
Willard Charles
Marjorie Alice   m. Charles Cinnamon. Child: Kenneth
Ardyce Josephine   m. Hedrick at Littleton;
Richard Harvey
Francis Wayne

1870 Boulder County Census:
121 A   St. Vrain – Burlington Post Office St. Vrain District 15 –
        5 July 1870
Brackett, Levi   45   TN   Farmer RE 2500 PP 1200

Record of Burials Lyons Cemetery:
Block 2 Lot 51 S1/2
Brackett, William L.   b. 17 Sep 1916   d. 04 Sep 2001

Record of Burials Hygiene Cemetery:
Row 13 Lot 72
Levi Brackett   d. October 7, 1898,
                         Aged 77 years "Heaven Is my Home"
Row 17 Lot 99
Frank Brackett   b. 1886   d. 1972
Maxine Brackett   b. 1910   d. 1919
Richard Brackett   d. at 6 weeks
Willard Brackett   b. 1916   d. 1991
Dale E. Brackett   b. April 26, 1952 d. January 23, 1997
                         (son of Francis) "In Loving Memory"
Floss Brackett   b. 1888   d. 1877

Charles Bradford

Charles Bradford   b. 07 June 1844 at Astoria, Long Island,
                       d. 13 January 1929 at Lyons,
                       m. #1Sarah White in 1868,
                       m. #2 Mary E. Robey 09 May 1926.

1870 Boulder County Census:
120 B   Upper St. Vrain – Pella; Burlington Post Office
         St. Vrain District 14 – 2 July 1870
Bradford, Charles   24   NY   Farmer Real Estate 700
                                       Personal Property 200
       , Sarah S.   26   IL   Keeping House

Held Patent 1278 for 3 North, 70 West, Hall Ranch, 13 Auguat 1881.

1885 Boulder County, Colorado Census:
Bradford, Charles   Farmer   MH   42   NY
       , Sarah   Wife   42   IL

Record of Burials in the Lyons Cemetery:
Block 2 Lot 87
Charles   b. 1844   d. 1929 Co. 1 3rd Ill. Cav.
Sarah S.   b. 1843   d. 1923

John C. Brodie

John C. Brodie, b. 16 aug 1861 at Furness, Scotland the son of
        John and Mary Campbell Brodie, d. 5 Aug 1940 at San
        Francisco, California. Interment is in the family plot at
        Crown Hill Cemetery, Denver, Colorado, m. Wife #1
        Angelina Sibson, Wife #2 Ella Baldwin on 7 Jul 1923.
Angelina Sibson Brodie, b. 24 Jan 1868 Isle of Guernsey, England
                        d. 21 May 1921 from sleeping sickness
                        at Denver, Colorado.
                        bur: Crown Hill Cemetery, Denver, CO

Children of John and Angelina Brodie:
John Charles Brodie, Jr., b. 4 Dec 1925 at Del Rapids, S D
        d. 8 Apr 1937, m. Mary Mc Coy 14 Dec. 1945 at SD
Peter Brodie d. as a baby. Bur: Hygiene Cemetery, Hygiene, CO
Mary Campbell Brodie b. 14 Dec 1890 at Del Rapids, SD,
        m. Charles Howard Webb, d. 15 Jul 1968.

William Earl Brodie, b. 2 Jan 1892 at Del Rapids, SD,
d. 20 Jan 1960 at Reno, Nevada.

Brown Family

Alfred Bennet Brown,   b. 01 Jun 1837,
       m. Linda Cloyd (01 Jun 1842– 11 May 1931),
       d. 21 Oct 1907 at home on Stickney Avenue.
       He built the house in 1899.

Children of Alfared and Linda Cloyd Brown:

Louise	b. 1862,	m. Newcomb
Maude,	b. 1865,	m. Evans
Frank	b. 1868,	d. 1907 in Alaska, US Signal Corps.
Mabel	b. 1875,	m. Higgens
Cloyd	b. 1876	

Harry Earl Jack b. 1878 at Friend, Nebraska, m. Susan Montgomery
       Murry 25 May 1915 at Golden, Colorado.
       Children: Imogene and Mary Jane. Imogene m. Victor
          Dick; two children: Vickie and Lynda
       Mary Jane m. Duane Krout;
          Two children: Susan and David

Vivien   b. 1882,   m. Hadley.

Fred Bucherdee

Bucherdee, Fred C b. Nov 1848 at Seymour, Indiana,
       m. 17 June 1875. Sarah E. Hutchinson, 15-year-old
       daughter of Joseph Hutchison at Left Hand by Rev.
       Nathan Thompson., d. 28 September 1909.
Sarah E. Hutchinson, b. 06 April 1860 at Oskaloosa, Iowa,
       d. 05 May 1950. Husband #2 Perry Morris in 1935
       at Boulder. Morris family. Bur: Lyons Cemetery.

1880 Census:

Bucherdee, Fred C.,   Age 30, b. IN,   Parents from Germany,
            Saloon Keeper in Jamestown.
   , Sarah (Hutchinson),   Age 19,   b. IA.

Record of Burials in Lyons Cemetery:

Block 2 Lot 86

Fred Bucherdee C.	b. 17 Nov 1848	d 28 Sep 1909
Morris, Perry James	b. 18 Feb 1876	d. 27 April 1936

Block 1 Lot 84

Morris, Sarah Eunice	b. 06 Apr 1860	d. 05 May 1950

Block 2 Lot 25
Morris, Shirley Ann   b. 16 Mar 1928   d. 01 May 1933

Obituary of Fred C. Bucherdee:
"The people of Lyons were badly shocked, Tuesday morning, when the word was passed around that Fred C. Bucherdee, an old resident of Lyons, had committed suicide. He had been afflicted with stomach trouble. He was born in Seymour, Indiana. Member of Odd Fellows and Red Men Lodges of Lyons."

Dr. O. M. Burhans
Record of Burials in the Lyons Cemetery:
Location of burial was never recorded
Burhans, Dr. O. M.   b. Aug 1845   d. 07 Sep 1910

John Peter Burness
John P. Burness b, 1854 in Sweden, d. 15 Aug 1922 at Lyons,
          m. Clara Sophia LaFalk (Falk) 1875 in Sweden.
          Occ. Stone Quarryman Arrived Lyons 1888.
Clara Sophia LaFalk,   b. 20 Aug 1853 in Sweden,
     (Falk)   d. 03 Jul 1936 in Lyons. Bur: Lyons Cemetery.

Children of John Peter and Clara Sophia LaFalk Burness:
Oscar Johnson, b. 1878 in Sweden, d. 1898 in Lyons. Came to Lyons
          With father in 1888. Never married.
Charles Burness Johnson,   b. 08 Aug 1880 in Sweden,
          d. 19 Jul 1949 in Denver, bur. Lyons, CO.
          Never married. Occ. Groceryman.
          Came to Lyons with father in 1888.
Anna Sophia Burness,   b. 14 May 1892 in Lyons, d. 26 Mar 1971 at
          Greeley. Bur: Greeley Sunset Gardens
          m. John W. (Mac) (d. 1943) in Fort Collins.
          No children.
Ida Burness,   b. 02 Apr 1894 at Lyons, d. 26 Dec 1975 at Las Vegas,
          Bur: Las Vegas, NE Memory Gardens.
          m. John E. Lall in Longmont 07 Jan 1920,
          witnesses: Selma and Niels Jespersen. No children.
John E. Lall,   b. 16 Sep 1893 at Longmont, d. 09 May 1955 in
          Denver, CO. Bur. Olinger Crown Hill Cemetary.
          Occ. Game Warden in Lyons in 1922.
Selmas Burness, b. 02 Jul 1897 in Lyons, D. 09 Dec 1971 at Las Vegas,
          Bur: Las Vegas Memory Gardens.
          m. Niels P. Jespersen in Lyons 30 May 1917

Birth of a Quarry Town

Niels Peter Jespersen   b. 21 Dec 1890, Snedsted, Denmark,
                          d. 30 Nov 1958 at Las Vegas NE,
                          Bur Las Vegas, Mr. View Memory Gardens.
                          Occ: Dairyman

Children of Selma Burness and Niels P. Jespersen:
Harold Burness Jespersen, b. 10 Jun 1921 at Lyons. m. Marie M.
        Steigerwalt 08 Dec 1945 at Bethlehem Lutheran Church,
        Lawrenceburg, IN. 4 children: David Nils, Carol Anne,
        Donald Paul;, Robert Car, b. Cincinnati, OH.
Charles Wilbur Jespersen, b. 07 Mar 1928 at Boulder, d. Jan 1976 in Salt
        Lake City, UT, Bur: Las Vegas, NE.
        m.. Jeanne Schultz 05 Sep 1948 in Las Vegas NE.
        5 children: Karen, Lynn, Terri, Marc, Tarl, b. Las Vegas, NE.

Record of Burials in Lyons Cemetery:
Block 2 Lot 46

Burness, Clara Sophia	b. 20 Aug 1853	d. 29 Jun 1936
Burness, John Peter	b. 1854	d. 15 Aug 1922
Johnson, Charles Burness	b. 08 Aug 1880	d. 19 Jul 1949
Johnson, Oscar W.	b. 08 Nov 1882	d. 17 Mar 1907

        (dates don't agree with notes from Harold B. Jespersen)

Jane Capson

Jane Capson   b. 21 February 1823 at Belfast, Ireland,
                d. 05 December 1914 at Lyons. Bur: Lyons Cemetery
                Widow. Aunt to Sarah Capson Welch.
                      Sister of Sarah's mother.
Children of Jane Capson:
Emma Capson Carvell and Leona Capson Scanlon.

Record of Burials in Lyons Cemetery:
Block2 Lot33
Capson, Jane   b. April 1823   d. 05 Dec 1914. (Cemetery Records)

Lewis Albert Carvell Family

Lewis Albert Carvell   b. 06 Aug 1864, m. Emma Capson 1924,
                        m. Katherine Urban Epley 1925,
                        d. 01 Sep 1953 at California.
Children of Lewis Albert and Emma Capson Carvell:
Arthur N.   b. 29 Jul 1885,
                m. Hilda S. Johnson (10 Sep 1883– 08 Feb 1952),
                d. 23 Nov1979.

Children: Donald A., b. 13 May 1910,
m. Mabel L. Brown;
Mildred, b. 16 Jan 1913, m. William R. Kincaid.

Ethel   b. 02 Dec 1888   d. 23 Feb 1976.
m. Theodore Schlapfer (11 Dec 1868–02 Mar 1970),
Children: Alma b. 28 Apr 1914, m. Eddie Smith, d. 20
Jan 1963. Elizabeth m. Gus German.

Bessie   m. Harvey Dreamer One adopted son, Lewis
William   b. 30 Aug 1895,
m. Marie Urban (03 May 1895–03 Feb 1965),
bur: At Walden, Colorado.
Children: Katherine, b. 30 July 1915 at Lyons,
d. Aug 1935.

Loraine   b. 71 Aug 1917 at Lyons.
William R.   b. 10 Jul 1926 at Lyons.
May L.   b. at Lyons.

Records of Burials at Lyons Cemetery:

Block 5 Lot 59

Carvell, Arthur N.   b. 29 Jul 1885 d. 23 Nov 1979
, Donald A.   b. 13 May 1910 d. 27 May 1985
, Hilda Sophia   b. 15 Sep 1883 d. 08 Feb 1952
, Mabel L.   b. 30 Mar 1915 d. 12 Dec 1998

Block 2 Lot 33

Carvell, Emma   b. 21 Jul 1865 d. 10 Oct 1924

Block 9 Lot 15 C 1 / 1th

Carvell, Katheryn Maxine b. 28 Jul 1915 d. 11 Aug 1934

Gilead P. Cheney

Gilead P.   b. 24 Mar 1838 at Virden, Illinois the son of
Murray Cheney

Heney   b. 1809 at Vermont   d. 1885
Caroline Pickett m. Emily C. Plowman 1860,
d. at his home in Noland, Friday, morning,
July 12, 1907 at the age of 69 years.

Children of Gilead P. and Caroline Pickett Cheney:

Charles M.   b. 03 Oct 1862, m. May Flansburg 16 Apr 1903,
d. 1936
Children: Dorthea, m. Rev. Snider of Brighton;
Margaret, m. Russell Glasgow; Emily, m. Ward Hawk.

John Plowman b, 16 Dec 1873, m. Sadie Jamison, d. 11 Apr 1928.
Children: Merad Grace, m. Fred Ballard;

William Robert, m. Martha Timken;
Catherine Louise Murphy.
Henry Edward
Mrs. E. N. Greene of Denver.

John George Cheney
John George Cheney   b. 1852,
     m. Amanda Eveline Maltby (17 Dec 1852–
      01 Feb 1918) 10 Mar 1873 at Virden, IL.
    Amanda bur: Mountain View Cemetery, Longmont, CO

Children of John George and Amanda Eveline Maltby Cheney:
Two died in infancy
Josephine   m. Byron Hall in 1904
Hazel   Never married, lived in Lyons all her life.
Howard   m. Johanna Schappler 25 Feb 1928.

Record of Burials in Lyons Cemetery:
Block 2 Lot 55
Emily Caroline   b. 14 December 1841,   d. 19 January 1917
Gilead P.   b. 24 March 1838,   d. 12 July 1907
John T. (Jonathan)   b. 10 December 1873,   d. 27 April 1928
Sadie J.   b. 21 September 1887,   d. 28 Nov. 1984
William,   b. 01 April 1856,   d. 04 May 1924.

Alexander Chisholm
Alexander Chisholm   b. 12 Mar 1855,
     m. Mary Hinkley (03 Feb 1837–15 Dec 1923 at
      Fort Collins),
     d. 24 May 1917 at Thermopolis, Wyoming.
Two sons: James and John

Record of Burials at Hygiene Cemetery:
Lot 4 Row 91
Chisholm, Mary Waltham   b. 03 Feb 1867   d. 15 Dec 1923
     , Alexander   b. 12 Mar 1855   d. 25 May 1917
     , James Alexander   b. 31 Dec 1893   d. 22 Jul 1958
     , John W.   b. 12 Jan 1897   d. 14 Aug 1966

James W. Collett
James W. Collett   b. Jul 1843, m. Tabitha Barr Mar 1866 in IN
     d. 05 Jan 1903.

Children of James W. and Tabitha Barr Collett:
Two children died prior to 1903;
others are: J. A., John W., Henry, Viola Osborne, Charles, George,
        Esther Twist, Grace Davis and Minnie Goodard.

Record of Burials at the Lyons Cemetery: BLock 7 Lot 29

Collett, James W.	b. 29 Jul 1843	d. 06 Jan 1903
, Tabitha Elma	b. 09 Jan 1849	d. 20 Dec 1939

Aquilla Cook

Aquilla Cook,	b. 1833,	d. 1868 in Colorado

Records of burial in the Hygiene Cemetery:
Lot 18 Row 3

Cook, Aquilla	b. 1833- 1868 (Is this same Cook?)
Cook Freeman	1863–1889 (question of relationship)

Cox Family

E. C. Cox   d. 16 Oct 1891. No record of burial in the Lyons or
                 Hygiene Cemeteries
Effraim [Ephrim, Efraim] C. Cox homesteaded at Noland in 1887.

Children of Efraim C. Cox:

Charles A.	b. 23 Jan 1866,	d. 11 Aug 1929 at Longmont.
Alice Bell	b. 03 Jan 1855,	m. Charles Kesler Hirschfeld,
	d. 24 Mar 1934.	

C. K. Hirschfeld b. 20 Apr 1854,   d. 19 Jan 1940.

Record of Burials in the Lyons Cemetery:
Block 2 Lot 54

Charles A.	b. 23 Jan 1866,	d. 11 Aug 1929
Minnie Floy	b. 01 Feb 1879,	d. 22 Mar 1935

James Robert Cunningham

James Robert Cunningham, b. 1865 in North Carolina,
             m. Minnie Bell Baker (1870–1948), d. 1953.

Children of James Robert and Minnie Bell Baker Cunningham:
Five children
Three born prior to 1900:
             William Robert, Mary Virginia and Edwin Everts.
Leonard Cecil,   b. 1903
Ruth Winifred,   b. 1906, m. Kenneth C. Brodie.

Seven children: Ruth, Mary, James, Charles,
Nicholas, Patsy, one child died.

<u>Record of Burials in the Lyons Cemetery:</u>
Block 5 Lot 21

Cunningham, James Robert	b. 19 Jan 1865	d. 19 an 1953
, Minnie Bell	b. 25 Dec 1870	d. 06 Sep 1948
, William R.	b. 24 Jan 1889	d. 29 Jun 1969.

Dr. E. S. Crona
Dr E. S. Crona, b. 28 Dec 1838, d. 02 Mar 1919, Bur. Longmont,
m. Eva R . Graham at Denver 25 Jun 1901.

Leonard Henry Dieterich
L. H. Dieterich   b. 26 Oct 1858 at Springfield, Ohio,
d. 13 Aug 1933 at Lyons
m. Gertrude (Genetta) A. Thomas,
b. 05 Sep 1861 at Lebanon, OH. d. 13 August 1933.

<u>Children of L. H. and Gertrude A. Thomas Dieterich:</u>
William   b. 22 Dec 1896 at Lyons,   d. Arizona
Howell   b. 03 Apr 1900 at Lyons in their new home
400 block of Stickney, m. Juanita Sprowl
d. November1962 at Lyons.
Henry Leonard, b. 16 Jul 1905 at Lyons, m., d. 21 December 1978
Bur: Lyons Cemetery.
Children: L. A. dietrich; Mrs. Blake (Margaret)
Patterson; Mrs. Al (Mary Ann) Hagen;
and Mrs. Shirley Merrill.

<u>Record of Burials in Lyons Cemetery:</u>
Block 7 Lot 14

Leonard Henry Dieterich	b. 26 Oct 1858	d. 13 Aug 1933
Gertrude A. Thomas	b. 05 Sept 1861	d. 15 Apr 1937
Henry Leonard	b. 16 Jul 1905	d. 21 Jun 1978
Howell Ferdinand	b. 03 Apr 1900	d. 05 Feb 1987

Charles Valtine Engert
Charles Engert b. 01 August 1861 to John Engert b. Germany
and Matilda Wernetle Engert b. Pennsylvania,
m. Sarah Ann Powell 28 September 1885,

d. 05 March 1949.
Sarah Ann Powell Engert
> b. . 07 Octobert 1861 in Effingham County, Illinois ,
> d. 28 Feburary 1933 at home.

Children of Charles V. and Sarah Ann Powell Engert:
Mrs. W. P. (Eugenia) Billings
Mrs. R. E. (Ora Annetta Grace) House, b. 07 April 1889 at Logan KS.
Mrs. C. F. (Lenora/Legora) May

Record of Burials in the Lyons Cemetery:
Block 7 Lot 53
Charles V.   b. 01 Aug 1861   d. 05 Mar 1949
Sarah Ann   b. 07 Oct 1870   d. 17 Feb 1943

Griffith Evans Family
Griffith J. Evans   b. 02 May 1832 in Wales,
> m. Jane Owens 1855 at Dodge County WI
> d. 05 July 1900 Boulder County,
> Bur: Jamestown Cemetery, Jamestown, CO.

Jane Owens   b. 20 September 1837 in Wales, d. 1921 in Boulder.

Children of Griffith J. and Jane Owens Evans:
Jennie   b. 1859, m. Deckster (Deck) Smith. They had 11 children.
Llewellen   b, 1862, m. Nellie Beach.
Evan   b. 1866, m. Margaret Davis.
Nell (Catherine Ellen)   b. 10 January 1869 near Burlington, CO
> m. Walter Clemens (b. 7 October 1861).
> Six children: Boyd, Paul, Jerone, Clinton, Douglass,
> and Quay.

George   b. 1871, m. Edith Greenlee (Greenley)
Florence   named after Isabella Bird.
John   b. 1876, m. Winnefrcd Owens.

1870 Boulder County Colorado Census:
Burlington post Office; St. Vrain District 19; Sheet 123A;
Evans, Griffith J.,   40,   b. Wales,   occ. Laborer,
> personal property $150

1885 Boulder County Census:
Enumeration District 2-Sheet 23-Lines 36–44, Lyons section
Evans, Griffith J.   54,   b. Wales,   occ. miner;
> 19 May 1879 (property ownership)

, Jane A.	47,	(wife) Wales
, Luellen	22,	WI, occ. rancher;
		(alternate spelling Llewellen)

, Evan, 19, CO; Nellie, 16, CO; George, 13, CO; Florence, 11, CO;
John, 8, CO.

Stanley, M   25,   MI, CAN, CAN, miner, bro. of Jane.

Ben Durr
Ben Durr   b. 04 Nov 1851 at Lohr, Bavaria   d. 28 Mar 1891.

Frank Brothers
Charles   m. Emma from Luxembourg 1896,
                d. 24 Jul 1935 at Goldfield, Nevada while working on
                    a mining claim,
                Bur: Santa Monica, California.

Emma   d. 23 Mar 1956.

One son: Bernhardt, b. 05 Jan 1898. U. S. Army WWI,
                Never married, d. 1957.

William Frank   m. Neva Holcomb, daughter of John and Eliza
                    Holcomb in 1894, d. 1957.Two sons:
                Lyle d. 07 Feb 1901 at age 3 of diphtheria
                Carl b. 29 Jan 1895, m. Zella Gilger 05 Oct 1917, d. 1957.

Nicholas Frank b. 25 Apr 1860 in Luxemberg Germany,
                    m. Ella Goodwin in 1907,
                    d. Jul 1911 3 miles west of Lyons.

Josiah Flynn
Josiah Flynn   b. Cass County, Illinois July 22, 1852.
                m. Martha S. (Mattie) Leonard December 11, 1876
                    at Indianola, Iowa.
                d. September 5, 1936.
                Bur: Linn Grove Cemetery at Greeley.

Children of Josiah and Martha S. Leonard Flynn:

Willie	b. 29 June 1978,	d. 20 July 1880
Edgar	b. 1 May 1880,	d. 19 August 1882
Grace	b. 27 May 1884 in Iowa,	

Grace (cont.)   m. Angelo French 08 August 1909,
                d. 19 November 1914 at Denver from goiter operation,
                bur. Greeley.

Warren   d. shortly after his birth in 1886.

Norean   b. April 14, 1893, m. Sydney Mayhew 25 Feb 1913 at
               Boulder, d. 1945. Child: Lavinia.
               #2 m. Noah Herbert Early at Berthoud.

Noami Lucile
Dorothy
Ruth
Joseph Benjamin   d. WWII
Roy Herbert   d. WWII.

Dr. George W. Gammon

1900 Colorado Census Record:

Gammon, George W.	Apr 1843	57	b. ME	Physician & Surgeon
, Addie	Jan 1852	48	b. ME	Dressmaker

b.

Record of Burials in Lyons Cemetery:

Block 2 Lot 75:

Dr. George W.	b. 22 Apr 1844	d. 13 Feb 1908
Addie	b. 14 Jan 1850	d. 21 Jul 1935

Gordon Family

J. C. R. Gordon   b. 1843 in Pennsylvania,
                  d. 1914 at the Lyons Post Office
                  Bur: Witherow Lot in the Mountain View
                        Cemetery at Longmont, Colorado.
Lizzie Baughman   b. 15 Apr 1840,   d. 05 Jan 1927
                  kept house & chores for Mr. Gordon
                  Bur: next to Mr. Gordon.

Charles Fullerton Gordon

Charles F. Gordon   b. 22 September 1863 at Shady Grove, PA
                  m. Barbra Negley Summer (28 October 1868
                     at Williamsport, Maryland—11 Sept 1948),
                  d. 25 January 1933.

Parents of Charles: Humphrey and Deborah Gordon
Parents of Barbra: Elias and Elmira Summer.

Children of Charles Fullerton and Barbra Negley Summer Gordon:

Bruce Edwin   b. 7 January 1891 at the Columbus Weese farm,
                  m. Blanche Young Goss of Hygiene.
                  Children: Margery, Goss, and Edwin d. in infancy.
Grace Carrie   b. 17 October 1892 at Longmont,

m. Ray R. Rushton 2 June 1915.
Children: Charles Eugene and Barbara Ann.

Roy Summer   b. 11 January 1895 on the farm southeast of Lyons,
m. Violet Dawe at Lyons, d. 14 December 1960.
Two Children: Aileen m. Roger Collinson
Patsy d. at 2 years in March 1932.

Elmira Deborah Gordon,   b. 18 June 1901 on the farm SE of Lyons,
m. Reuben G. Sjogren at Fort Collins 21 April 1923,
d. 1978,   bur. Longmont Cemetery.
Child: Barbara Marie, m. Aldro Steadman of Longmont.

Anna Jean   b. 7 March 1907, m. Leslie L. Gibbons on 16 June 1930.
Children: Myrna Jean, m. Don Packard; Patricia
Frances, m. Gary Doughty; Bruce Leslie Gibbons
of Fort Collins.

William Griffith Family

1885 Boulder county Census
June 1885 Ed 3, SH 59, L 46

Griffith, William D.	53	CT RI RI	tone Cutter
, Harriette	49	CT RI RI	
, Lizette	dau	16	CT CT CT
, William A.	son	13	CT CT CT
, Dora M.	dau	12	CT CT CT
, Emma F.	dau	6	CT CT CT

Children of Dora M.:

Flora   m. William Noyes.

John   m. Ethel, an English war bride.
Four children: Flora Ann, David, Tommy, and Bill.

David   m. Barbara Four children: Amy, Sara, John, child died.

Land Patent:

Griffith, William O. Sec. 13, Twp. 3N, Range 71 dated 24 Sept. 1884.

Rec ord of Burials in the Lyons Cemetery

No Record

Harriet F.   d. 28 Feb 1907
Block 2 Lot 21

Mike Dennis,   b. 02 June 1914,   d. 21 August 1983
Block 5 Lot 23

Susan Elizabet b. 22 July 1899,   d. 18 March 1994

William Alex,   b. 13 January 1897,   d. 23 February 1969
Block 9 Lot 2

William O.   b. about 1832
Block 9 Lot 4
Jake
Rhoda   b. 12 march 1864,   d. 28 July 1934

Hall Family
Marriages:
John Bigland Hall m. Hannah Roberts 28 March 1878 (1877) Chicago.
Charles Byron Hall   m. Josephine Cheney of Lyons 06 Jun 1904.
Madge Hall   m.Robert Stoll August 1940.
Chester Bigland Hall   m. Nellie Mae Morris 21 June 1911.
Lois Hall   m. Frederick Lamb
George   m. Lucille Humphrey
Madge   m. Robert Stoll movedto Washington

Children born to J. B. Hall and Hannah Roberts Hall:
Charles Byron   b. 19 August 1879 at Chicago,   d. 27 April 1944.
Madge   b. 24 February 1915,   d. 10 Nov 1984.
Chester Bigland b. 24 October 1881,   d. April 1965
Lois   b. 21 July 1888 at Lyons,   d. 11 Oct 1980.
George & Mable   d. 22 April 1907.

Children born to Charles Byron and Josephine Cheney Hall:
George   b. 31 March 1911 at Lyons
Madge   b. 24 February 1915 at Lyons

Children born to Chester and his wife:
Maureen and Wilbur

Children born to Lois and Frederick Lamb:
Jack, Donald, and Kenneth.

1885 Boulder County Census Records:
Hall, John B.   Farmer   37   b. Scot
  , Hannah   25   b. WI Parents: Wales
  , Charles B.   son   5   b. IL
  , Chester   son   4   b. IL
  , Roy   son   2   b. CO
  , Mathew,   Brother   30   b. Scot
                          occ. Carriage Maker
Roberts, Mary   Sister-in-Law 27   b. WI
Forbes, William Nephew   23   b. Scot
Roberts, David E.

Father-In-Law 72   b. Wal occ. Shoe Maker

1900 Boulder County Census Records:

Hall, John B.	June 1848	22	Stock raiser Scotland
,Hannah Roberts	Apr 1860	22	b. WI Parents: Wales
, Charles B.	Aug 1879		b. IL Stock Herder
, Chester B.	Oct 1881		b. IL
, Lois T.	July 1888,		b. CO
Lee, Charles A.	Oct 1863		b. MO Hired Hand

Record of Burials in the Lyons Cemetery:
Block 2 Lot 50

C. Maurine	b. 03 March 1915, d. 26 April 2000
Hannah Roberts	b. 16 April 1860, d. 02 June 1939
	b. at Cambria, Wisconsin (Welch descent)
John Bigland	b. 20 June 1847 (1946), d. 14 April 1934
Block 1 Lot 42	
George & Mable	b. ?, d. 22 April 1907.

Halliday, Annia (Anna)

1885 Boulder county Census:

Halliday, Annia	M ay 1860	20	b. Sweden. Dressmaker
, Ana L.	Mar 1884		b. SD
, Mable C.	July 1886		b. SD
, Elsie R.	Nov 1888		b. SD

Hirschfeld Family
Charles Kesler Hirschfeld   b. 20 Apr 1854 at Philadelphia, PA
            m. Alice Belle Cox (dau. of E. C. Cox) at Mesopotamia,
            OH 22, Feb 1883,
            d. 19 Jan 1940.

Children of Charles Kesler and Alice Bell Cox Hirschfeld:
Floss,   b. 13 Jun 1888, m. Frank Brackett, d. 10 May 1977.
            Children: Merle, William, Willard, Marjorie, Ardith, Francis.
Belle,   b. 20 Apr 1891.
Dewey (female), b. 01 Apr 1898,   m. Gibson

Record of Burials in the Lyons Cemetery
Block 2 Lot 54
Alice Bell   b. 03 Jan 1855,   d. 24 Mar 1934

Charles Kesler   b. 20 Apr 1854,   d. 19 Jan 1940
Charles J.   b. 28 Aug 1870,   d. 05 Dec 1925.

Charles J. Hjertquist

Charles J. Hjertquist,   b. 28 Aug 1870 at Hyortsberga Smaland,
        Sweden to John P. and Stina K. Swenson, ,Never married,
      d. 1925 from heart failure after rescuing miners from a mine
      in Nederland.
      Changed his name from Swenson to Hjertquist when he was
      discharged from the Swedish Army.

Siblings of Charles J.
S. M. Johnson of Lyons
Mrs. Emma Johnson of Frederick
Mrs. Amanda Sealander of Cascade.

Record of Burials at the Lyons Cemetery:
Block 2 Lot 24
Charles J.   b. 28 Aug 1870   d. 05 Dec 1925
His parents:
Swenson, John P.   b. 22 Aug 1834 d. 22 Nov 1908
Swenson, Stina K.   b. 21 Jul 1877   d.17 Aug 1967

John Bradley Holcomb

John B. Holcomb,   b. 27 Nov 1845 in Wayne County, Indiana,
                m. Eliza Cook in 1868,
                d. 04 Jan 1922. Civil War Veteran
Eliza Cook   b. 24 May 1850 in Ohio.
      Eliza's widowed mother, Jane m. J. D. Sanford, lived in
        Muggin's Gulch with dau. Catherine
Catherine   m. A Spaulding

Children of John B. and Eliza Cook Holcomb:
Neva   b. 15 March 1872 at Somerset Indiana, m. William Frank
          in 1894.
        Children: Lyle who died in childhood and Carl
          b. 29 Jan 1895, m. Zella Gilger 05 Oct 1917.
Carl   b. 05 Nov 1875 at Maine, Indiana.
Twin boys   b. Lyons d. as babies
Rossie   b. 24 April 1887at Lyons,
        m. Arthur Stiles 11 Oct 1905 at Lyons.
        Children: Arthur Clair b. 06 Oct 1906, d. 29 May 1917
          and Freida

Nadine   b. 15 Jun 1908.

Albert Edward Howe
Albert Edward Howe   b. November 1868,
                        d. 6 March 1944 at Boulder.
Marriages:
  A. E. Howe m. Lura Dean McFadden, daughter of
        Thomas P. McFadden 3 March 1897 Old Stone Church, Lyons

Children of A. E. Howe:
Alberta E.   b. Jan 1897 at Lyons,   m. John C. Oliver,
                d. 12 November 1958.
Virginia   b. mar 1898 at Lyons,   m. Charles S. Lough
Norman R.   b. 27 September 1901 at Lyons, m. Helene Knoefler
                  24 Nov 1937 at Boulder,
                d. 23 Jan 1993 at Boulder,
                Bur: Mountain View Cemetery, Longmont
Theodore E.   b. 26 Jan 1903 at Lyons, m. Goldene Copeland
                  31 May 1936,
                d. 24 Feb 1986 at Boulder, bur. Green Mountain Cem.
George Whitfield b. 11 Apr 1904 at Lyons, m. Rubye C. Ahlberg
                  15 June 1927 at Denver,
                d. 03 May 1978 at Boulder,
                Bur: Green Mountain Cemetery, Boulder
Rosa   b. 26 Dec 1905 at Boulder,   m. Chris G. Barbarino.
Carl Wayne   b. 01 July 1907 at Boulder,   m. Dorothy Scanlon
                  Tremmel,   d. Apr 1960,
                Bur: Green Mountain Cemetery, Boulder, CO
Emma Beatrice   b. 31 July 1909 at Boulder,   m. Criss C. Hedge,
                d. 19 Feb 1979 at Boulder.

1900 Boulder County Census Records:
Howe, Albert E.   Nov 1868 31   b. Can-Eng Hotel Keeper
    , Leura McFadden Feb 1880 28   b. KS
    , Alberta E.   Jan 1897   3   b. CO
    , Virginia   Mar 1898   2   b. CO

William Newton Hubbell
W. N. Hubbell   b. 06 Aug 1849 in Minnesota,
                d. 09 Feb 1908.
                m. Ida Melvina Gilbert(1857–1888) Brown Cty, MN

Wife #2: wd. Lillian Sigler Stiles, 09 Jun 1889 at
Lyons,   d. 1949 at CA. She had one living son,
Arthur Stiles from

previous marriage, who m. Rossie Holcomb in
1922,   d. 1958 in California.
Lillian Sigler Stiles Hubbell   m. John Smith in 1918.

Children born to William Newton and Ida Melvina Gilbert Hubbell:
Amanda Melvina   b. 24 Nov 1876,   d. 11 Jun 1877
William Henry   b. 20 Feb 1878 at Winona, Minnesota,
                    m. Rose Zella Funkhouser (15 Mar 1886 in
                      York County, Nebraska)at home
                    Children: 1) Ida Ellen 09 Feb 1904 at Lyons,
                          m. Carl StenmarkSep 1923.
                    2) Leona Lillian 30 Mar 1911 at Denver,
                      m. Verne Deas 27 Mar 1935.
                      One Child: Patricia Joan (1937–1950)
                    3) Wanda Gwendolyn, b. 10 May 1920,
                      m. Elmer Gauthier 20 Aug 1938.
                      Children: Judith Annett, b. 12 May 1939;
                      Joseph William, b. 03 Apr 1945.
Louis Herbert,   b. 06 Feb 1880 at Winona, Minnesota,
                 d. 08 Feb 1959 at a Denver Hospital.
Dwight,   b. 03 Sep 1884, d. 08 Oct 1885.

Alfred Jamison
Alfred Jamison,   b. 19 December 1850 of stone cutters consumption,
                 m. Catherine Hedges, d. 05 January 1914.
Catherine Hedges, b. 24 August 1852,   d. 1930.

Children of Alfred and Catherine Hedges Jamison:
John,   b. 27 December 1877 at McPherson, Kansas, m. Anna Bassett
          Wilcox 12 June 1902,
          d. 05 June 1962.
          Child: Helen Roberts Jaison Newman.
Ralph,   b. 26 May 1879,   d. childhood of diptheria.
Grace,   b. 07 May 1881,   m. D. S. Rich 09 March 1904 at Lyons
                                  Congregational Church.
          Three children: Anna Blanch, Edgar Ralph, David Russell.
Frank Percy,   b. 08 January 1883, d. childhood of diptheria.
Mary,   b. 09 March 1885,   d. childhood of diptheria.
Sarah (Sade), b. 21 Sep 1887,   m. John Cheney.
          Three Children: Merab Grace Cheney Ballard, William

Robert, Catherine Louis Cheney Murphy.
William Fred, b. 31 August 1890,
> d. self inflicted gunshot wound.
Catherine (Kitty) May,   b. 14 April 1896, m. Lon Parker in 1927
> (he died of the flu in 1928). No children.

Record of Burials in the Lyons Cemetery:
Block 2

Lot 53 Anne	b. 12 Jun 1877	d. 01 Jul 1958
John	b. 27 Dec 1877	d. 05 Jun 1962
Lot 73 Francis V.	b. 24 Oct 1857	d. 26 Mar 1915
BLock 1 MA Lot 41		
Katherine	b. 24 Aug 1852	d. 08 Jul 1930
Block 4 MA Loc 39		
Frank	b. abt 1883	d. 10 Jul 1890
Mary	b. abt 1885	d. 15 Jul 1890
Ralph	b. abt 1879	d. 22 Jul 1890
Tom	b. abt 1853	
William Fred	b. 31 Aug 1890	d. 26 Jul 1913

James S. Johns
James S. Johns   b. in Warren County, Iowa,
> m. Louisa Flynn 31 December 1879, (d. 21 Sepr 1941 at
> home in Lyons)
> d. 1943 at Lyons.
Children of James S. and Louisa Flynn Johns:
Boy   child born and buried in Iowa
Eva   b. 05 December 1889 in Iowa, m. Claude Stevens Sept 1904,
> d. 21 March 1964 in Lyons.
> > Two children: Fern Louis, m. Virgil Rigdon of Lyons;
> > Ila Fay, m. Willard Kirk.

Record of Burials in the Lyons Cemetery:
Block 2 Lot 11

James S.	b. 20 February 1861	d. 31 October 1943
Louisa	b. 27 June 1865	d. 21 September 1941

Erick Johnson
Erick Johnson   b. 02 april 1855, m. Gustave Albertina Ostrum at
> Umea, Sweden, d. 1923 at Steamboat Springs,
> Bur: Steamboat Springs.
Gustave Albertina Ostrum,
> b. 03 April 1854, d. 16 January 1947 at Hayden,

Colorado, Bur: Stamboat Springs.

Children of Erick and Gustave Albertina Ostrum Johnson:

Jonas "Ole",   b. 29 March 1881 at Unea, Sweden, Never
married, d. 17 July 1947 at Steamboat Springs, CO.

Hilda Sophia   b. 10 September 1883 at Sioux Falls, South Dakota,
m. Arthur N. Carvell, d. 08 February 1952.
One Child: Donald A. Carvell, b. 13 May 1910 at
Steamboat Springs, m. Mabel L. Brown.

Ellen Albertina, b. 07 June 1884 at Del Rapids, South Dakota,
m. Don M. Leckenby,   d. 23 August 1941.
Three Children: Don M., Mary Ellen, Robert Erick.

Teckla   b. 1886, d. 1891, drowned in St. Vrain River at Lyons.

Lillian Charlotte,   b. 13 November 1888 at Sioux Falls, S D
m. Alonzo Edgar Cook, d. 10 July 1976.
Four Children: Edgar Alonze, Myrtle Marie, Thelma
Charlotte, Leonard Johnson.

Charles Frechot b. 06 Jun e 1891 at Lyons,   m. Arlene Stickles,
d. 02 October 1928.   One Child: Marvin Charles

Christine Wilhelmina   b. 10 July 1893 at Lyons,
m. Rudolph F. Lindbert.
Two Children: Edna Mae and Susan

Swan Magni (Swenson) Johnson

John P. Swenson b. 22 Aug 1834 at Hjortsberga, Smaqland, Sweden
m. Stina K. (21 Feb 1837 at Hjortsberga, Smaqland,
Sweden– 03 Apr 1913 at Lyons,
d. 22 Nov 1908 at Lyons.
Son of John and Stina:

Swan M. Johnson   b. 03 Apr 1863, m. Amanda Augusta Carlsson
(04 Nov 1866–23 Jan 1933), d. 30 May 1938.

Children of Swan M. and Amanda August Carlsson Johnson:

Carl Emil,   b. 13 Nov 1888,   d. 01 Feb 1949

Ernest,   b. 24 Feb 1890 at Denver, d. Spring 1907

Emma,   b. 09 Jan 1892 at Lyons, d. Jun 1915 at Topeka, KS

Anna,   b. 07 Aug 1893, m. Russell Wayte of Leadville, CO
in 1917, d. 26 Nov 1918 at Minturn, influenza
epidemic of 1918.
Child: Russell Wayte. At 10 months old went to
live with grandparents, Swan Johnson,
m. Josephine Hansen in 1938.

Other Births:

Russell   b. 1939 and Pamela Jane, an adopted daughter,

	David,	b. 1943.
Rudolph,	b. 04 Mar 1896, d. Spring 1907 of typhoid fever
Baby boy,	b. & d. Feb 1900
Ellen,	b. 1902,	d. 1905
Thelma,	b. 15 Jan 1904, d. 22 May 1918
Gertrude,	b. 28 Mar 1907, d. 01 May 1922.
Edwin,	b. 09 Mar 1898.
Jennie,	b. 21 Apr 1909, Lives in Lakewood, CO
Walter,	b. 14 Jul 1912, m. twice, d. 1999.

Thomas Lavridson
Thomas Lavridson m. Mary Madison Jan 1891.

    1896 Lyons City trustee & quarryman
    1904 Lyons stone contractor

1900 Boulder County Census:
Lavridson, Thomas   Dec 1866   33 b. Denmark,
                        Landlord & Stone Cutter
    , Mary P. Madison   b. Jan 1871 29 at Denmark
    , Anna m.   b. Oct 1891 8 at Colorado

Laycook Family
John S. and Zillah W. Laycook settled in Hygiene in 1873.

Children of John S. and Zillah W. Laycook:
Joseph B. Laycook   d. 03 November 1945 in San Bernardino, CA
Robert S.;   Elvis;   and Fred.

Children of Francis M. and Nancy Laycook :
Mrs. Susie Kimbell
Mrs. Beth Holden

Lowe Family
Brothers Thomas and James Lowe of Lyons
Brothers William and Alfred of Boulder
Four sisters:
    Anna Combs of Denver, Mrs. Mary A. Livingston of Golden,
    a sister in California and another in Wyoming.

Record of Burials in the Lyons Cemetery:
Block 9 Lot 29
Thomas Lowe   b. 17 Mar 1867   d. 04 Jun 1911
Ella Lowe   b. 15 Feb 1872   d. 21 Jan 1962

Block 3MA Lot 39
James Lowe   b. 01 Mar 1865   d. 05 May 1923

Lyon Family

Parents of Edward S. Lyon:

Thompson Lyon,   b. 05 Dec 1793, m. Elizabeth Weeks,
                           d. 27 Apr 1859
Elizabeth "Eliza"
  Weeks Lyon,   b. 08 Oct 1808, d. 1847.

Children of Thompson and Elizabeth Weeks Lyon:
Nathan, Susan, Esther, and Ellen.
Edward S. Lyon,   b. 02 Sep 1843 at Windham County, CN
                 d. 4 Jan 1931 at California, bur. San Diego, CA

Marriages of Edward S. Lyon:
#1 Caroline Evangeline Barrett, b. 1864, m. 1864 at Woodstock, CT
                          d. 1873.

        Four Children:
        Lillie Eliza   b. 1864, d. 1873, m. T. J. Thorne 1884 at
                      Longmont.
        Leonard Cutler b. 1868, d. 1905, m. Alice C. Sosey 1889
        Eva   b. 1879, d. 1944, m. William Thorne (brother
                      of T. J. Thorne)
                      Two Children: Harold and Mabel
        Frank Lyon   b. 1873, d. 10 Oct 1945, m. Ollie Hunter
                      (d. 28 Jun 1956) at North Park, CO 1892.
                      Two children;
                          Della, b. 07 Mar 1901, m. Frank Kerfoot,
                              d. 1971 in an airplane accident.
                        Eunice Caroline, b. 15 Nov 1903,
                              m. George Roxburgh, d. 1968, heart
#2 Adeline Sherman   b. 1873, d. 1889
                      One son died shortly after he was born.
#3 Carrie Boyd   m. 02 Sep 1890 at Denver, Colorado
                      Two-year-old son died in house fire.
#4 Dora Griffith   m. Mar 1900 at California.

Children of Edward S. and Caroline Barrett Lyon:
Lillie   b. 1866 at Putnam, Connecticut,
                      m. T. J. Thorne 02 Jul 1884 at Lyons.
Leonard Cutler   b. 17 Mar 1868 at Putnam, Connecticut,
                      m. Alice C. Sosey 06 Jun 1889 at Lyons,

                d. Dec 1905 at Lyons.
                Child: Clarence Austin, b. 23 Apr 1890,
                    m. Natalie Netta Coombes 05 Sep 1911.
                Two Children:
                Jane Alice, b. 24 May 1917, m. Bob Grimshaw
                  Two children: Carolyn and Martha.
                Donald Leonard, b. 29 Jan 1925.
                Myrtle May, b. 25 Jun 1892, m. Norman Lombard
                Fern Elizabeth, b. 11 Sep 1899, m. Daniel Pickett
Eva   b. 1870

Children of Leonard Cutler and Caroline Barrett Lyon:
Myrtle   b. at home at 435 Reese Street, Lyons,
                m. Norman Lombard.
Clarence Austin   b. 23 Apr 1890
                m. Natalie Netta Combes 05 Sep 1911.
                Children: Jane Alice and Donald Leonard
Fern Elizabeth   m. Daniel Pickett, d. 1981.

Ed McCall
Ed McCall ,   b. 16 Apr 1883, d. 17 Mar 1956

1885 Boulder County Census:

McCall, Thomas	Farmer MH	58	Ohio
Elizabeth	Wife	45	Wales

Children of Thomas and Elizabeth McCall:
                Clara 18; Wilbert 17; Thomas 15; May 14; Eleanor 12;
                Theodore 10; Bessie 8; **Edward 2.** All born in Colorado.

McConnell Family
Hugh   b. 1852 at Ireland, d. 1918 Walla Walla, WA
                m. Emily McCann (1830 at New York–1894
                  at south Dakota) 14 June 1851. Nine children.

Children of Hugh and Emily McCann McConnell:
William,   b. 1854, m. Emma Lightburn at Cripple Creek, CO
                Emma d. in childbirth at Eastlake, CO in Feb 1912.
James Albert   b. 7 Aug 1860 at Conway, Ontario,
                d. 30 Mar 1932,
                m. 31 Dec 1892 to Bertha Jane Reese,
                bur: Hygiene Cemetery.
Elizabeth b. 1853; Jennie b. 1856; Fannie & Jennie b. 1864;

Vincie b. 1867; Hugh e. b. 1869; John MS b. 1872.

<u>Children of James Albert and Bertha Jane Reese McConnell:</u>

Ethel	b. 09 Oct 1893(4) at New York
	m. John Woods
	d. & bur: at Klamath Falls, OR.
Orville	b. 26 Dec 1895 at Hygiene, CO
	m. Opal Compton
	d. & bur: Greensb urgh, LA.
Lenore	b. 13 Dec 1896 at the McConnell Farm near Hygiene
	m. John Foster
	d. Madison, Wisconsin; Bur: Ft. Collins, CO
Bernie LaVern	b. 25 Feb 1900 near Eastlake, CO,
	m. Irene Emmerling (20 May 1923–20Apr 1976). Emmerling was a Schoolteacher in Brantner near Henderson, CO.
	d. & bur: at Lyons 26 Sep 1988.

<u>Children of Bernie L. and Irene Emmerling McConnell:</u>

Berene Rose,	b. 21 may 1925, m. William C. Sullivan, Two children: Rosamond and Floyd.
LaVern Maxine,	b. 23 Feb 1927, m. F. LaVerne Johnson, Two Sons, Gerald and Ronald
Violet Ann,	b. 06 May 1930, m. Albert Betz Three children: Barbara Jean, Debra, and Leann
Herbert Reese,	b. 03 Aug 1936, m Linda Keppen Children : Terri and Tracey. d. In Lyons while at work 31 Aug 1995
Sharon Dee,	b. 24 May 1943, m./div. Two Children: Scott Leiding and Laura Leiding
Byron Ray,	b. 28 Jun 1944, m. Sharon Pigeon Two daughters: Kelly and Jackie

<u>Record of Burials in the Lyons Cemetery:</u>

Block 3MA Lot 17

McConnell, Bernie LaVerne	b. 25 Feb. 1900	d. 26 Sep 1988
, Irene Marie	b. 06 Jan 1902	d. 20 Apr 1976
, Herbert Reese	b. 03 Aug 1936	d. 31 Aug 1995
, Linda L.	b. 23 Oct 1938	d. 07 Nov 2000

<u>Record of Burials in the Hygiene Cemetery:</u>

Lot 9 Row 53

Bertha Jane	b. 1870	d. 1958

Donna Mae   b. 02 Jul 1936   d. 10 Jan 1939 (Dau of Orville McC.)
James Albert   b. 07 Aug 1860   d. 30 Mar 1932

McFadden Family
Thomas Pierce , b. 1839, m. Virginia Alice David (d. in Kansas
            abt 1901 – 43 y) ,
            d. 1894 at Lyons,. Drowned trying to save his twelve
            year old son Howard from the St. Vrain River.

Children of Thomas Pierce and Virginia Alice David McFadden:
Lura,   b. 08 Feb 1880 at Logan County, Kansas,
            m. A. E. Howe 03 Mar 1897 at Lyons,
Charles W.,   b. 1874,
            m. Nettie Spaulding (07 Apr 1873–19 Apr1966)
              Oct 1900,
            d. 05 Jul 1930.
Rose   m. Jack Hawkins
Carl   b. 04 Apr 1891,
            m. Jennie Archie 29 Sep 1915 at home in Lyons,
            d. 16 Feb 1964.
            Left in the care of Mrs. Katie Blubauagh at death of
              his mother in 1901. One child: Marjorie.
Alice   Left with an aunt after the death of her mother in 1901.

Child of Charles W. and Nettie Spaulding McFadden:
Charles Thomas,   b. 27 Jul 1902,   m. Roberta Calloway,
            d. 05 Feb 1968.
            Children: Charlotte, Charles, and Janet.
         Francis, John, Leota, m. Ralph Marshall, Marley

Record of Burials in the Lyons Cemetery:
Block 2 Lot 13
Charles Thomas,   b. 27 July 1902,   d. 5 February 1968.
Charles William,   b. 16 October 1874, d. 5 July 1930.
Nettie B.   b. 7 April 1873,   d. 19 April 1966
Block 2 Lot 26
Jeanette Blanche   b. 7 April 1873,   d. 19 April 1966.
Carl A.   b. 4 Sept 1891,   d. 15 February 1964.
Block 2 Lot 28
Esther Mae   b. 12 August 1907, d. 18 June 1954.

Records of Burials in Hygiene Cemetery:

Lot 88 Row 15

Thomas P.,	b. 1839,	d. 1958
Howard J.,	b. 1884,	d. 1895
Kattie,	no dates	

Lot 95 Row 16

Lucy,	b. 1916,	d. 1963.

Charles Miller Family

Charles Miller b. 1840 as one of thirteen children,
m. Susan Brown (b. 1856) Oct 1877, d. 1915
Elizabeth Brown grew up in a foster home in Illinois with Susan

Children of Charles and Susan Brown Miller:

Todd Miller Children: Francis Miller Landeau and Dean Miller
Mayme Miller Barnes Child: Orval Barnes
Bessie

Montgomery Family

William M. b. 1898 in Maryland,
m. Mary Elizabeth Dawson (1816 in Virginia–1881),
d. 1890.

Children of William M. and Mary Elizabeth Dawson Montgomery:
Born at York County, Virginia

Child	died at birth	
Sarah,	b. 1835,	m. Stephen Conroy in 1855, d. 1873
Willia	m A, b. 1838,	d. 1911
Alexander,	b. 1840,	d. 1931 *See below*
Lucy A.,	b. 1842,	m. George Walker 1861 in IA, d. 1879
Henrietta,	b. 1844,	m. William Richardson, 1840 in IA, d. 1915
Franklin,	b. 1846,	m. Mary Hall 1879, d. 1932. Child b. at Pella, IA, d. in infancy
Robert	b. 1848,	m. Clara Chapman in 1879, d. 1924 at Lyons. Eight children.
Cyrus	b. 1859,	m. Dora Hedges in 1884, d. 1945. Three children.
Alexander,	b. 1840 at Virginia	m. Emma Peel Ferguson (1855 in IL–1912) 23 Apr 1871 at Niwot, CO d. 12 Jun 1931 at Colorado Springs, CO.

Birth of a Quarry Town

Children of Alexander and Emma Peel Ferguson Montgomery:
William Gilbert, b. 23 Jan 1872 at Lyons, d. 25 July 1879 of diphtheria.
Mary Helen,   b. 13 Aug 1873 on the Montgomery Farm,
                 m. William Hansen 22 Aug 1897, d. 30 Aug 1949.

Children of Mary Helen and William Hansen:
Harry   b. 06 Oct 1892   d. 20 Dec 1970.
Margaret   b. 18 Jul 1898   d. 11 Oct 1975
Emma   b. 12 Aug 1905
William   b. 20 Jan 1913   d. 03 Oct 1963
Myrtle   b. 19 Sep 1909   d. 25 Dec 1980
Robert   b. 05 Dec 1917
Myrtle Elizabeth, b. 01 Sep 1876,
                 m. Charles Frank Clinton (23 Feb 1876–24 Jul 1939)
                    01 Apr 1907, #2 m. Robert Scanlon in 1970s,
                 d. 10 Sep 1964.
John Washington, b. 13 Feb 1879 on the Montgomery Farm,
                 m. Maude May Brown Bradford 25 Dec 1899 Lyons,
                 d. 27 Sep 1954.

Children of John Washington and Maude May Brown:
Born in Lyons
Charles   b. 14 Jun 1900   d. 16 Apr 1972 in California
Susan   b. 01 Aug 1902
Orvice (Jack)   b. 15 Sep 1904   d. 24 Nov 1972 in California.
Raymond   b. 17 Mar 1908
John Bradford   b. 01 Oct 1910   d. 8 Apr 1962 at Reno, Nevada
Lucille   b. 17 Jun 1912
Bernice   b. 07 Aug 1914
Margaret (Maxine) b. 26 Jan 1923
Susan Savannah,   b. 19 Nov 1882 on the Montgomery Farm,
                 m. William Murry 1902, Divorced 1904.
                 Child: Maude
Leona.   m. Harry Earl Jack Brown 25 May 1915 at Golden,CO
                 Children: Imogene Cloyd and Mary Jane Linda.
Roy Phillip   b. 18 Sep 1891 on the Montgomery Farm,
                 m. Marie Woodruff 16 Aug 1917 at Steamboat Springs,
                 d. 19 Sep 1969.
                 Children: Melroy 15 May 1918; Lois, 20 Apr 1925;
                    Phillip 04 Apr 1932; Donald 02 Jan 1937.
Robert Bruce Montgomery
                 b. 28 Oct 1848 in Marion County, VA

m. Clara Chapman of Chapman Switch in 1879,
d. 29 Jul 1924

Children of Robert Bruce and Clara Chapman Montgomery:

Harvey Bruce,   b. 19 Apr 1880,   d. in infancy

Pearl Olive,   b. 18 Oct 1881,
        m. Thomas Wallace (07 Dec 1875 at Union County,
           Iowa–12 Dec 1944),
        d. 18 Apr 1912.
        Three Children: Pearl Estella b. 23 Sep 1905 at
           Brush, CO, m. Jack Ross 07 Apr 1928 at Seattle, WA

Frank Robert,   b. 16 Aug 1883,
        m. Ruth Humphries (23 Oct 1883–04 Jul 1956),
        d. 04 Jul 1941
        Two children in Fort Collins.

Florence Ethel b. 02 Jan 1886,
        m. Albert Schwilke 21 Aug 1907,
        d. 15 Aug 1962.

Children of Frank Robert and Ruth Humphries Montgomery:

Arthur Ewing, b. 07 Jul 1889, m. Pearl Hodgell #2 Katherine Howard,
        d. 16 May 1948.
        Two children with Pearl and one child with Katherine.

Martha Iva,   b. 18 Mar 1892 at Lyons,
        m. Fared McLaren 03 Aug 1919,
        d. 09 Feb 1966. They had six children.

Charles Edwin, b. 04 Jan 1894 at Lyons, Never married, WWI,
        d. 10 Dec 1975 on father's farm.

Ruth Estella   b. 06 Nov 1897 at Lyons.

1885 Boulder County Census:

Name	Relation	Status	Age	M/S	State
Montgomery, R. B.	Farmer	MH	35	M	IA
, Clara		Wi	23	M	CO
, Pearl		Da	3	S	CO
, Frank		So	1	S	CO
Montgomery, A. W.	Farmer	MH	45	M	VA
, Emma		Wi	30	M	IL
, Mary H.	Da	11	S	CO	
, Murty		Da	8	S	CO
, John W.		So	6	S	CO
, Susan		Da	2	S	CO
, William		Fa	76	W	MD

Montgomery, B. F.	Farmer	MH	38	M	VA
, Louisa		Wi	32	M	Swe
, Carrie J.		Da	5	S	CO
, Elizabeth		Da	3	S	CO

Record of Burials for the Hygiene Cemetery:
Row 1 Lot 3
William Montgomery   d. Oct. 8, 1890 in Lyons
            Aged 81 yrs. 10 mo. "Rest In Peace"
Mary Wife of William   b. August 14, 1916,
        d. November 26, 1881,
            Aged 65 yr. 3 mo. 12 days,
            "Blessed are the dead who die in the Lord"
Row 6 Lot 33
Mrs. Mary S. Montgomery d. September 1, 1866, Aged 17 yrs 2mo
Row 9 Lot 54
W. G. Montgomery   b. January 25, 1872,
        d. July 25, 1879, Age 7 yrs 6 mos

Record of Burials in the Lyons Cemetery:
Block 2 Lot 27
Alexander W.   b. 13 Jan 1840,   d. 12 Jun 1931
Emma F.   b. 22 Apr 1855,   d. 10 Oct 1912
No Record
Robert Eugene   b. Nov 1919,   d. Dec 1919

Jacob Clifford Moomaw
Jacob (Jack) Clifford Moomaw   b, 18 Jun 1892 at Mirage Flats, NE,
        m. Lila Weese 05 Jun 1915 at Douglas, Wyoming,
        d. 10 Jan 1975 t Longmont.

Children of Jacob Clifford and Lila Weese Moomaw:
Patricia   b. 01 May 1925,   m. Forrest Burron,
        d. Jan. 1948 of a cerebral hemorrhage.
Mrs. Helen B. Button Motley,   b. 1946

Siblings of Jack C. Moomaw alive after his death:
Two brothers: John of Longmont and Joseph of Denver
Four sisters: Mrs. Emma Hutchins of San diego, California,
        Mrs. Alice Flannery of Cheyenne, Wyoming,
        Margaret Coyle of Albuquerque, New Mexico d. 2000),
        Mrs. Maude Beasley of Longmont.

Record of Burials at Hygiene Cemetery:

Lot 3 Row 90

Moomaw, Jacob Clifford	b. 1892	d. 1975
, Lila Weese	b. 1893	d. 1961

Lot 84 Row 6

Moomaw, Charles Ward	b. 1900	d. 1913

Ohline Family

Record of Burials in the Lyons Cemetery:

Block 9 Lot 19

Golda Marie Brown	b. 15 Jul 1906,	d. 01 Aug 1988

Block 9 Lot 20

Arthur E., Sr.	b. 09 Aug 1897,	d. 04 Aug 1972
Arthur, Jr.	b. 03 Jul 1926,	d. 30 Jun 1973

Block 9 Lot 22

Anna	b. 14 May 1868 at Sweden, (mother of	
	Arthur, Sr.),	d. 11 Feb 1847
Custer Gerald	b. 14 Oct 1901,	d. 29 Aug 1952
Olaf	b. 07 Oct 1856,	d. 14 December 1934

Reese Family

John Reese   b. 12 Jan 1831,
        m. Catherine Cornelia (Kate) Gifford,
        d. 21 Oct 1887.

Catherine Cornelia Gifford
        b. 19 Feb 1835 at Greenwich, Ohio,
        d. 13 Oct 1911. She was one of seven children.
        Parents Jane Jenny and Humphry Gifford. She was the
        first teacher at the Montgomery School east of Lyons.

Children of John and Catherine Cornelia Gifford Reese:

Bertha Jane Reese   b. 31 Oct 1870, m. Albert McConnell.
        Children: Ethel, Orville, Lenore, and Bernie b. 25 Feb 1900
        at Eastlake, Colorado, m. Irene Emmerling on 28 May 1923
        at Henderson, Colorado, d. 28 Sep 1988.
Frank Lewis Reese   b. 31 Oct 1872, d. Nov 1928.

Marriages:

John Reese to Catherine E. Gifford 11 Nov 1869
James Albert McConnell to Bertha J. Reese 31 Dec 1892

1870 Boulder County, Colorado State Census:

120B Upper St. Vrain – Pella; Burlington Post Office

St. Vrain District 14 – 2 July 1870
Reese, John   39   PA   Farmer
           Real Estate Value 2000 Personal Property 300
Kate C.   32   OH   Keeping House
1880 Boulder County, Colorado United States Census:
Reese, John   49   Farmer PA PA PA
   , Kate C.   44   OH MA MA
           Maiden name: Gifford
   , Bertha   9   CO PA OH
   , Frank Lewis 8   CO PA OH
   , Lewis   7   CO PA OH
       (Census taker error. Lewis was not a family member)

1900 National Census: **Reese Family**
Enumeration District 165, Sheet 8, Lines8 & 9
Kate C. Gifford   63 Feb 1835 wd OH MA MA   Farm
Frank L.   Oct 1872   CO PA OH   farmer

Record of Burials in the Hygiene Cemetery: Reese Family
Row 9 Lot 53
John   b. Jan, 12, 1881,   d. May 10, 1887
Catherine C. Gifford   b. Feb. 19, 1835,   d. Oct. 13, 1911
Frank Lewis   b. 1872   d. 1928

Michael John Scanlon Family
M.J.   b. 21 November 1866 at New Britain, Connecticut
       m. Leona Elizabeth Capson b. 08 May 1866 at St. Johns,
          New Brunswick, d. 16 April 1956. at Denver 1891
       d. 11 January 1941 at Lyons, Colorado.

Parents of John Scanlon:
John Scanlon,   d. 07 November 1910, bur. St. Mary's Cemetery,
          New Britain, Connecticut.
Margaret Golden Scanlon   d. 09 September 1880 ,
          Bur: St. Mary's Cemetery, NewBritain, CT.
Children of Michael J. and Leona Capson Scanlon:
Leona,   b. 30 June 1893 at Lyons, m. George W. Dunbar
               Children: 3 sons, 1 daughter.
Marguerite,   b. 28 April 1895 at Lyons, m. C. A. Garrett of Longmont.
               Daughter Joan b. Silverthorne.
John Capson,   b. 06 May 1900 at Lyons, d. 08 July 1962,
               m. Margaret J. Newby of Lyons. Child: Son John

William Donald b. 20 August 1902 at Lyons,
              m. Aurelia Murphy late in life.
              d. 02 January 1965, at Hartford, Connecticut
Robert,   b. 24 July 1905 at Lyons,
              m. #1 Edith Nelson Connecticut;
              Two children, Michael and David.
              Wife #2 Myrtle Lea Clinton.
Dorothea   b. 24 May 1907 at Lyons,
              m. #1 Robert Trimble of Ft. Collins.; #2 Carl Howe;
              Daughter, Judith Lea
Helen Valentine b. 14 February 1911 at Lyons,
              m. W. K. Evert of Longmont (1906-07 Oct 1999)
              d. 07 Oct 1999.
Note: Information supplied by a family member.

Schwilke Family
Record of Burials in Hygiene Cemetery:
Row 3 Lot 84
Gottabine Dorthea Mohl Schwilke   b. 1850   d. 1902

Record of Burials in Lyons Cemetery:
Block 2 Lot 66:
Gottlob Frederich Aldinger, husband of Minnie Schwilke.
        b. .in Felbach, Wurtenberg, Germany
        Bur: in Lyons Cemetery   01 Nov 1859–20 May 1928
Minnie Schwilke Aldinger, Sister of Jacob Schwilke
        b. Felbach, Wurtenberg, Germany
        Bur:in Lyons 20 Sep 1863–07 Mar 1926

John A. Sealander
John A. b. 01 December 1868 in Sweden,
         m. Amanda Swenson 27 June 1902,
         d. 1932,
         Bur: Lyons Cemetery.
Amanda b 03 August 1875 in Hjortsberga, Smaland, Sweden,
         d. 28 Feb 1961, Bur: Lyons Cemetery.
Children of John A. and Amanda Swenson Sealander:
Harry b. 28 July 1903 at Lyons, m. Joyce Smidle.
         One child: Laurel
Carl O. b 24 February 1906 at Lyons,
         m. Della Golden on 26 June 1938 at Denver, d. 1980
Victor b. 10 June 1908, U S Army WWII,
         d. 27 December 1966 at San Francisco, CA,

Birth of a Quarry Town

Bur: Crown Hill Cemetery in Denver.
Irvin L. b. 20 November 1910, m. Thelma H. Larson of Denver,
    d. 1975 at Riverside, CA.
    Three children: John, Norman, and Sara.

Record of Burials in the Lyons Cemetery:
Block 2 Lot 37
Sealander, Amanda A   b. 03 Aug 1875   d. 28 Feb 1961
Sealander, John A.   b. 1866   d. 1932

Sigler Family
Children of Mascheck and Sophronia Sigler:
Lillian B.   b. 08 Aug 1862 at Memphis, Missouri,
    m. Wellington Stiles in 1878 (he died 1885),
      #2William N. Hubbell, Estes Park Stage Line.
    d. 1949.
    Sons: James, unknown, Dalison, Walter b. 1856, d. 1881.

Record of Burials in the Hygiene Cemetery:
Lot 6 Row 29 North
Sigler, Sophronia   Mother, Wife of M. Sigler, d. 18 Oct 1891,
    Aged 67y 5 mo 5 d.
Sigler, Walter M.   son of M and S. A. Sigler, d. 21 Feb 1882,
    Aged 17y 3 mo 16 d.

William Sites Family
1870 census:
Upper St. Vrain/Pella area
Sites, William, 36   occ. Farmer   Maine
    Personal Property $800.
  , Ester, wife, 28   Keeping House. Missouri

1880 Census:
Sites, William 46   he and parents born in Maine, farmer in the Pella area
  , Ester 37   b. Missouri, F. MA M. OH
George 9   b. Colorado;
Jessie (dau) 3   b. Colorado;
Bessie 3   b. Colorado.

1885 Census:
Sites, William 51   stock raiser
  , Ester J. 42
  , George W. 14

228

, Jesse (son) 8   See 1880 Census: Jessie, dau

, Bessie   8

Four boarders:

    W. Clark, H. H. Lunker, F. H. Lunker, and J. Rorder.

<u>1900 Census:</u>

Sites, Ester,	b. September 1841, (died July 1912), a widow and stock raiser
, George W.	b. April 1871, stock raiser
, Bessie	b. October 1876

One boarder:

    Ollin Shenefield   b. September 1860 in Indiana, occ. Tending irrigation ditch.

On the back of the census card a note by Boulder Genealogical Society Genealogist, Mary McRoberts: W. H. Sites died in Lyons 28 April 1894, aged 60 years 4 months. "Another good man felled by his 4-legged workers." [A horse kicked William.]

<u>1910 Boulder County Census:</u> 147 Bross

Sites, Esther J. (misspelled), 68, a widow, occ. Cook, own income

  , Bessie   33, music teacher, b. Iowa.

  , Jessie (grandson),   6, b. Colorado, father b. Colorado.

<u>Record of Burials for the Hygiene Cemetery:</u>

Row 3 Lot 18

W. M. Sites	d. April 28, 1894, Aged 60 years 4 mo.
Esther Cook Sites	b. Sept. 27, 1841 d. Jul. 2, 1912

John G. Sjogren

John G. Sjogren,   b. 26 October 1859 in Sweden,
                  m. Charlotte Marie Johnson in Denver,
                  d. 26 May 1930.

Charlotte Marie Johnson, b. 21 January 1861, d. 09 June 1923.

<u>Children of John G. and Charlotte Marie Johnson Sjogren:</u>

John Gunnar,   b. 1890 at Lyons, Never married, d. 1935 at Lyons.

Reuben George, b. 24 February 1893 at Lyons,   m. Elmira D.
               Gordon 12 April 1923,   d. 22 October 1924.
               Children: Barbara Marie,   b. 24 December 1923.

Ernest Victor,   b. 17 February 1895 at Lyons, m. Thelma,
               d. 19 October 1949 at Estes Park.
               One child: Shirley.

Ruth T.,   b. 23 May 1902,   d. 16 July 1902.

Dan Slaughter
Dan Slaughter, b. 1855 in Illinois,
                     d. 25 August 1923 during surgery in Longmont.
Brother   William Henry.

Record of Burials in the Lyons Cemetery:
No Record of locations

Daniel	b. abt 1855	d. 27 Aug 1923
Dollie	b. abt 1868	d. 08 Dec 1928
William Henry	b. Sep 1852	d. Feb 1907

Smead Family
Chester L. Smead   b. 27 Feb 1822 at Weybridge, Vermont,
                     m. Mary Portwood in 1848, d. 01 Jun 1915.
Mary Portwood,   b. 1824, d. 28 Sep 1905.

Children of Chester L. and Mary Portwood Smead:
Emma,   b. 1864, m. Charles W. Bird (1861–1947),   d. 1919
Warren   m. ?, Two children, Herbert and Lillie Marion
Nancy   d. 1926 automobile accident.
Mary   d. 1859 age of 12 years, fell from the wagon on the
                 way to Colorado.
Omah (dau)   m. Mott. One child, Vinney.

Marriages:
Thomas Barr to Maggie Smead 31 December 1886
Richard R. Brown to Oma Smead 4 July 1877.
Charles L. Goddard to Emma C. Smead of Longmont 4 July 1881
        at ME parsonage in Boulder.
Emma C. Smead Goddard to Charles W. Bird 1890.
C.C. Smead to Hattie Rippley 16 May 1892
James L. Smead to Laura E. Chapman 29 June 1876
Brown, Richard R. m 4 July 1877 Oma Smead in Boulder
Mott, Henry S. m 18 July 1886 Anna Smead at home of bride's
        parents in St. Vrain by Justice C P Wilcox.

Children of Emma Smead and Charles Goddard:
Lyman,   b. 1882,   m. Grace Rowely
Charles,   d. at birth in 1884
Lloyd,   b. 1886,   m. Minnie Collett.

Children of Emma Smead Goddard and Charles W. Bird:
Ora Elva,   b. 1892,   d. 1959 buried Cheyenne, Wyoming.

m. Dan Sauer.   Children: Elva, Marian and Ida.
Marion Russell, b. 1894,   d. 1934,   m. Imo Kenney,
          Children: Charles and Francis.
          Held title to Patent Number 4252, 3 North, 70 West,
            Heil Ranch, August 24, 1896.
Linnie E.,   b. 1898,   d. 1938,   m. Arthur Fisher
Raymond   d. in his first year 1901
Julius H.,   b. 1902,   d. 1963,   Bur: Laramie, Wy,
          m. Elizabeth Coen in 1934;
          Children: Emma Caroline b. 1935; Ann Elizabeth,
          b. 1938;Linnie Jewel b. 1941; Thomas Russell, b. 1946.
James W.   b. 1906,   m. Dorothy Coen 1934,
          Children: James d., Glenna, Marian, Danna, Janice.

Divorces:
Goddard Emma Caroline (Smead) vs. Charles Louis Goddard –
desertion, custody of 2 youngest children. *Boulder News* 31 Oct. 1889:4.

1860 National Census:
Lyman_Smead   38   b. Illinois,   occ. farmer.
  , Mary,   26,   wife
      Children: son Chester, 12; dau Marion, 5 and dau Anna, 2,
      (Name is Oma, not Anna).

1870 National Census:
118A St. Vrain district 10, Burlington PO; Lines 16-23
Smead, Chester S.   48   b. VT   Farmer
     Real Estate $600; Personal Property $600 (Pella 1800)
Mary A.   38   b. MO   Keeping House;
Chester L.   21   b. Il   Farm hand
Children: Marion,   13   b. IL
        Oma   11   b. IL
        Warren   8   b. CO
        Emma   4   b. CO
        Rufus   1   b. CO.

1880 National Census - Pella
C. L. Smead,   58,   b. VT, father b. VT, mother b. VT, occ. Miner,
Mary   55,   b. MO
Children:
  Marion (son)   22,   b. IL
  Warren,   18,   b. CO;
  Emma   16,   b. CO;
  Rufus   11,   b. CO.

<u>1900 National Census</u>
Ed 165 Sh 8 L14–28.

Smead, Chester L.	78	b. Feb 1822, m., Occ. Farmer	b. VT MA MA
Maryann	72	b. Jan 1828, m	b. MO KY KY
Rufus H.	29,	June 1879,	b. CO VT MO;
Warren A.	38,	Feb 1862, m.,	b. CO VT MO, farmer;
Lusindia	24,	Dec 1875, m.,	b. NE IN IN
Herbert W.	15,	Oct 1884,	b. CO CO NE
Lillie L.	13,	Apr 1887,	b. CO CO NE
Bird, Charles W. 3	7,	Feb 1863, m, PA UNK ,plasterer, Son-in-law	
Emma Smead	35y 9m,	July 1864,	b. CO VT MO
Goddard, Lyman H.	18,	Apr 1882,	b. CO IL CO Stepson
Loyd H.	14,	Sept 1885,	b. CO IL CO Stepson
Jessie	11,	Sept 1888,	b. CO IL CO Stepdau
Bird, Ora E.	7,	July 1892,	b. COL PA CO Dau
Marion R.,	5,	Nov 1894,	b. CO PA CO Son
Sylinda E.	1,	June 1898,	b. CO PA CO.

<u>Record of Burials in the Hygiene Cemetery</u>:
Row 6 Lot 31

| Chester L. Smead | d. Dec. 19, 1882, Aged 33 yrs. 9 mos. 22 days; Senior died 21 January 1915. | |
| Mary Ann Smead | b. 1826 | d. 1906 (1905?) |

<u>Record of Burials in the Lyons Cemetery</u> :
(Warren Smead, son of Chester)
Block 12 Lot 67

Henry C. Smead	b. 1875	d. 1964
Sarah G. Smead	b. 1883	d. 1922
Baby Smead		d. 1915
	(father Warren Smead, son of Chester L.)	
Ewing Smead	b. 1905	d. 1909
Laura Eva Smead,	b. 5 Sep 1898	d. 6 May 1931 Mother
Mary Ann Smead	b. Jan 01 1826	d. Sept 5 1906
Donovan Smead	b. 1986	d. 1987

William Sosey Family
William Sosey m. Arminta Shinkle at State Center, Iowa in 1869.

Parents of Arminta Shinkle Sosey:
Charles   b. 1830 in Ohio,   d. 1884
Eliza   b. 1833,   d. 1888.
Children of William and Arminta Shinkle Sosey:
John,   m. Winnie Ham in Boulder, attended University of
            Michigan. Worked for the Kellogg Company.
Fred,   m. Ida Prospect in Lyons. Worked for the Pasadena
            Electric Short Line.
Floyd   d. 1902 of from influenza.
Alice,   m. Leonard Lyon (son of E. S. Lyons) 1889. Three children.
            Adopted Hazel and Olive.

Charles A. Spaulding
Charles A. Spaulding, b. 21 December 1843 at Hillsdale, Michigan,
                m. Flora Catherine,
                d. 22 June 1905.

Children of Charles and Flora Catherine Spaulding:
Frank and Harry
Mrs. Jennie Logan and Mrs. Nettie McFadden.

Record of Burials in the Lyons Cemetery:
Block 2 Lot 14
Charles A.   b. 21 Dec 1843   d. 22 Jun 1905
Flora Catherine   b. abt 1847   d. 15 Jul 1925

Stiles Family
Wellington   b.1858 in Iowa, m. Lillian Belle 26 Sigler Aug 1878
                        at Cheyenne, Wyoming,
                        d 02 May 1885. of blood poisoning

Sigler Stiles   b. 08 Aug 1862 at Memphis, MO
                       d. 1949
Lillian remarried, William N. Hubbell 11 Jun 1889 at Boulder, CO
        Child: William Newton Hubbell 10 Dec 1899.

Children of Elwood Wellington and Lillian Belle Sigler Stiles:
Henry Elwood   b. 02 Sep 1880 at Lyons,
                       d. 02 Mar 1881 at Lyons.
Arthur M. Stiles   b. 02 Jul 1883 at Lyons, m. Rossie Holcomb
                        (24 Apr 1887 at Lyons–12 Jay 1978 at
                         California) 11 Oct 1905 at Boulder, CO
                       d. 17 Jul 1958

Children of Arthur M. and Rosie Holcomb Stiles:
Arthur Clair   b. 02 Oct 1906,   d. 29 May 1917 at 10 years.
Freida Nadine   b. 15 Jun 1908,   m. Alfred Douglas Johnson
                (11 Feb 1906 at Baja California, Mexico,
                d. 26 Nov 1961) 28 Jul 1929 at National City, CA
                Child: Trudy Ann b. 14 Aug 1937, m. Ralph Hartung
                Chs: Audery Lynn, Gary Douglas,and Renee Annette

Record of Burials in the Lyons Cemetery
Block 1MA Lot 40
Stiles, Arthur Claire   b. 02 Oct 1906   d. 29 May 1917.

John P. Swenson
Record of Burials in the Lyons Cemetery:
Block 2 Lot 24
Swenson, John P.   b. 22 Aug 1834   d. 22 Nov 1908
Swenson, Stina K.   b. 21 Jul 1877   d. 17 Aug 1967

Sherman S. Swift
Sherman S.   b. 15 Apr 1867 in Indiana,
              m. Anna Phillipena Bohn 10 May 1894,
              d. 16 Mar 1934.
Parents George B. and Martha Everett Swift.

Children of Sherman S. and Anna Phillipena Bohn Swift:
Eloise, George, Herbert, Verna, Charles P., and Sheridan born at Lyons

Record of Burials in the Lyons Cemetery:
Block 6 Lot 10
Swift, Child
Block 7 Lot 2
Swift, Sherman S.   b. 15 Apr 1865   d. 17 Mar 1934
Swift, Anna P.   b. 21 Jul 1877   d. 17 Aug 1965
Block 8 Lot 20
Swift, Charles Phillip   b. 14 Oct 1914   d. 20 Jun 1998

Thomas Jefferson Thorne
T. J. Thorne   b. 13 May 1857 at Ohio,
              m. Lillie Lyon, daughter of Edward S. Lyon,
                 founder of Lyons, Colorado 02 Jul 1884,
              d. 11 Mar 1904 of pneumonia at Fort Collins, CO.

Siblings of T. J. Thorne:
Three brothers:
Bill   m. Lillie's sister Eva.
George, an attorney who lived in Lyons in 1891
John,   lived in Albuquerque, NM at one time
One sister: Mary (no information)

Children of T. J. and Lillie Thorne:
Edward Raymond (Ray) b. 1886 at Lyons, m. Ida Fuller
                (1884 Mystic, Iowa–05 Mar 1978 at Longmont, CO)
                       d. 29 Jan 1956, bur. Walden.
Thomas J. Thorne   b. 16 Nov 1900 at Lyons,   d. 1970.

Children of Edward Raymond and Ida Thorne:
Mabel Eliza,   b. 30 Dec 1913, m. Vyrl Schilling, 01, Jun 1935 at
                     Cowdrey, CO,   d. Feb 1961.
                 Two children:
                     Luella, b. 27 Nov 1937, m. Frederick Lindquist
                     Bert, m. Kathy Ketchenson 14 Nov 1970.
Margaret Isabell, b. 07 Jul 1915,   m. Clayton Rich.
                 Three children:
                     Mabel LaVerne, m. Floyd Naylor.
                     Ray, professor at University of New Mexico
                     John, m. Donna Headley
Edward Raymond, Jr. b. 17 Mar 1921,   d. 1970,   Never married.
Ida Beth,   b. 21 Dec 1922,   m. Russell Crowder.
                 Three children: Karen Eileen, m. Don Hakonson.
                     Kent, Kathy, m. David Coffey.

1885 Boulder County Census:
Ed 3 Sheet 60 Line 9 & 10
Thorne, Thomas J   MH   28 m. OH occ. Blacksmith
           Lillie E.   Wife   19 m. CT
Records of Burials in the Lyons Cemetery:
Block 6 Lot 9
Mabel   b. 12 July 1891,   d. 03 July 1901
Block 6Lot 23
Thomas J.   b. 13 May 1857,   d. 11 march 1904

Thorne's mother, Cornelia Thorne lived in Longmont in 1900.
ThreeChildren:
        Will   m. Eva Lyons

George lived in Lyons in 1891. He was an attorney with the
      Department of Justice in Washington, D. C. & CO.
Mary

William Tilton
William Tilton,   b. 11 Apr 1866 at Deep River, Iowa,
        m. Cora Flowers (22 Aug 1865–05 Aug 1951)
           11 Nov 1888,
        d. 22 Feb 1914.

Children of William and Cora Flowers Tilton:

Lester B.,	b. 10 Aug 1889 at Bellevue,	d. in Fort Collins
Jasper,	b. 12 may 1892 at Bellevue, 18 Mar 1925	m. Louise Durrett
Allen E.	b. 18 June 1895 at Bellevue, Bur.:at Winnemucca, NV	

Charles True
Charles True (Charley) b, 11 Aug 1833 at Caledonia CountyVermont,
        d. 21 May 1894 of dropsy at the age of 60y 7m.
Marriages:
Charles C. True to Lydia A. Davis 15 Feb 1867
Edwin C. True to Lizzie m. Wellman 1894 at the parsonage at Hygiene
    by Rev Griffith.

Children of Charles and Lydia True:
Three children: two sons and one daughter.

1870 Boulder County Census:
120 A – in and beyond Pella area – Burlington Post Office
    St. Vrain District 13 - 2 July 1870.

True, Charles C.	37	b. VT,	occ. Farmer,
		Real Estate $2500,Personal Property $1000	
Lydia A.	19,	b. IA	Keeping House
Edwin	1	b. CO.	

1880 Census:

True, Charles C .	47	b. VT , farmer (Pella)	
, Lydia	28	b. IN, wife	
, Edwin S.,	10	b. CO	
Roy	1	b. CO	
Celia, dau		b. CA 1872 missing from census.	

236

The obituary states a burial in the Hygiene Cemetery; however there is no record of a True burial at the cemetery.

John William Tumbleson

John William Tumbleson   b. 1843 in Ohio,
                                      m. Sarah Weese 12 Apr 1877,
                                      d. 28 Mar 1917.

Children born to John William and Sarah Weese Tumbleson:
Charles, Maggie, John , Arthur d. 25 Jun 1890 at 9yr 5mo 11 d
Mrs. A. C. Smith, Mrs. Grace Martin.

Record of Burials in the Hygiene Cemetery:
Lot 11 Row 65 North
Tumbleson, Arthur   d. 25 Jun 1890 at 9yr 5mo 11
        "At Rest our Loved One" Son of J. W. and S. E. Tumbleson.

John Walker Family

John Walker,   b. 14 November 1861 at Wapello County, Iowa,
                m. Clara McCall on 10 Mar 1887,
                d. 04 June 1940 at Estes Park, Bur: Lyons Cemetery.

Children of John and Clara McCall Walker:
Ida Walker,   b. 22 December 1887 in Kentucky,
                m. Alpha Blynn Gaddis (01 October 1879—27 October
                    1911) on 12 December 1906,
             d. 1978 at Estes Park, Bur: in Boulder.
               Child: Elma May Gaddis b. 11 February 1911 at Lyons,
               m. Maurice Willard West 08 Sep 1932, d. 28 Jul 1978.
            Husband #2 Carl Piltz, stone mason on 04 April 1916,
                 d. 06 July 1926.
            Husband #3 Joseph P. Morris, d. 26 August 1955.
Thomas Walker b. 26 December 1889, d. 07 October 1891.
Laura Walker   b. 18 December 1892, d. 02 April 1893
May Walker   b. 14 October 1894,
                m. Frank Dexter (20 October 1884—12 Spril 1953)
                17 February 1912,
                d. 31 March 1961
                Five Children:
                    John Francis 12 May 1913—15 November 1922
                    Donald J. b. 05 October 1915
                    m. Myrtle Vitry 19 July 1936, d. 10 June 1971
Three Children: Robert Jay, Eleanor May, and Clinton John.

Edward Jay	b. 28 January 1899, Never married, d. 01 October 1958, Bur: at Lyons.
Theodore Robert ,	b. 16 May 1901, d. 10 June 1911.
Beulah Mildred	b. 08 September 1904, m. Edward Haberl 24 October 1925, d. 29 June 1960 Child: Nannetta Alice b. 01 April 1928, m. Norman Prescott.
Russell McCall Walker,	b. 21 March 1901, m. Nona Amsden Manaugh 16 Sep 1930.

Record of Burials in the Lyons Cemetery:
Block 7 Lot 24

| Jay E. Walker | b. 28 Jan 1899 | d. 01 Oct 1958 |

Block 7 Lot 25

John D. Walker	b. 14 Nov 1861	d. 04 Jun 1940
Clara Walker	b. 15 Sep 1866	d. 30 May 1951
Theodore Walker	b. 16 May 1901	d. 10 Jun 1911

Jeremiah C. Wamsley Family

| J. C. Wamsley | b, 1849, m. Dica, | d. 1901. |

Children of Jeremiah C. and Dica Wamsley:

Otto,	b. Illinois, m. Jessie Goddard in 1906, #2Abbie Adams in 1916, d. Fort Morgan 1942.
Lee	lived in Lyons
Luther	d. 1904 in North Park
Walter,	lived in North Park
B urk,	lived in North Park
Earl	lived in North Park
Mrs. Bertha Wamsley Hansen,	d. 1940 in Denver
William,	b. 1881at Clarinda, Iowa, d. 1946.

Record of Burials in the Lyons Cemetery:
Block 9 Lot 14

Wamsley, Dica Ann	b. 1858	d. 26 Nov 1928
, Jerry C.	b. 28 Dec 1849	d. 30 Jul 1901
, Otto H.	b. 1883	d. 22 Jun 1942
, Walter W.	b. 23 Jan 1881	d. 22 Sep 1946

Block 3MA Lot 1

| Wamsley, Katherine | b. 1833 | d. 1899 |

George Washington Webster
Children of George Washington and Melinda Jane Baker Webster:
Alvin,   b. 16 September 1883, m. Bessie Miller, d. 1947
Lila,   b. 1894, m. Jack Moomaw, d. 1961.
                       Dau. Patty; Granddaughter Helen Motley.

Marriages:
George W. Webster to #1 Mary Wisner, 22 Apr 1865.
George W. Webster to #2 Mollie Johnson, 7 Dec 1881.

1870 Boulder County Census:
120 A – in and beyond Pella area – Burlington Post Office
       St. Vrain District 13 - 2 July 1870.
Webster, George   36,   b. PA,   occ. Blacksmith
               Real Estate $3000, Personal Property $200.

Record of Burials in the Hygiene Cemetery:
BLock 5 Lot 29
George Webster   b. 1834   d. 1904
Mary E. Webster   b. 1840   d. 1869

Weese Family
James Samuel Weese   m. Permelia Susan Howard.

Children of James Samuel and Permelia Susan Howard Weese:
Mellisa Jane   m. Norman Johnson, a contractor
Lula   m. Carl Peterson, an Erie farmer

Christopher Columbus Weese, a cousin of Levi Brackett.
       b. 1845 in Green County, IL,   m. Melinda Jane Baker 1882.

Children born to Columbus and Melinda Weese:
Alvin Weese,   b. 16 Sep 1883,
               m. Bessie Miller (dau. of Charles Miller),
               d. 1947.
Lila Weese,   b. 1894,   m. Jack Moomaw,   d. 1961.

Children born to Alvin and Bessie Weese:
Doyle Weese   Child: Doyle Jr.,
Grace Weese Harbin,   Two children: Carol and P.
Sylvia Weese Ward,   Three children: Larry, Harry, Debra
Farice Weese Miller,
Ethel Weese Seahorn,   b. 1935 at Lyons.

Birth of a Quarry Town

Sylvia Weese Bradford
> Children: Jerry Bradford and Darlene Bradford Nix

Norville Weese
> Children: Norma Weese Conway, Ronald Weese, DickWeese m. Judy. Both were shot to death in NV June 1977.

Glen & Leonard

1885 Boulder County Census Records:

Weese, C. C.	Farmer	38	b. IL
, Matilda	Wife	30	b. AR
, Alvin	Son	1	b. CO
Williams, Thomas J.	Stepson	8	b. TX
Baker, Mary	Sister-in-Law	16	b. CO
Wachter, H. C.		27	b. NY Farm hand & boarder

Record of Burials in the Hygiene Cemetery:

Lot 2 Row 89 North

Father Christopher C. Weese	b. 1846	d. 1916
Malinda J. Weese	b. 1859	d. 1932

Lot 2 row 90 North

Lila M. Weese	b. 1893	d. 1961

Lot 4 Row 23

John Weese	b. 1841	d. 1912
Rosa Weese	b. 1848	d. 1925
Deckie, son of J. & R. Weese,	d. 18 Au 1876, Aged 4 y, 7m.	

Lot 11 Row 66 South

Doyle Weese	b. 1902	d. 1979

Lot 17 Row 66 South

Lempi Weese	b. 1896	d. 1972

Lot 13 Row 77 South

James Weese,   b. 10 Sep 1837, d. 14 Jun 1882, "Say Nothing but Good of the Dead"

Rebecca Weese,   d. 17 Nov 1881,
> "Dearest Mother: Thou has Left Us and the Loss We Deeply Feel But this God Who Has HereLeft Us He Can All Our Sorrows Fill"

Lot 17 Row 100 South

Albert (Abe) Weese	b. 1915	d. 1983
Buford Weese	b. 1890	d. 1941
Laura Weese	b. 1882	d. 1960

Thomas Weese	b. 1910	d. 1978
Lot 17 Row 102 South		
Bessie E. Weese	b. 1879	d. 1949
Alvin Weese	b. 1883	d. 1947
Elsie Weese	b. 1909	d. 1918
Glenn Weese	b. 1916	d. 1979
Leonard C. Weese	b. 1905	d. 1979
Willard Weese	b. 1904	d. 1915

William "Billy" A. Welch Family

Aristides Welch, m. Henrietta

Aristides owned the Erdenheim Stock Farm in Chestnut Hills,
    Philadelphia, Pennsylvania home of the Kentucky Derby
    winner, Iroquois. His horses also won the Prekness, and
    the Belmont Stakes.

Children of Aristides and Henrietta Welch:

William A. Welch	b. 1861 in Tennessee, m. Sarah Billings, d. 1938 (1944) in Denver.
Robert	b. about 1860 at Washington, D. C.
James A.	b. about 1864 at Pennsylvania

1870 National Census: p.80 Div. 285. Whaitemarsh Township, Montgomery County, PA August 28, 1870 Post Office Plymouth Meeting:

Welsh, Aristides	57	Farmer b. PA
		Real Estate 80,000 Personal Estate 80,000
, Henrietta	54	Keeping House b. Tennessee
, Robert	10	At home b. District of Columbia
, William	8	b. PA
, James	6	b. PA

12 other people are listed as residing at the residence.

Note: spelling of last name is Welsh, not the accepted Welch.

1880 National Census p240C Whitehmarsh, Montgomery, PA FHL film #1255159, Nat'l Archives #19-1159:

Welch, A.	68	Widower	Farmer b. PA
		mother and father b. PA	
Welch, Robert	20	Single b. DC	Medical Student
Welch, William	18	Single b. PA	Law Student

14 other people are listed as workers and domestic servants.

Birth of a Quarry Town

1900 Boulder County Census Records:
Welch, William Aug 1861 38   b. PA Hotel Keeper (Resort)
     , Sarah   Feb 1862 38   b. MA
Boarders:
Chee, Tue Hem Jul 1851   48   b. China Cook
Sam, Young   July 1851 48   b. China Laundryman
Born a son   15 May 1908, J. E. Welch

Record of Burials in Olinger Crown Cemetery, Denver, CO:
Block 24 Lot 222 Section 56
Welch, Sarah Elizabeth   bur. July 28, 1936
Welch, William S.   bur. May 31, 1938.

Wilcox Family
1885 boulder County Census Records:
Wilcox, Charles P.   Farmer   43   b. MI
     , C.(Cynthia)   M. Wife   42   b. OH
     , Ralph   Son   9   b. MI
Hardy, Henry   Father-in-Law   70   b. OH
                            Retired Farmer
     , Maria   Mother-in-Law   68   b. PA

Record of Burials in the Hygiene Cemetery:
Lot 11 Row 49 north
Wilcox, Ralph L.   b. 06 Apr 1876   d. 24 Mar 1895
     , Cynthia M.   b. 05 Mar 1843   d. 26 Apr 1928

Record of Burials in the Lyons Cemetery:
Block 2 Lot 73
Wilcox, Charles James, Jr. b. 23 Jan 1917   d. 24 Mar 1963
Block 2 Lot 8
Wilcox, John E.   b. 10 Nov 1845   d. 14 Sep 1930
     , Melissa M.   b. 04 May 1847   d. 23 Aug 1939

APPENDIX II

INVENTORY OF ITEMS RECEIVED AT FORT ST. VRAIN 1838

Inventory of Items Received at
Fort St. Vrain 1838

Ft. Lookout Oct. 24th 1838, received of Able Baker Jr. of Ft. Jackson with its merchandise, Peltreis, Live Stock formerly belonging to Messrs Sarpey & Fraeb–Bent, St. Vrain & Co.

No. 1 One box containing
      56 lbs Blue Seed Beads
      60 lbs White Seed Beads
      8 Blue chiefs Coats
      3 Scarlet chiefs Coats
No. 2 One bbll. Containing
      22 2/3 doz best Wilkinson Scalping Knives
      18 doz 2nd quality Scalping Knives
      27 2/3 doz. 6 inch Butcher Knives
      8 doz 7 inch Butcher Knives
      1 11/12 doz green handle Cartouch Knives
      1 11/12 doz inland fancy handled Knives.
No. 3 one box containing
      2 green Blanket Capotes, 1 damaged by mice
      13 masses white Rickaree Beads
      1 pr Salampoon Calico 16 yds
      1 dox Black silk hdkfs
      2 damaged green Table Covers
      4 Cotton hdkfs, 3/4 cotton
      Shawls damaged by mice
      7 1/2 masses Blue Rickaree
Beads
      24 1/4 lb Vermillion
      180 pr Large Ear Bobs
      200 pr small Ear Bobs
      14 masses white Barleycorn Beads
      3 masses red Barleycorn Beads
      12 bunches white Barleycorn Beads Small
      4 masses imitation wampum wg 2 lbs
      2 groce gold Coat Buttons
      1 3/4 groce finger rings
      11 packs small Hawks Bells

2 packs Large Hawks Bells
2 setts pieced B roaches
3 setts embossed Broaches
10/12 gross Indian Awls
10/12 doz fine Ivory combs
1 M Brass Tacks
No. 4 One Box Containing
1 ps Cotton plaid 38 yds
1 ps Cotton stripe 13 yds
remant bleached shirting 17 1/2 ys cost 11 cts
11 11/12 Doz crambocombs
1 Dox paper covered pocket
Looking Glasses
1/2 Dox 7 inch Butcher
Knives (rusty)
1/2 Dox 7 inch Burcher
Knives perfect
1/6 Dox 6 inch Burcher Knives
7/12 Dox 5 inch BurcherKnives
Beads
42 bunches Blue Cut Glass
3 1/4 Doz Black Cut Glass
54 5/12 Doz Yellow Cut
Glass
3 3/4 bunches green Cut glass
10/12 Doz pocket knives 'blade
3/12 Doz pocket knives
2 blades damaged
1/2 m gun flints
4 lb Linen Thread,
Assorted colors
No. 5 Box containing
Beads
9 strands pigeon egg Beads wg 4 lbs.
1 mass Blue oblong glass
1 doz white oblong glass
1 3/4 doz white Barleycorn
2 1/4 doz white Agate or
Rickaree

1 1/4 doz yellow Barleycorn
2 doz Red or Coral
10 strands Large Blue
Barleycorn
17 doz do white Barleycorn
1/2 mass smallest white
Barleycorn
4 doz striped fancy
Barleycorn
4 strands flat white
Barleycorn
1 4/5 masses garnett
Barleycorn
1/2 lb Blue & white seed
1 2/5 setts wampum money
32 Ticquois shells bought in the country cost 25 cts
each in goods
3/4 Doz fire steels
3 Doz 7 inch handsaw files
2/3 doz 5 inch whipsaw files
1/2 doz. 9 inch whipsaw file
1/6 doz half round rasps
1/6 doz flat rasps
1/4 doz Bastard flat Rasps7"
1/3 doz Bastard flat Rasps 13"
1 gross Indian Awls
No. 6 Cow Skin Balecontaining
3 green Blanket Capotes
1 doz best Wilkinson
Scalping Knives
2 1/2 doz 2nd quality
Scalping Knives
1 11/12 doz white handled
Cartouch Knives
1 pr furn. check 46 1/3 yds
1 remenant furniture check
5 1/4 yds
5 Madras Hdkfs
2 x 8/4 cotton Shawls

2 rem. cotton plaid 27 yds
1 remant cotton strip 23 yds
1 rem. Red grd. calico 3 yds
1 remant Scarlet cloth 1 yd
2 rem. Blue cloth 9 1/2 yds
5 Red Flannel Shirts
6 woolen caps
1 Blue Chiefs Coat
1 Scarlet Chiefs Coat
1/2 lb Linen thread
1 doz Red Cock Feathers
1 doz Foxtail Feathers
6 1/4 doz gilt Coat Buttons
No. 7 Cow Skin Balecontaining
1 pr 3 pt green Blankets
1 pr 3 pt blue Blankets
1 pr 3 pt Red Blankets
1 pr 3 pt white Blankets
2 pr 2 1/2 pt white Blankets
1 pr 2 pt white Blankets
1 pr 1 1/2 pt white Blankets
3 Brittannea Lookin
Glasses No. 4 Largest
4 Brittannea Looking Glasses No. 3 3rd size
No. 8 Cow Skin Balecontaining
Green Blanket Capotes
Blue Blanket Capotes
Blue Chiefs Coats
Scarlet Chiefs Coats
Red flannel shirts
Cotton check shirts
Cotton plaid shirts
1 woolen vest
5 woolen caps
No. 9 Cow Skin Balecontaining
3 1/2 prs 3 pt Red Blankets
1 pr 3 pt Green Blankets
1 pr 3 pt Blue Blankets
1 pr 3 pt White Blankets

1 pr 2 1/2 pt White Blankets
1 pr 2 pt White Blankets
1 pr 1 1/2 pt White Blankets
1 pr 1 pt White Blankets
No. 10 Cow Skin Baleontaining
1 1/2 prs 3 pt Blue Blankets
1 pr 3 pt Red Blankets
1/2 pr 3 pt White Blankets
1 pr 3 pt Green Blankets
1/2 pr 2 1/2 pt White Blankets
1 pr 2 pt White Blankets
1/2 pr 1 1/2 pt White
 Blankets, damaged
1 pr 1 pt White blanket,
perfect
4 Red flannel shirts
Beads
1/2 mass white Rickaree
1/4 mass white Barleycorn
3 masses Fancy striped
1 lb White seed Beads
1/2 lb Blue seed Beads
300 Sewing needles
2 pr goggles
200 Trout fish hooks
1 yd bleached sheeting
No. 11 Cow Skin Bale containing
1 rem. Blue Sattinett 7 3/4yd
4 remant Blue cloth 14 yds
1 remant Red moleting
11 1/4 yds
4 rem. Scarlet cloth 20 1/2yd
1/2 gross w/2 pieces quality binding
5 B attle axes
5 powder horns
1 ps Scarlet cloth 17 1/4 yds
No. 12 Buffalo Robe Bale containing
3 ps Scarlett Cloth 51 1/2 yd
1 pr woolen gloves

No. 13 Buffalo Robe Bale containing
 4 ps Blue Lisle cloth 76 3/4 yds
No. 14 Buffalo Robe Bale containing
 4 ps Blue Lisle cloth 76 3/4 yds
No. 15 Buffalo Robe Bale containing
 1 ps Scarlet cloth 18 1/3 yds
 1 ps Blue Lisle Cloth 19 1/4 yds
 1 ps Blue Strand cloth 20 yd
No. 16 Buffalo Robe Bale
 2 ps Blue Strand 40 yds
 1 ps Blue Lisle cloth 18yds
No. 17 Buffalo Robe Bale
 1 ps Blue Lisle Cloth 20 yds
 1 ps Scarlet Cloth 10 1/4 yd
 1 ps Scarlet Cloth 18 yds.
No. 18 1 Bale Tobacco wb.
 Gross 84 lbs
No. 19 1 Box containing
 29 1/2 doz clay smoking pipes
No. 20 1 Bag containing 78 lbs Trade Balls
No. 21 1 Bag Trade Balls w/nett 35 lbs.
No 2 1 Box containing
 4 shaving Boxes
 3 Collins Axes
 2 1/2 packs Largest Hawk Bells
 5 packs 2 size Hawk Bells
 2 Doz box combs common quality
 1/2 doz Crambo combs
 1 1/2 gross gun worms
 1/2 m gun flints
 3 1/2 Doz shaving soap
 3/4 lb candle wicking
 3/4 lb Dutch pipes
 1 Scythe Stone wg 1/2 lb
 3 Doz Indian Awls
 1/4 Doz 7 inch handsaw files

Unpacked Goods & Used tools from Ft. Jackson, Oct. 6th, 1838:

Kitchenware included:
    3 Large Mess pans tin
    4 2nd size pans tin
    5 small pans tin
    11 Iron Spoons
    2 Table Knives
    6 Table Forks
    1 Coffee Pot
    4 Sheets iron
    1 Brass Kettle
    6 Pewter plates wg 5 lbs.
Livestock:
    1 yoke oxen
    1 Heifer
    6 Mules in good condition
    6 Horse in good condition
    1 Mare lame
    Robe Trade Of Fort Jackson Since April Last
    14 Buffalo Robes N"1 of best quality
    20 Buffalo Robes N"2 2nd quality
    69 Buffalo Robes N"3 3rd quality
    36 Apishemoy
    4 Calf skins
    12 Dressed cow Skins 1st Qualities
    4 Dressed cow Skins 2nd qualities
4 Beaver skins weighing 5 3/4 lbs that were taken
    in payment of debts that were contracted last year.

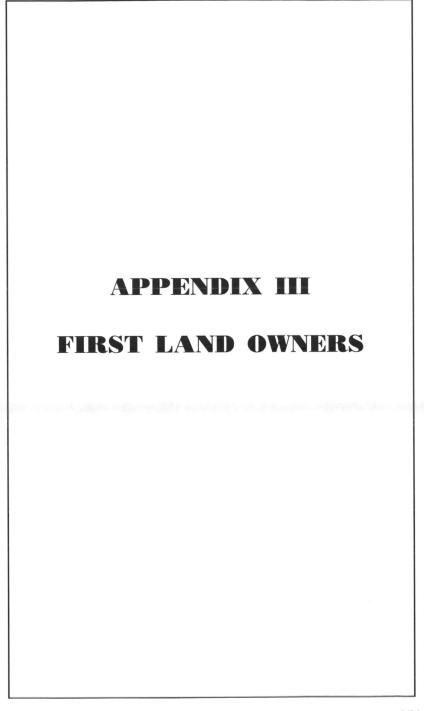

APPENDIX III

FIRST LAND OWNERS

First Land Owners
Section 1-36, Township 3N, Range 70W

Name of Owner	Section	Acres	Date of Proof
Ackerman, James	24	80	24 August 1880
Alber, Chas A.	21	120	19 November 1864
Andrew, Chas F.	2	80	17 July1918
Baker, Wm.	22	80	03 March 1866
Baker, Wm	27	80	03 March 1866
Barclay, Carrie	14	160	20 December 1886
Becker, John	3	200	06 November 1917
Becker, John	4	120	06 November 1917
Bennett, Hiram P.	14	160	25 April 1871
Benson, Alfred	4	160	01 April 1890
Bergen, George H. Van	33	160	06 November 1884
Bishop, Theophilus	8	160	26 September 1883
Blair, Benjamin J.	12	160	22 January 1914
Boiney, Chas.	31	200	16 November 1921
Boot, Henry	33	160	21 February 1878
Boot, Wm H.	33	160	28 October 1876
Botts, Osburn	19	40	27 April 1891
Botts, Osburn	30	120	27 April 1891
Boyce, James	22, 23	80, 40	23 September 1871
Bradford, Charles	19	160	30 January 1880
Breach, Henry	5	160	20 January 1883
Brown, Chas.	4	80	27 May 1907
Brown, Robert J.	26	4	01 June 1866
Brown, Robert J.	22, 23;	40, 40	01 June 1866
Carlow, Edward T.	20	40	18 March 1892
Carter, Jno. H. C.	36	80, 80	22 February 1865
Carter, Jno. C.	27	160	01 March 1867
Chandler, Walter	15	160	01 February 1889
Chapman, Eri W.	28, 29	120, 40	12 March 1877
Chapman, Joshua E.	27	120	03 November 1869
Cheney, Charles M.	6	160	03 December 1888
Cheney, George J.	8	160	03 March 1897
Cheney, Gilead P.	6, 7	80, 80	07 July1892

Name of Owner	Section	Acres	Date of Proof
Chicago Colorado Colony	32	240	02 February 1871
Chicago Colorado Colony	34	40	02 February 1871
Clark, Wm.	19	40	07 September 1885
Colson, Oscar E. P.	6	120	24 March 1903
Condit, Wm. L.	14	40	23 December 1874
Cox, Ephraim C.	5	40	27 September 1888
Culver, Cary	1	160	24 July 1869
Cummings, Robert E.	9	160	01 April 1890
Davis, Joseph	35	80	05 August 1869
Denver Pacific RR Co	25	40	24 April 1875
Dewey, Joseph	30	80	12 February 1890
Dewey, Joseph	31	160	13 December 1886
Dow, Jas. E.	21	160	28 July 1869
Elliott, Moses	36	80	02 September 1865
Emler, Daniel T.	28, 33	80, 80	21 September 1878
Evans, Griffith J.	18	160	19 May 1879
Fairchild, Jno.	24	80	01 August 1874
Florey, Wm H.	14, 23	40, 40	06 September 1882
Foster, Nathan	32	80	19 December 1881
Franklin, Benjamin A.	21	80	21 October 1869
Franklin, Benjamin A.	28	80	21 August 1869
Gifford, Wm. H.	34	160	07 February 1871
Goss, Jno. W.	24	80	14 July 1876
Goss, Percy D.	27, 34	120, 40	28 September 1870
Hamblin, Chas. P.	26	80	14 July 1876
Hansen, Andrew J.	12	160	29 November 1891
Hardesty, Thos.	28	160	21 February 1871
Hartshorn, Charles	17	80	13 November 1889
Hartshorn, Charles	8	80	13 November 1889
Hauck, Wm H.	18	160	25 March 1879
Hershman, David	36	160	17 October 1865
Iverson, H. C.	12	160	No Date
Johnson, Jos. D.	25, 26	80, 80	10 Sept. 1867
Kelly, Geo C.	5	40	29 Nov. 1882
Kiley, Richard	19	80	16 June 1919
Kiley, Richard	29	80	16 June 1919
Kiley, Richard	30	120	16 June 1919
Kites, Wm.	17	160	25 May 1883

Name of Owner	Section	Acres	Date of Proof
Lamson, Jno. W.	34, 35	120, 40	13 January 1874
Lane, Albert	15	160	26 October 1885
Levey, Roxana	8, 9; 80, 8006		July 1888
Lewis, Barber	18	40	26 June 1882
Likens, David J.	2	160	24 July 1869
Lincoln, Jarius	32	160	22 Nov. 1887
Lykins, David J.	3	160	20 October 1882
Loukonen, J. Wm & Meaney, Thos	6	120	06 January 1902
Lyons, Edward S.	7	160	30 April 1889
Lyon, Edward S.	18, 19	80, 40	26 June 1882
Marchtin, Emory	34	160	04 May 1877
Marchtin, Hamilton C.	24	80	14 July 1876
Marchquardt, Franz A.	28, 33	40, 80	09 December 1878
Marchquardt, Franz A.	34	40	09 December 1878
Mason, Geo. W.	25	160	17 January 1867
Mathews, Andrew A.	5, 6	80, 80	09 May 1882
Mathews, Orson P.	9	160	18 October 1887
McCall, Theodore J.	7	80	27 December 1916
McCall, Thos.	26	160	10 May 1870
McCaslin, Matthew L	26, 35, 35	80, 80, 80	03 November 69[2], 9 September '02
McLaugusthlin, Cyrus H.	2	160	26 January 1871
McLAugusthlin, Cyrus H.	2	80	12 February 1871
Miller, David W.	25	160	04 Nov. 1867
Miller, Edwin J.	17	40	09 April 1905
Monks, Michael	6	40	08 July 1890
Montgomery, Alexander W.	26	40	13 May 1873
Montgomery, Wm. A.	23	160	08 July 1869
Moomaw, Lila Weese	10	80	16 March 1920
Oetter, Robena	4, 5	240, 240	06 April 1923
Parsons, Wm L.	20, 21	120, 40	15 December 1867

Name of Owner	Section	Acres	Date of Proof
Patterson, Joseph	3	40	14 October 1889
Patterson, Joseph	4, 9;	40, 80	14 October 1889
Perkins, George N	22	80	30 December 1887
Perkins, Geo. N.	23	160	20 April 1877
Phillips, John H.	36	80	19 Sept. 1865
Pounder, John	7	160	15 May 1883
Powers, Minerva	20	80	01 June 1910
Rannells, Jno R.	20	160	07 March 1878
Ransom,			
Albert Bacon	22	80	20 August 1890
Rebstock, James S	30	160	28 July1890
Reed, John	15	160	04 January 1886
Reese, Jno.	19, 20	80, 80	09 December 1879
Reese, John	19	40	06 July1886
Reese, John	30	120	06 July1886
Rhodus, James B.	7	80	14 February 1889
Ripley, Frank	26, 35	120, 160	01 December '84, 19 August '67
Richardson, Frederic		21	8026 August 1865
Richardson, Fred.	28	80	26 August 1865
Richardson, Isaac	22	80	20 February 1866
Rowainen,			
Lorres Peter	29	160	04 August 1910
Rowland, Geo	29, 30	40, 40	30 October 1919
Rowland, Geo	31, 32	200, 40	30 October 1919
Runyan, Isaac	36	160	01 February 1865
Sanford, Albert C.	31, 32	40, 120	04 May 1886
Sawyer,			
Hiram F.	17, 18	120, 40	28 Dec. '81[2]
Sawyer,			
Hiram F.	18	160	28 January '79
Scobey, Daniel	17, 20	80, 40	06 December 1879
Scobey, Daniel	21	40	06 December 1879
Scott, Caroline L.	20	40	18 October 1881
Scott, Caroline L.	29	160	18 October 1881
Sigler, Mashenk	21	80	26 August 1865
Smith, Dexter A.	7	80	15 May 1883
Spath, Charley H.	12	160	22 January 1914
Short, Elisha B.	24	80	08 January 1878
Sigler, Mashenk	22	80	26 August 1865
Smead, Marchion W.	29	160	01 June 1896

255

Name of Owner	Section	Acres	Date of Proof
Smith, Justus B.	24	80	06 Sep. 1873
Smith, Justus B.	24	80	30 April 1880
Stanley, Daniel	27	80	18 December 1869
Stanley, Daniel	28	80	18 December 1867
Stiles, Hy C.	19	160	30 January 1880
Stiles, Lilian B.	17	160	31 December 1888
Taylor, Geo. W.	25	80	02 January 1868
Thorne, Thomas J.	9	160	07 Sep. 1885
Truxton, Scott	5, 8	40, 120	10 August 1883
Tumbleson, Jno.W.	22	160	24 March 1873
Tumbleson, Silas T.	15, 22;	80, 40	16 February 1871
Tumbleson, Silas T.	21	40	16 February 1871
True, Charles C.	34	40	03 March 1866
Union P. RR Co	1	160	08 Nov. 1881
Union P. RR Co	1	320	10 May 1883
U. P. RR Co	13	640	08 Nov. 1881
U. P. RR Co	23	160	08 Nov. 1881
U. P. RR Co	25	40	0 8 Nov. 1881
Webster, Geo. W.	26, 27, 35	40, 80, 40	04 March 1865
Webster, Geo W.	35	160	02 Sep. 1875
Weese, Christopher	10, 11	40, 120	13 July1914
Weese, Lila	3, 10	160, 80	20 June 1919
Weese, Jno.	24	80	28 July1880
White, Perry	36	80	04 Nov. 1865
Wockman, Wm H.	2	80	20 January 1885
Wolpert, David	10	320	27 May 1871
Wolpert, David	10	120	06 June 1885
Wynkoop, Wm. C.	34	40	10 March 1871
Zimmerman, John W.	14	160	05 April 1888

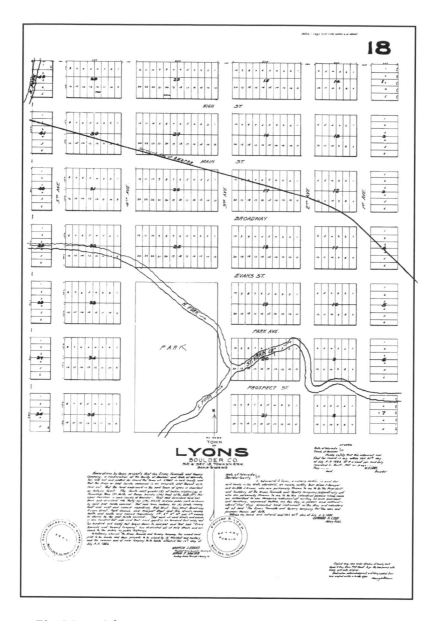

Plat Map of the Town of Lyons, Colorado, Girffith J. Evans,
Hiram F. Sawyer, and Edward S. Lyons July 12, 1882,
altitude 5380 feet. From the Boulder County Clerk and
Records Plat Books, Boulder, Colorado.

First Property Owners Lyons, Colorado 1885-1899

Listed by date of Sale

LOT	BLOCK	SELLER	TO	DATE
PT Sec 18	T3N R70W	Lyon, Edward S & Adeline A.	Putnam, Thomas G.	03/04/1882
PT Sec 18	T3N R70W	Lyons, Adeline A	Evans Townsite & Quarry	06/24/1882
PT Sec 18	T3N R70W	Lyon, Edward S	Evans Townsite & Quarry	06/28/1882
PT Sec 18	T3N R70W	Lyon, Edward S & Lewis, Barber	Evans Townsite & Quarry	06/28/1882
PT Sec 18	T3N R70W	Putnam, Thomas G.	Lyons, Adeline A	07/18/1885
9 etal	28	Putnam, Thomas G	Reese J	10/02/1885
PT etal	23	Putnam, Thomas G	Gilbert, H S	10/06/1885
PT 13	15	Putnam, Thomas G	Mangan, P A	10/14/1885
11 etal	25	Putnam, Thomas G	Flander, William P &	10/20/1885
11 etal	25	Rice, William A		
PT Sec 18	T3N R70W	Putnam, Thomas G	Denver Utah & Pacific RR	11/21/1885
PT Sec 18	T3N R70W	Evans Townsite & Quarry Co	Denver Utah & Pacific RR	11/21/1885
6	31	Putnam, Thomas G	Eddy, Mary Ellen	01/22/1886
1	40	Putnam, Thomas G	Billings, George S.	01/25/1886

259

LOT	BLOCK	SELLER	TO	DATE
14	19	Putnam, Thomas G	Putnam, Thomas G & Stiles, Lillian B	02/05/1886
6 etal	29	Putnam, Thomas G	Evans Townsite & Quarry	04/15/1886
7 etal	35	Putnam, Thomas G	Parson, Mary E	05/13/1886
PT etal	33	Putnam, Thomas G	Wilson, Winfield S	05/24/1886
1 etal	23	Putnam, Thomas G	Gilbert, Henry S.	10/01/1886
1 etal	32	Putnam, Thomas G	Dillion, Henry C. Trustee	10/15/1886
PT 7	32	Putnam, Thomas G	Meily, Luther M	11/01/1886
8	31	Putnam, Thomas G	Robbins, O	12/01/1886
PT 10	31	Putnam, Thomas G	Klasen, John	1 2/28/1886
2	33	Putnam, Thomas G	McKinley, Charles S	03/17/1887
7	40	Putnam, Thomas G	Gammon, Addie	05/06/1887
PT 1	34	Putnam, Thomas G	Whitehead, Lydia	05/31/1887
PT 1 etal	38	Putnam, Thomas G	09/25/1889	
PT 12	26	Putnam, Thomas G	Castor, Tobias	10/24/1889
1 etal	30	Putnam, Thomas G	Roblyer, Benjamin	11/20/1889
PT 11 etal	8	Putnam, Thomas G	Pounder, Emily E	11/25/1889
PT	17	Putnam, Thomas G	Denver Utah & Pacific RR	01/17/1890
PT	32	Lyon, Edward S & Evans Townsite & Quarry Co	Putnam, Thomas G.	01/27/1890
7	34 P	Putnam, Thomas G	Lyon, Edward S	01/27/1890
PT 14	30	Putnam, Thomas G	Dannels, William	02/03/1890
PT 13	30	Putnam, Thomas G	Brechel, William J	02/10/1890
PT 15	30	Putnam, Thomas G	Thorne, Thomas J	02/12/1890

LOT	BLOCK	SELLER	TO	DATE
PT 5	38	Putnam, Thomas G	Morey, O E	02/21/1890
PT 13	30	Putnam, Thomas G	Brechel, William J	03/06/1890
PT 4 etal	40	Putnam, Thomas G	Kimball Red Sandstone CO	03/26/1890
PT 15	33	Putnam, Thomas G	Merrill, Diantha L	04/07/1890
PT 1	38	Putnam, Thomas G	Fitting, August	04/18/1890
PT 1	35	Putnam, Thomas G	Drew, David	04/29/1890
PT 1 etal	31	Putnam, Thomas G	Knoth, Catharina	05/05/1890
PT 1	34	Putnam, Thomas G	Manning, James	06/03/1890
PT 9	30	Bradford, Charles	Putnam, Thomas G.	06/04/1890
PT 11	30	Putnam, Thomas G	Scanlon, Michael J	06/16/1890
PT 5	41	Putnam, Thomas G	Eddy, Herbert	07/04/1890
20	25	Putnam, Thomas G	Ash, Jennia R	07/28/1890
PT 9	30	Putnam, Thomas G	Costello, James	08/02/1890
5	31	Putnam, Thomas G	Crona, Ewald S	08/05/1890
22	25	Putnam, Thomas G	Durbin, Carl J	08/29/1890
Inc.	Legal	Putnam, Thomas G	Runyon, Louisa J.	08/29/1890
4	31	Putnam, Thomas G	Pence, Dora C	08/30/1890
23	25	Putnam, Thomas G	Runyan I B & I S	08/30/1890
PT 7	31	Putnam, Thomas G	Lippert, Elizabeth A	09/04/1890
PT 8 etal	19	Putnam, Thomas G	Gilroy, Mary A	09/08/1890
PT 15	19	Putnam, Thomas G	Hubbell, Lillian B	09/16/1890
PT 11	35	Putnam, Thomas G	Bradley, Joseph	10/09/1890
3	40	Putnam, Thomas G	David, Lucy J. & Blubaugh, Katie E.	10/13/1890

LOT	BLOCK	SELLER	TO	DATE
6	41	Putnam, Thomas G	Foy C C	10/22/1890
3	38	Putnam, Thomas G	Day, Mary A & EW Estate	11/06/1890
PT 9	33	Putnam, Thomas G	Hair, William B &	11/26/1890
PT 9	33	Harper, John R		
PT 8	34	Putnam, Thomas G	Rockwell, Moses B.	12/01/1890
4	38	Putnam, Thomas G	O'Dell, E L	12/01/1890
1	33	Putnam, Thomas G	Bucherdee, Sarah E	12/05/1890
Inc.	Legal	Putnam, Thomas G	Burcherdee, F C	12/19/1890
16	30	Putnam, Thomas G	Hewes, John M	12/27/1890
PT 9	23	Putnam, Thomas G	Dannels, William	01/05/1891
PT 12	26	Putnam, Thomas G	Skelton, Henry	02/20/1891
PT 12	18	Putnam, Thomas G	James, Effie M.	02/20/1891
13 etal	22	Putnam, Thomas G	Conefield, William	02/24/1891
12	33	Putnam, Thomas G	Lall, John &	02/27/189
12	33	Malberg, Matt		
PT 12	30	Putnam, Thomas G	Scanlon, Michael J &	03/04/1891
PT 12	30	Brice, Jame L.		
PT 13 etal	18	Putnam, Thomas G	Burghardt, William	03/06/1891
PT11	33	Putnam, Thomas G	Elison, John &	04/16/1891
PT 11	33	Anderson, Severin		
PT 5	34	Putnam, Thomas G	Davison, Jeptha	04/20/1891
PT 21	25	Putnam, Thomas G	Runyon, Louisa J.	05/07/1891
PT 16 etal	23	Putnam, Thomas G	Robbins, Elmer	05/18/1891
2	34	Putnam, Thomas G	Sjogren, Charlotte	06/24/1891

First Property Owners, Lyons, Colorado

LOT	BLOCK	SELLER	TO	DATE
PT 3	19	Putnam, Thomas G	Mumford, J. M.	06/27/1891
10	23	Putnam, Thomas G	Miller, Henry	07/01/1891
18	25	Putnam, Thomas G	White, Mary B	07/06/1891
PT 17	24	Putnam, Thomas G	Joy, S. A. Mrs.	07/22/1891
13	27	Putnam, Thomas G	Thompson, Zora C.	07/25/1891
PT 10	19	Putnam, Thomas G	Martindale, J. W.	07/27/1891
10	35	Putnam, Thomas G	Miller, Charles	08/10/1891
4	19	Putnam, Thomas G	Hubbell, William L.	08/13/1891
19	25	Putnam, Thomas G	Ash, Jennie R.	08/14/1891
16	25	Putnam, Thomas G	Warner, lillie M.	08/31/1891
PT 15	35	Putnam, Thomas G	Davison, Jeptha	09/02/1891
PT 10 etal	30	Putnam, Thomas G	Bradford, Charles	09/03/1891
PT 16	24	Putnam, Thomas G	Larson, Rasmus	09/14/1891
PT 14	33	Putnam, Thomas G	Sandy, Mary	10/19/1891
PT 13	33	Putnam, Thomas G	Johns, Elisha	10/19/1891
PT 1	30	Putnam, Thomas G	Parsons, Mary E.	12/07/1891
PT 2	19	Putnam, Thomas G	Doudna, Anna	01/23/1892
4	31	Putnam, Thomas G	Pence, dora C.	01/28/1892
PT 7 etal	26	Putnam, Thomas G	Donovan, J A & D C	02/06/1892
PT 3	33	Putnam, Thomas G	Montgomery, A. W.	02/18/1892
PT 11	19	Putnam, Thomas G	Montgomery, A. W.	
PT 12	19	Putnam, Thomas G	Montgomery, A. W.	
PT 3	31	Putnam, Thomas G	Lall, John &	
PT 3	31	Putnam, Thomas G	Maalberg, Matt	02/25/1892

LOT	BLOCK	SELLER	TO	DATE
PT 5	29	Putnam, Thomas G	Gilroy, Thomas G.	03/16/1892
PT 15	27	Putnam, Thomas G	Burhans, Orman M.	03/17/1892
PT 11	18	Putnam, Thomas G	Flynn, Mattie	03/24/1892
PT 6	42	Putnam, Thomas G	Town of Lyons	05/03/1892
6	42	Putnam, Thomas G	Town of Lyons	05/11/1892
PT Sec.18	T3N R70W	Lyons Rock & Lime Quarry Co	Murphy, Hugh	06/07/1892
9	10	Putnam, Thomas G	Wamsley, J. C.	06/29/1892
PT 1 etal	19	Putnam, Thomas G	Morey, O. E.	07/26/1892
4	30	Putnam, Thomas G	Lyon, Carrie B.	08/23/1892
9	26	Putnam, Thomas G	Blair, James E.	09/23/1892
PT 6	34	Putnam, Thomas G	Smith, Joseph L.	11/27/1892
2	33	Putnam, Thomas G	Robbins, Hannah	12/09/1892
PT 6	41	Norton, E. E.	Town of Lyons	12/15/1892
19 etal	19	Putnam, Thomas G	Janssen, Frenich	01/07/1893
8	23	Putnam, Thomas G	Burnside, John	01/09/1893
13 etal	24	Putnam, Thomas G	Norton, E. E.	01/17/1893
7 etal	33	Putnam, Thomas G	Sargent, Anna	01/17/1893
PT 8 etal	24	Putnam, Thomas G	Norton, E.E.	01/28/1893
2 etal	21	Putnam, Thomas G	Gammon, Addie	04/18/1893
13	21	Putnam, Thomas G	Crow, James	08/13/1893
2 etal	30	Putnam, Thomas G	First Congregational	02/10/1894
	#399	Church Society	First Congregational	02/10/1894

LOT	BLOCK	SELLER	TO	DATE
12	21	Putnam, Thomas G	Gross, Christopher C.	09/05/1894
16 etal	27	Putnam, Thomas G	Day, Mary A.	04/20/1895
7 etal	23	Putnam, Thomas G	Daniels, David K.	11/02/1895
3	28	Putnam, Thomas G	Allen, Georgie	09/15/1896
PT 15	24	Putnam, Thomas G	Larson, Laurence	05/10/1897
PT 16	33	Putnam, Thomas G	Blair, Samuel	01/12/1898
PT Sec 18	T3N R70W	Lyons Rock & Lime	Town of Lyons	04/06/1898
Quarry Co				
PT 9	30	Putnam, Thomas G	Bradford, Charles	09/26/1898
6 etal	29	Putnam, Thomas G	Brown, A. B.	10/20/1898
3 etal	28	Putnam, Thomas G	Dwyer, Ella	04/10/1899

PT=Partial

Boulder County Courthouse Records, Boulder, CO

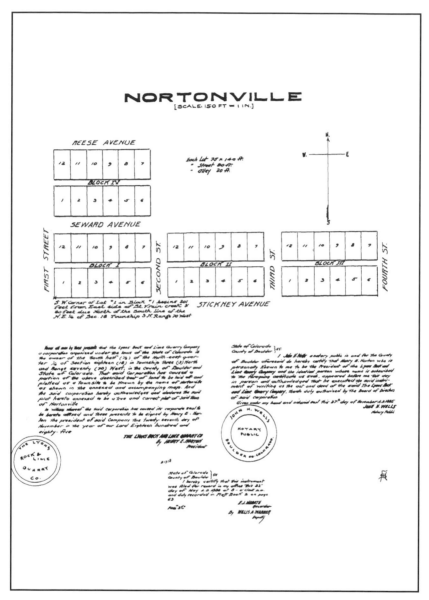

Nortonville original plat map created by The Lyons Rock and Lime Quarry Co. by Henry E. Norton, President, John N. Wells, Notary Public November 27, 1885. From the Boulder County Clerk and Recorders Office plat maps, Boulder, Colorado.

FIRST PROPERTY OWNERS
NORTONVILLE 1886-1895
SELLER - LYONS ROCK & LIME QUARRY COMPANY
Listed by Date of Purchase

LOT	BLOCK	SOLD TO	DATE	DOC #
1		Spaulding, Catherine	09/01/1886	80092506 add.
1	2	Dowling, James C	04/06/1887	80109171
5	1	Day, Edwin W	06/11/1889	80122423
6	4	Stickney, Frank H	07/12/1889	80122467add.
2	1	Lyon, E. S.	09/04/1889	80122524
9 etal	4	Fittings, Ellen	09/04/1889	80122525
7	1	Miller, L C		
6	1	Buchanan, George	05/16/1889	80122385
2	4	Wilson, Frank	07/16/1889	80122473
12	4	McCall, Eliza A	07/31/1889	80122483
		SW Corner of Reese & 5th		
12	1	Thorne, Lillie	08/29/1889	80122513add.
8 etal	1	Chisholm, Alexander	11/27/1889	80137078add.
		Stone House		
5	5	Miller, L C	10/22/1890	80151220
7	1	Walsh, U C	10/23/1890	80151229add.
11	1	Griffiths, William O	11/11/1890	80151260
7	1	Walsh, U C	11/14/1890	80113504add
4 etak	7	Milley, Mary A	11/19/1890	80151279add.
5 ctak		Currie, M	11/18/1890	80151281add.
PT 6	4	Wild, George	11/25/1890	80151298
11	2	Wright F E	12/09/1890	80151327add.
1	7	Matthews J S	12/10/1890	80151331add.
3	2	Tiech, Matthew	01/02/1891	80151383add.
2	7	Thorne, Carrie E	02/05/1891	80151456add.
5	2	Allen, Ada B	07/09/1891	80155231
11 etal	4	Lyon, Leonard	07/30/1891	80155262add.
4	1	Wright, John	10/07/1891	80155401add.
10	2	Miller, David W.	10/17/1891	80155427add.
6	7	Loule, James	10/30/1891	80155462add.
5	3	Hendricks, Louisa	05/05/1892	80156253add.
3 etaL	4	Cunningham, J R	05/11/1892	80156265add.
		Sw Corner of 5th&Seward		

Birth of a Quarry Town

LOT	BLOCK	SOLD TO	DATE	DOC #
7etal	2	Fuller, Jessie M	05/23/1892	80156283 add./Stickey
1	4	Totten, C	08/30/1892	80156469add.
4	2	Dubech, Fred	05/04/1893	80158385add.
9	2	Carlson, Oscar E p	07/02/1894	80163224add.
1	3	Hinkson, Sallie J	07/09/1894	80163235add.
7	4	McFadden, T P	06/12/1895	80176103add. NE Corner of 4th&Seward

Boulder County Courthouse Records
Boulder, Colorado

1800s Known Burials
Lyons Cemetery, Lyons, Colorado

NAME	BIRTH	DEATH	PLOT
Hoag	28 Jun 1888	No Record	
McDermid, Son of Hugh	abt 1881	26 Feb 1889	No Record
Tucker, Son	abt 1879	08 Oct 1889	No Record
Caruthers		05 Jan 1890	No Record
Sites, Sherman	abt 1886	28 May 1890	No Record
Jamison, Frank	abt 1883	10 Jul 1890	Blk4MA Lot39
Jamison, Mary	abt 1885	15 Jul 1890	Blk4MA Lot39
Jamison, Ralph	abt 1879	22 Jul 1890	Blk4MA Lot39
Jamison, Tom	abt 1853		Blk4MA Lot39
Smede, A.		26 Aug 1890	No Record
Christ, son of Peter	abt 1886	04 Sep 1890	No Record
Tucker, child of M.		06 Sep 1890	No Record
Hartline, Son of		21 Oct 1890	Blk10 Lot11
Billings, Gracie	abt 1881	30 Oct 1890	No Record
Peterson, Augusta	abt 1871	02 Nov 1890	No Record
Hill, B. L.	abt 1850	16 Nov 1890	No Record
McDermid, Hugh's Child	abt 1883	09 Dec 1890	No Record
Rugren, Charles. B.		15 Dec 1890	No Record
Warner, G. W.	abt 1886	01 Feb 1891	Blk1MA Lot43
Porter, Edwin Blanchard		07 Feb 1891	Blk2 Lot87
Blevins, John's child		10 Feb 1891	No Record
Hayden, Ben		17 Apr 1892	No Record
Sandford, Mary J.		26 Aug 1893	Blk1MA Lot40
Sandford, Jane		27 Aug 1893	Blk4MA Lot14
A'Hearn, Irene M.		06 Dec 1893	No Record
Hutchinson, James A.	07 May 1893	20 Sep 1894	Blk1MA Lot40

NAME	BIRTH	DEATH	PLOT
Schields,			
Charles	26 Feb 1828	01 Jan 1895	Blk4MA Lot14
Runbarg,			
Gjord	22 Feb 1895	11 Jun 1895	Blk10 Lot4
Gibson,			
Charles E.		19 Jul 1895	Blk10 Lot20
Bohn,			
Georgie	17 Aug 1895	18 Sep 1895	Blk10 Lot22
Bohn,			
Amelia L.	20 Feb 1892	29 May 1897	Blk10 Lot22
Jensen, Louis	05 Aug 1860	12 Feb 1899	Blk7 Lot3
Otis, Ida	21 Apr 1887	11 May 1899	Blk9 Lot16
Blair,			
Matthew M.	14 Dec 1825	28 Aug 1899	Blk3MA Lot59
Service, James	03 Jul 1864	16 Nov 1899	Blk7 Lot20
Wamsley,			
Katherine	1833	1899	Blk3MA Lot1

In the cemetery there are 106 Babies from 0–5 years of age that have been identified. Twenty-four of these interments have no records other than obituaries or family remembrances.

The above information was collected from obituaries, news articles, cemetery records, and funeral home records in Boulder, Longmont, and Lyons, Colorado.

Colorado Revised Statues
State of Colorado 1876

Agricultural, Public Land, Water, and Property Protection of Livestock Article 40 Predatory Animals—Control

35–40–108. Scalps produced, claimant. (1) Any person claiming any premium shall produce the scalps, including the entire ears, to the county treasurer of the county in which the wolf or coyote was killed, within three months after the killing, and shall take or subscribe the following oath (or affirmation) before the treasurer: "I do solemnly swear (or affirm) that the scalp (or scalps) here produced by me this day is (or are) of a wolf, or coyote (as the case may be, giving number), within the county of _____ and that the said animal (or animals) was (or were) killed by _____ within the boundaries of the state of Colorado."

Further the county treasurer was directed to pay for such scalps: $1 per coyote and $2 per wolf and keep a suitable separate book for recording the killings.

> Mountain lion bounty history:
> 1881 – Colorado enacts a bounty of $10
> 1885 – Bounty repealed
> 1889 - $10 bounty reinstated
> 1893 – Bounty reduced to $3
> 1920–1935 – *Denver Post* offers a bounty of $25 for adult
> animals, $10 for kittens
> 1965 – bounty repealed, mountain lion declared "game."

Reference:
Baron, David H. letter and several telephone conversations
July 2001.
Colorado Revised Statues,State of Colorado 1876, 2000,
Volume 10, Title 35–38, Annotated.
Division of Wildlife paper, photocopy received from
David Baron.

1800   Boulder County Bounty Affidavits
7 Aug 1889 to 17 Jun 1895

NAME	N0.	SCALP	DATE	KILLED BY
Reuban Allen	1	Coyote	August 7, 1889	
Malcomb J. Nelsom	2	Coyotes	September 27,1889	
Fred Tyler	1	Coyote	October 23,1889	
Edwin Bohnenberger	1	Coyote	December 23,1889	
J. B. Smith	1	Coyote	December 24,1889	
W. S. Mitchell	5	Coyotes	December 30,1889	
Geo. W. Webster	1	Coyote	December 30 ,1889	
Edwin Bohnenberger	1	Coyote	January 10, 1890	
Fred Runienschneiaer	1	Coyote	Janiuary 16, 1890	
John Noake	1	Coyote	January 28, 1890	
Alfheus Bashor	6	Coyotes	February 3, 1890	brother
C. E. Sheldon	6	Coyotes	February 4, 1890	
Harry White	1	Wolf	February 15, 1890	
John J. Fleck	4	Wolves	February 17, 1890	
James White	1	Wolf	February 19, 1890	
John Bloom	1	Coyote	March 8, 1890	
John Doran	1	Wolf	March 8, 1890	
A. F. Ta(o)tter	1	Coyote	March 10, 1890	
John Murphy	1	Coyote	March 13, 1890	
D. J. Crow	1	Coyote	March 14, 1890	
J. A. King	1	Coyote	March 24, 1890	
Edwin Bohnenberger	1	Coyote	March 28, 1890	
Edwin Bohnenberger	1	Coyote	April 5, 1890	
A. Reed	1	Coyote	April 5, 1890	
Frank Bacher	1	Coyote	April 15, 1890	
Fred Affolter	1	Coyote	April 23, 1890	Xed out
C. J. Stewart	1	Coyote	May 2, 1890	
I. S. Stapp	1	Bear	May 8, 1890	
Lafayette Chapman	1	Coyote	May 8, 1890	

NAME	NO.	SCALP	DATE	KILLED BY
Edward Slaten	4	Coyotes	May 15, 1890	
Joel Plumber	1	Coyote	May 17, 1890	
T. S. Peck	1	Coyote	May 19, 1890	
A. J. Bliven	1	Coyote	May 22, 1890	
John N. Cushing	1	Coyote	June 13, 1890	
J. P. Johnson	1	Coyote	June 16, 1890	
Geroge Hepner	6	Coyotes	June 28, 1890	
Levi Allen	6	Coyotes	June 28, 1890	
Frank Wolcott	2	Coyotes	June 30, 1890	
William Rhyne	1	Coyote	July 12, 1890	
Ted Hixon	13	Coyotes	July 17, 1890	
Ben Jain	1	Coyote	July 21, 1890	
John (Jno.) Murphy	1	Coyote	July 21, 1890	
Fred Owen	5	Coyote	July 30, 1890	
C. K. Blauton	1	Coyote	August 5, 1890	
W. H. Rowley	2	Bear	August 6, 1890	
George Buchanan	2	Coyotes	August 19, 1890	
George Buchanan	1	Mtn. Lion	August 19, 1890	
Edward Faivre	1	Coyote	September 12, 1890	
Guy Miller	4	Coyotes	September 13, 1890	
William (Wm.) Blake	1	Bear	September 24, 1890	
Marshall Long	2	Coyotes	October 11, 1890	
Ted Hixon	1	Coyote	October 17, 1890	
W. Horry	1	Coyote	November 10, 1890	
Charles Nelson	1	Coyote	November 15, 1890	
Charles Healy	1	Coyote	November 19, 1890	
Graham Shaw	2	Bears	November 21, 1890	
J. M. Rowley	1	Coyote	November 22, 1890	
G. M. Dryden	1	Wolf	November 24, 1890	
F. J. Royer	1	Wolf	December 12, 1890	
M. McCaslin	2	Coyotes	December 24, 1890	
Mrs. A. C. Sanford	3	Coyotes	December 27, 1890	
John Blake	1	Coyote	January 15, 1891	
William Blake	1	Wolf	February 2, 1891	
Peter LeFevre	4	Coyotes	February 12, 1891	

Birth of a Quarry Town

NAME	NO.	SCALP	DATE	KILLED BY
James B. Tourtellot	1	Wolf	February 13, 1891	
R. E. Allen	1	Coyote	February 13, 1891	
A. N. Morgan	1	Coyote	February 19, 1891	
John A. Nelson	2	Coyotes	February 21, 1891	
William Blake	4	Coyotes	February 26, 1891	
C. Thorkolson	1	Coyote	February 26, 1891	
C. E. Sheldon	1	Coyote	March 3, 1891	
Peter LaFever	1	Coyote	March 6, 1891	
John Blake	1	Coyote	March 9, 1891	
C. C. Tru(e)	1	Coyote	March 9, 1891	
Fred W. Kohler Jr	2	Coyotes	March 9, 1891	
W. F. Bennett	8	Coyotes	March 10, 1891	
James F. Jones	1	Wolf	March 13, 1891	
William Reed	1	Wolf	March 14, 1891	
Levi Allen	5	Coyotes	March 19, 1891	
Reuban Allen	1	Coyote	March 24, 1891	
William Blake	1	Coyote	April 1, 1891	
Ed Allen	1	Coyote	April 2, 1891	
C. F. Stewart	1	Coyote	April 9, 1891	
Mrs. Sarah Boot	1	Coyote	April 14, 1891	
Charles Nelson	1	Coyote	April 14, 1891	
J. B. Tourtellot	1	Coyote	May 7, 1891	my son
Richard Voges	1	Coyote	May 23 , 1891	
J. D. Steele	6	Coyotes	June 1, 1891	
John A. Webber	2	Coyotes	June 1, 1891	
Samuel Harrop	2	Coyotes	June 9, 1891	
W. S. Henderson	5	Wolves	June 11, 1891	
William Sites	2	Coyotes	June 15, 1891	my son
James B. Tourtellot	1	Coyote	June 15, 1891	
David Spicer	1	Wolf	June 19, 1891	
Arthur Crees	1	Coyote	June 26, 1891	
James A. Walker	1	Mtn. Lion	July 1, 1891	
J. M. Taylor	1	Wolf	July 8, 1891	
David Spicer	4	Wolves	July 13, 1891	
C. D. Johnson	1	Wolf	July 28, 1891	
M. Jacobson	1	Wolf	July 28, 1891	
John Allen	1	Coyote	August 3, 1891	

1800s Boulder County Bounty Affidavits

NAME	NO.	SCALP	DATE	KILLED BY
Mrs. A. C. Sanford	2	Coyotes	August 21, 1891	
John L. Brinsing	2	Coyotes	August 31, 1891	
Charles Simonds	1	Wolf	September 7, 1891	
A. J. Bliven	1	Coyote	September 7, 1891	
John A. Webber	2	Coyotes	September 12, 1891	
E. S. Crona	1	Coyote	September 23, 1891	
William Reed	12	Coyotes	September 24, 1891	
James A. Walker	1	Coyote	September 30, 1891	
James Shanahan	1	Coyote	October 15, 1891	
Peter LeFever	1	Coyote	October 16, 1891	
John Lawton	2	Coyotes	October 21, 1891	
				Made a
Mark F. H. McMillan	3	Bears	November 7, 1891	
Chas. K. Springsteel	1	Coyote	November 10, 1891	
E. B. Lewis	2	Wolves	November 25, 1891	
Mrs. A. C. Sanford	4	Coyotes	November 27, 1891	
Samuel Harrop	1	Coyote	November 28, 1891	
W. R. Blo(u)re	4	Coyotes	November 20, 1891	
Joseph Koerler	1	Wolf	December 1, 1891	
T. W. Wagner	2	Coyotes	December 7, 1891	
Thomas Fitzhaugh	1	Coyote	December 7, 1891	
Ben Harrop	1	Coyote	December 15. 1891	
Alfheus Bashor	3	Coyotes	December 19, 1891	
Edw. H. Heath	1	Coyote	December 19, 1891	
J. O. Maddox	1	Coyote	January 5, 1892	
Frank Waggner	1	Coyote	January 12, 1892	
William Blake	4	Coyotes	January 21, 1892	
Garry E. Brown	1	Coyote	January 25, 1892	
Marshall Long	1	Coyote	January 29, 1892	
Samuel Harrop	1	Coyote	January 30, 1892	
Peter Haldi Jr	2	Coyotes	February 1, 1892	
C. G. Bickerdike	4	Coyotes	February 2, 1892	
W. W. Wolf	3	Coyotes	February 13, 1892	

NAME	N0.	SCALP	DATE	KILLED BY
J. A. King	1	Wolf	March 3, 1892	
William Blake	2	Coyotes	March/12/1892	
Levi Allen	4	Coyote	March/12/1892	
John A. Webber	1	Coyote	March/16/1892	
J. H. Springsteel	1	Coyote	March/19/1892	
William Sherwood	1	Coyote	March 23, 1892	
William Blake	1	Coyote	April 8, 1892	
Fred Long	3	Coyotes	April 12, 1892	
J.D. Bashor	7	Coyotes	April 12, 1892	
R. B. Montgomery	5	Coyotes	April 13, 1892	
L. Chapman	1	Coyote	April 1, /1892	
Mrs. A. C. Sanford	5	Coyotes	April 26, 1892	
E. T. Hill	6	Coyotes	May 16, 1892	
W. R. Blo(u)re	7	Coyotes	May 24, 1892	
A. J. Hansen	8	Coyotes	May 24, 1892	
Geo. Laughlin	5	Coyotes	June 2, 1892	
Frank LaFever	5	Coyotes	June 4, 1892	
A. P. Larsen	2	Coyotes	June 11, 1892	
John Henderson	2	Wolves	June 27, 1892	
J. J. Fleck	1	Wolf	July 2, 1892	
J. H. Leach	6	Coyotes	July 13, 1892	
D. C. Fonda	1	Coyote	August 2, 1892	
F. H. McMille(a)n	1	Bear	August 4, 1892	
William Sites	2	Coyotes	August 20, 1892	
Mrs. A. C. Sanford	2	Coyotes	August 22, 1892	
T. J. Trevarton	1	Coyote	August 26, /1892	
Peter LaFever	1	Coyote	September 3, 1892	
Andrew Reed	1	Wolf	September 7, 1892	
Tom McNarnara	3	Coyotes	October 22, 1892	
John Doran	1	Wolf	October 2, 1892	No Affidavit
Fred L. Buchanan	1	Bear	October 31, 1892	
T. F. Spicer	1	Wolf	January 20, 1893	

1800s Boulder County Bounty Affidavits

NAME	N0.	SCALP	DATE	KILLED BY
Judson Baylan	1	Wolf	January 30, 1893	
Clyde Balton	1	Wolf	July 3, 1893	
Benjamin Harro	4	Wolves	July 26, 1893	
R. C. Morrison	1	Wolf	August 5, 1893	
Martin Parsons	1	Wolf	August 8, 1893	
Herbert Hardy	1	Wolf	August 9, 1893	
Joseph Roehnl (?)	1	Coyote	August 15, 1893	
Sylvester Binesley	1	Coyote	August 24, 1893	
Joel Plumber	1	Coyote	September 9, 1893	
Hiriam Prince	2	Coyotes	September 9, 1893	
Peter Haldi Jr	1	Coyote	September 26, 1893	my father
Thomas Lousidson (?)	2	Coyotes	September 28, 1893	
Marshall Long	1	Coyote	October 4, 1893	
James A. King	1	Coyote	October 7, 1893	
James Githers	1	Coyote	October 12, 1893	
H. Orr	1	Wolf	October 16, 1893	
S. A. Ritter	4	Coyotes	October 18, 1893	
James A. King	3	Coyotes	October 19, 1893	
O. N. Reed	2	Coyotes	November 17, 1893	
James A. King	1	Coyote	November 19, 1893	
George Jones	1	Coyote	November 21, 1893	
A.C. Sanford	1	Coyote	October 7, 1893	
H. L. Orr	3	Coyotes	December 6, 1893	
Otto Noreen	1	Coyote	December 9, 1893	
R. B. Montgomery	4	Coyotes	December 12, 1893	
J. C. Butler	5	Coyotes	December 14, 1893	
Gelbert Knott	1	Coyote	December 18, 1893	
Otto Noreen	2	Coyotes	December 21, 1893	
Peter Haldi	3	Coyotes	December 23, 1893	
Thomas Dodd	1	Wolf	December 29, 1893	
Thomas Dodd	3	Coyotes	December 29, 1893	
Samuel Hassop	1	Coyote	February 5, 1894	
W. Springsteel	3	CoyotesF	ebruary 8, 1894	
Mrs. E. Williams	1	Coyote	February 12, 1894	Roy Romane

NAME	N0.	SCALP	DATE	KILLED BY
Peter Haldi Jr	2	Coyotes	February 12, 1894	
Peter Haldi	2	Coyotes	February 17, 1894	Son
Levi Allen	8	Coyotes	February 21, 1894	
Peter Haldi Jr	1	Coyote	March 10, 1894	
Johthan Allen	2	Coyotes	March 9, 1894	
Frank Harrop	1	Coyote	March 24, 1894	
Peter Haldi Jr	1	Coyote	March 31, 1894	
Levi Allen	8	Coyotes	April 28, 1894	
Wm. Crosby	6	Coyotes	June 9, 1894	
Wm. Arbuthnot	4	Coyotes	June 9, 1894	
James M. Shaw	3	Coyotes	June 15,1894	
Harry Baldwin	1	Coyote	August 6, 1894	
Peter Haldi	1	Coyote	August 25, 1894	Adolph Haldi
John Hale	1	Coyote	November 10, 1894	
Peter Haldi Jr	4	Coyotes	January 5, 1895	
Ben Hassop	1	Coyote	January 7, 1895	
Peter Haldi Jr	1	Coyote	January 19, 1895	Father
Clyde Bolton	5	Coyotes	April 17, 1895	
C. G. Bickendike	1	Coyote	April 27, 1895	
Fred Jacobson	5	Coyotes	June 6, 1895	
Louis Sawhill	6	Coyotes	June 6, 1895	
G. H. Rowe	1	Coyote	June 11, 1895	
O. N. Reed	1	Coyote	June 13, 1895	
James A. King	8	Coyotes	June 17, 1895	

Coyote Premium $1.00
Wolf Premium $1.00
Bear Premium $10.00
Mountain Lion Pre. $10.00

Count Treasurer: D. R.   McNaughton

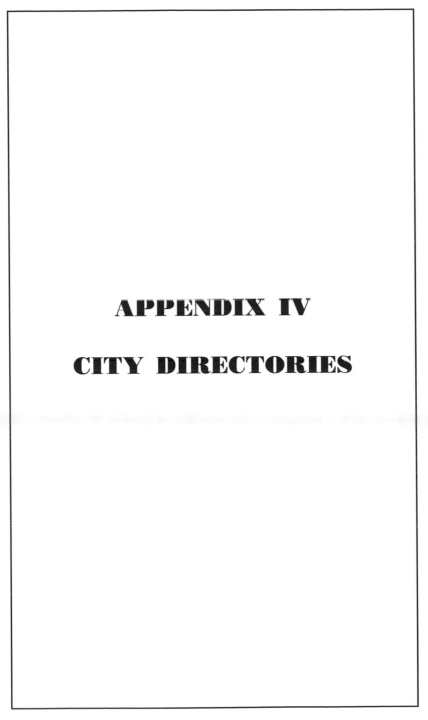

APPENDIX IV

CITY DIRECTORIES

City Directory 1890
Colorado Business Directory
Listing for Lyons, Colorado

B
Ballinger, H. F.	Shoemaker
Billings, George	Saw Mill
Bird, C. W.	Plasterer
Bradford, Charle s	Saloon
Brooks, Wm.	Wheelwright
Buchanan, George	Saw Mill
Burnside & Bucherdee	Saloon

C
Cartright, J. J.	Agent B & M RR
Chisholm, A.	Blacksmith
Corlow, Ed	Painter
Crona, E.	Physician

D
Daniels, William	Saw Mill
Day, Ed	Carpenter
Driskell, D.	Plasterer

E
Eddy Hubert	Blacksmith
Edmans, J. B.	Hay & Grain

F
Foster, Henry	Wheelwright
Frank, Nicholas	Meat Market

G
Gammon, G. W.	Physician, Drugs
Griffith, William	Stone Mason

H
Hubbell, W. N.	Livery, Coal, & Stage Line

K

Keotch, Mat	Blacksmith
Kimball Red Sandstone CO	Geo. L. Kimball, Gen. Mgr.

L

Lall & Co	Saloon
Lightbourn & Co	Lime Burn's
Lyons, E. S.	Postmaster
Lyons House	E. S. Lyon, Prop.
Lyons Rock & Lime Quarry Co	E. S. Lyon, Mgr.

M

McFadden, Charles	Transfer
May, J. A.	Saloon
Morrey, H. N.	General Merchandise

P

Pounder, J.	Stone Quarry

R

Rucker, M. T.	Contr'tor Jeweler
Runyon, A.	Saw Mill

S

Sites & Buell	Stone Quarry
Smart, B. B.	Carpenter
Sosey, Wm.	Carpenter

T

Thorne, T. J.	Meat Markey, Coal

W

Warner, W.	Transfer
Watt, Wm.	Livery
Wild, George	Hotel
Wright, F. E.	Carpenter

City Directory 1892

Lyons is a town of about 600 inhabitants, located on the line of the B. & M. Railroad, eleven miles west of Longmont, at the base of the Rockies. The principal industry is the quarrying of sandstone, which furnishes employment to a large number of men.

-A-

Ahearn Thomas,	quarryman
Anderson Andy,	lab.
Anderson S. S.	car cleaner
Appleton F. G. Rev.	
Armstrong Robert	
Armstrong & Johnson,	saloon

-B-

Baldwin Ned	
Ballinger H. F.	Shoemaker
Barnard J.	telegraph operator
Billings F. D.	lab
Blair James J.	
Blair M. M.	
Blair M. M. Jr.	quarryman
Blair S. H.	drayman
Bradford A. A.	carriage maker
Bradford Charles	saloon
Bradford H. J.	foreman road house
Brice J. L.	storekeeper
Browers Fred	
Brown A. B.	car repairer
Brown Harry	Emp. H. M. Morey
Brown James	
Bucherdee F. C.	saloon
Res 4th bet Evans and Park Av.	
Burhand O. M.	phys. druggist
Main bet 4th & 5th	
Burnside Oscar,	
res. Evans bet 4th & 5th	

Bushy George car repairer,
bds A. B. Brown

-C-

Caldwell E. H.,
emp M. N. Hubbell
Chrisholm Alex blacksmith
Churchill W. D. merchant
Clark W. J. lab– 1885 Census
Coates C. E.
Coffee James clerk
Collins B. E. Emp J. Pounder
Colvin Joel engineer
Crist Peter blacksmith
Crona E. S. druggist
Crosley C. H. clerk
Crow James stone quarry
Cunningham Robert

-D-

Dannels David sawer
Dannels Shelbey blacksmith
Dannels William sawer
DeLaney Joseph compositor
Dell J. F. (Dell & Small), res
Longmont
Dell & Small groceries
Deubach Fred mason
Dooley John fireman
Drew Frank
Drew J. F. bakery
Durbin Car saloon
Dutro C. R. clerk
Dyer W. C. merchant

-E-

Eads J. D. hostler
Eads, J. M. hostler

-F-

Fitting John
Flanders William
Flynn J. C.

Fondhen Peter	flag cutter
Foote George	switchman
Foster E. A.	hotel
Frank Bros	meat market
Frank C.	(Frank Bros.)
Frank N.	(Frank Bros.)
Frank W.	(Frank Bros.)
Freeman Elmer	
Freeman E.	barkeeper

-G-

Gammon G. W.	physician and druggist
Gilroy Thomas	clerk
Gilroy William	lab
Griffiths W. O.	
Ground I. B.	
Ground I. B. & Son	feed
Ground R. E.	

-H-

Haff George C.	clerk
Haka John	
Halliday A. Mrs.	
Hanson H.	cook
Hendricks Edward B.	
Hendircks H. O.	
Holdredte Ell A.	supt public works
Hubbell W. N	livery

-J-

James John M.	
Jansen L.	lab
Johns E. S.	lab
Johns J. S.	
Johnson Emil	paving cutter
Johnson C. F.	
Johnson Peter	(Armstrong & Johnson)
Jonstone I. C., lab	
Joy Sarah A. Mrs.	

-K-

Kerr F. P.	carpenter
Kerr W.	

Killman Allie Miss	cook

-L-

Lakelan Robert	painter
Larson L	plasterer
Leonard F. Mrs.	
Lichty M. W.	telegraph operator
Lippert J. H.	stone hauler, res
Park Ave bet 2d & 3d	
Lippert J. W.	
Litchey Miles	
Lollar E. B.	editor and propr
	Long's Peak Rustler
Lowe James	paving cutter
Lowe Thomas	paving cutter
Lungrain William	drug clerk
Lyon Leonard C.	quarryman
Lyons E. S.	hotel

-M-

Maltdy Mary Mrs.	
Mandan M.	saloon
Marlburg Thomas	
Matthews W. D.	physician
Merrill J. M.	hotel
Miller C. B.	street comr
Miller J. E.	engineer
Mill John	
Miller William	compositor
Morey H. N.	general merchandise
Murphy Hugh	quarryman

-Mc-

McCall M. C. Mrs.	
McCall Thom	rock hauler
McClaren Charles	
McFadden Charles	
McFadden Thos. P.	water hauler
McIntyre George	barber
McIntyre George P.	barber
McLaren C. A.	

-N-
Nelson R.   carpenter
Norton E. E.   broker
-O-
O'Dell Ellison   carpenter
O'Harrie Thomas
-P-
Palm Frank   quarryman
Parsons Frank   teamster
Pickett W. L.   agent B. & M. RR
Poily W.
Pounder John   quarryman
                                     supertendent of quarry

-R-
Raynolds F. A.   expressman
Robbins Elmer
Robertson Lizzie Miss   cook
Robson Dan
Rogers J. T.
-S-
Sandy F. D.
Sanford   livery
Scanlon M. J.   clothing
Service Samuel   teamster
Shannon M.
Shilling B. P.
Shippey Edward
Small M.   (Dell & Small)
Smith Charles C.   quarryman
Smith Joseph L.   drayman
Smith William
Spaulding C. A.   car repairer
Spaulding Frank   yard master
Spragg Fred   livery
Sprague F. H.   livery stable
Stanley Henry
St. Clair Harry   clerk
Swift Sherman   bartender

-T-

Thorne C. Mrs.
Thorne M. A. Miss — teacher
Thorne William — bartender
Tucker M. T. — miner

-W-

Walker John — teamster
Walch U. C. — wagon maker
Walters W. M. — fireman
Walton Charles — hostler
Wamsley J. C. — marshal
Watt L. S. — barber
Watt William — livery
Western Union Telegraph Co.,
  B. & M. RR depot
Wilcox, C. P. — grocer
Wilcox Frank N. — clerk
Wiskerson Robert — switchman B & M RR
Woodside R. W. — pastor Christian Church

City Officers

Mayor—H. N. Morey
Clerk & Recorder—E. E. Norton
Treasurer— E. S. Lyons
Police Magistrate,.C. P. Wilcox
Marshal—J. C. Wamsley
Street Commissioner – C. B. Miller
Trustees—
W. C. Dyer, James Lowe,
Alex Chrisholm,
F. C. Bucherdee,
W. M. Hubbell,
R. B. Ground.

Church

Christian Church
  Main bet4th & 5th
  R. W. Woodside, pastor

Express Company
Wells Fargo Express Co—W. L. Pickett
  Agt; office at depot

Newspaper
Long's Peak Rustler—E. B.
  Lollar, prop Est. 1890
  Weekly. Main bet 4th and 5th

Post Office
High bet 4th & 5th E. S. Lyons,
postmaster; C. W. Thomas, asst.

Railroad
B. & M. Depot on Broadway
  bet 4th & 5th

Societies
P O S of A; E. B. Meeker, pres.
  Chas. Bradford, secy.
P C U, Branch 59 of Paving
  Cutters' Union; Jas
  Hargraves, prest
  Jas. Lowe, secy.

Telegraph Company
Western Union—W. L. Pickett,
  mgr. Office At depot.

YELLOW PAGES
Barbers: George Mc Intyre;
            George P. McIntyre;
            L. S. Watt
Baker: J. F. Drew
Blacksmith & Horseshoers:
            A. Chisholm; Peter Crist;
            Shelbey Dannels

Boardinghouses:
>A. B. Brown;
>J. M. Merrill

Carriage Maker:
>A. A. Bradford

Druggist:
>E. S. Crona

Feed:
>I. B. Ground & Son

Flour & Feed:
>I. B. Ground& Son

General Merchandise:
>H. N. Morey

Grocers:
>J. T. Dell & M. Small;
>C. P. Wilcox

Hostler:
>J. D. Eads; J. M. Eads;
>Charles Walton

Hotel:
>E. A. Forster;
>E. S. Lyon

Livery:
>Sanford;
>Fred H. Sprague;
>William Watt
>**Marshall:** J. C. Wamsley

Meat Market:
>Frank Brothers
>(C., N. & W.)

Newspaper
>Longs Peak Rustler:
>E. B. Lollar, prop.

Physicians & Surgeons:
>O. M. Burhans;
>G. W. Gammon;
>W. D. Matthews

Printer – Book & Job:
>   E. B. Lollar

Saloons:
>   Armstrong & Johnson;
>   Charles Bradford;
>   F. C. Bucherdee;
>   Carl Durbin;
>   M. Mandan

Shoemaker:
>   H. F. Ballinger

Stables – Livery, Feed & Sale:
>   W. N. Hubbell;
>   F. H. Sprague;
>   W. Watt

Telegraph Operator:
>   J. Barnard
>   M. W. Lichty

Undertaker:
>   I. B. Ground & Son

City Directories can be found at the Carnegie Branch Library, Boulder, Colorado.

1896 Lyons City Directory
Boulder County Directory p287

Note: This was the only listing for Lyons in the Boulder County Directory for 1896.

Baker:	Emma S. Durbin
Barber Shop:	Labano S. Watt
Billiard & Pool Parlors:	Frank Burt
	Lyons Billiard Hall,
	Chas. Bradford, prop.
Blacksmith & Horsehoers:	Alex Chisholm
Boots & Shoes – Dealers:	Lyons Golden Rule Store
	H. N. Morey
Churches:	FirstCongregational
Clothing – Men & Boys':	Lyons Golden Rule Store
	H. N. Morey
Confectioners:	Lyons Golden Rule Store
	H. N. Morey
Dressmakers:	Mrs. Annie Halliday
Druggists & Chemists:	E. S. Crona; M. J. Gerdes
Dry Goods:	Lyons Golden Rule Store
Estes Park Stage Line:	Mrs. A. Chapman
Flour & Meal:	Lyons Golden Rule Store:
	H. N. Morey
Funeral Directors &	
Undertaker / Embalmers:	R. B. Ground
Gatekeeper:	M. E. Bashor
General Merchandise:	Mrs. D. S. Ground
	Lyons Golden Rule Store;
	H. N. Morey
	C. P. Wilcox
Grocers:	Lyons Golden Rule Store,
	M. H. Scanlon, propr.

Halls:	I. O. O. F.
Hardware/cutlery:	H. N. Morey
Hay, Grain , Feed:	Lyons Golden Rule Store
	H. N. Morey
Hostler:	S. S. Bechtolt
Hotels:	Lyons Hotel,
	Leonard H. Dieterich,
	Mrs. Etta A. Dieterich,
	manager
Laundry:	Mrs. Maggie Shields (wid)
Livery and Stage Line:	W. N. Hubbell
Marshall:	Willima H. Fogg
Meat Market:	J. L. Smith
Mill Goods:	Lyons Golden Rule Store
Milliners:	Mrs. Lea Scanlon
Opera House:	Lyons Opera House,
	Thos. Lavridson, Prop.
Physicians & Surgeons:	G. W. Gammon
Quarries – Stone:	Thos. Jamison;
	Thos. Lavridson;
	St. Vrain Red Sandstone
	Quarries
Queensware:	Lyons Golden Rule Store;
	H. N. Morey
Saloons:	The Arcade Saloon,
	Frank Burk, propr.;
	Charles Bradford
Saw Mills:	Clark & Dannells
Schools:	Chas. R. Dutro, principal
	Lyons school
Societies:	I O O F

Stage & U. S. Mail Lines:	Estes Park Stage Line—
	Schedule Lv. Lyons 12m,
	Ar. Estes Park 5 p.m.;
	Lv. Estes Park 7a.m
	Ar. Lyons 11 a.m.;
	A. Chapman, prop.
	P. O. Morain,
	Frank Pample, mgr.
Stage Line:	Lyons, Allenspark and
	Grandview Stage Line
	F. L. Hornbaker,;
	Estes Park Stageline,
	stable Lyons
Tin & Agateware:	Lyons Golden Rule Store &
	H. N. Morey
U. S. Mail:	Ar. Depot in Boulder to
	Lyons (daily)
	Ar. 4:10 p.m.
	Mail closes 9 a.m.
Undertaker:	R. B. Ground & Son
Vegetable & Fruit Pedlar:	Michael Cavanaugh
Water Works:	Willima Fogg, supt.

The 1896 City Directory can be found at the Carnegie Branch Library, Boulder, Colorado.

Coroners
Boulder County, Colorado
1877–Present

Seth D. Bouker
1877-1881

E. B. Trovillion
1891-1892

O. M. Burhous
1892-1893

John G. Trezise
1893-1901
1908-1912

Jackob Campbell
1889-1897

D W King
1881-1889

Albert E. Howe
1914-1916
1920-1922
1924-1934

Frank Buchheit
1901-1908

Leslie B. Kelso
1912-1914
1916-1920
1922-1924

George W. Howe
1934-1954

Norman Howe
1954–1970

William B. Howe
1970–1982

Rodney A. Ahlberg
1982–1986

John E. Meyer
1986–Present

Lyons Municipal Organization
1891—1899

1891

Mayor	J. M. Hews
Clerk	E. E. Norton
Treasurer	M. J. Scanlon
Attorney	H. M. Minor
Str.Cm'r	M. D. Rockwell
	C. B. Miller
Supt. W. W.	
Marshal	W. M. Thorne
Magistrate	J. J. Cortright
Trustees	J.A. Donovan, J. L. Brice, F. L. Drew, U. C. Walsh, W. N. Hubbell, Jas. Lowe.

1892

Mayor	H. N. Morey
Clerk	E. E. Norton
Treasurer	E. S Lyon
Attorney	F. P. Secor
Str.Cm'r	C. B. Miller
Supt. W. W.	
Marshal	J. C. Wamsley
Magistrate	C. P. Wilcox
Trustees	W. C. Dyer, Alex Chisholm, Jas Lowe, W. N. Hubbell, R. B. Ground, F. C. Bucherdee

1893

Mayor	H. N. Morey
Clerk	E. E. Norton
	E. B. Loller
Treasurer	E. S Lyon
Attorney	F. P. Secor
Str.Cm'r	C. B. Miller
Supt. W. W.	J. C. Wamsley
Marshal	J. C. Wamsley
Magistrate	C. P. Wilcox

| Trustees | Alex Chisholm, Jas. Lowe, W. N. Hubbell, R. B. Ground, W. C. Dyer, F. C. Bucherdee |

1894

Mayor	Alex Chisholm
Clerk	E. E. Loller
Treasurer	E. E. Norton
Attorney	F. P. Secor
Str.Cm'r	T. P. McFadden
Supt. W. W.	J. C. Wamsley
Marshal	J. C. Wamsley
Magistrate	G. W. Gammon
Trustees	L. H. Dieterich, Jas. Lowe, E. H. Erickson, R. B. Ground, F. C. Bucherdee, W. N. Hubbell

1895

Mayor	G.W. Gammon
Clerk	E. B. Loller
Treasurer	E. E. Norton
Attorney	F. P. Secor
Str.Cm'r	L. C. Lyon
Supt. W. W.	L. C. Lyon
Marshal	L. C. Lyon
Magistrate	O. M. Burhans
Trustees	C. A. Spaulding, Samuel Service, Nicholas Frank, L. H. Dieterich, E. H. Erickson, Jas. Lowe

1896

Mayor	F.C. Bucherdee
Clerk	E. B. Loller
Treasurer	M. J. Scanlon
Attorney	H. M. Minor
Str.Cm'r	W. H. Fogg
Supt. W. W.	W. H. Fogg
Marshal	W. H. Fogg
Magistrate	G.W. Gammon

Trustees J. R. Cunningham, J. S. Johns,
Thos. Lavridson, C. A. Spaulding,
Samuel Service, Nicholas Frank

1897
Mayor Samuel Service
Clerk E. B. Loller
Treasurer R. B. Ground
Attorney H. M. Minor
Str.Cm'r John Miller
Supt. W. W. John Miller
Marshal John Miller
Magistrate O. M. Burhans
Trustees T G. Gilroy, J. N. Flynn, Jno. Sjorgren,
J. R. Cunningham, Thos. Lavridson,
J. S. Johns

1898
Mayor J. R. Cunningham
Clerk L. H. Dieterich
Treasurer R. B. Ground
Attorney H. M. Minor
Str.Cm'r J. N. Miller
Supt. W. W. J. N. Miller
Marshal J. N. Miller
Magistrate W.H.H. Lewis
Trustees Jacob Blubaugh, J. S. Johns,
Thos. Lavridoson, Thos. Gilroy,
J. N. Flynn, John Sjogren

1899
Mayor M. J. Scanlon
Clerk L. H. Dieterich
Treasurer R. B. Ground
Attorney H. M. Minor
Str.Cm'r J. N. Miller
Supt. W. W. J. N. Miller
Marshal J. N. Miller
Magistrate W.H.H. Lewis

Trustees E. A. Rathbone, Erick Johnson, Thos. Lavridson, Jacob Blubaugh, J. S. Johns, J H. Hutchinson

Colorado State Business Directory

1884

A mining camp in Boulder County. Summer population 300, winter uncertain.

Butler & Co. lumber
Dwyer, H. Mines & Mining
Gilroy, T. hotel
Gilroy, Wm. contractor

Lyon, E. S. postmaster
Parson, Wm. mines & mining
Reese, John, farm & mdse
Thorn, T. J. blacksmith

1887

Terminus of the D. U. & P. Ry., in Boulder County. Population, 100.

Billings, Geo. S., sawmill
Bradford, Chas., cattle
Brown & Fogg, saloon
Butler & Co, lumber
Farmers & Merchants Ins
  1130 15th, Denver
Gilbert, S. H., Estes Park
  Stage Line
Gilroy, Thos., boarding
Bammon, G. W., drugs and
  physician
Johnson & Smith, saloon

Morey, H. M., gen. mdse &
  postmaster
Parsons, Mrs. Wm., boarding
Pounder, John, stone quarry
Putnam House, E. S. Lyons, Mgr
Stiff & Co., J. W., lime kiln
Thorne, T. J., gen. mdse
U. P. Ry. stone Quarry
Vanbergon & Watt, saloon
Watt, Wm., hotel and restaurant
Wright, F., feed stable
McFadden, Geo. B. Station agt.

APPENDIX V

NEWS,
ADVERTISEMENTS,
SCHOOL ATTENDANCE

History of Newspapers
in
Lyons, Colorado

Lyons became established as a growing community with incorporation in 1891. There developed a need to dispense local, state, and national news with the influx of workers, visitors, and businessmen from across the country and world. A continuous series of newspapers served the town, beginning in 1889, except for a twenty year period 1947–1967.

1889—*Dampinouhatitis*, June, 1889—the first paper published in Lyons. Only one issue was released. It was technically an advertisement edited and published by H. N. Morey, merchant.

05 March 1890–1891—a paper called the *Lyons News* was started at Lyons by Miss Carrie Boyd, lately of Bellbrook, Ohio.

In 1891–1893—the *Lyons News* became the *Long's Peak Rustler*, under the editorship of Benjamin Durr with offices upstairs from the Lyons Golden Rule Store.
   "A newspaper is a tower of strength and influence to any place," said Jay A. May [saloon owner] at a Lyons public meeting in December of 1890.
   He urged his fellow businessmen to support the *"Longs Peak Rustler,"* new to town, but on the hustle for Lyons' good.

1892—*Longs Peak Rustler*— E. B. Lollar, proprietor. Established 1890 – weekly $1.50/year, $1.00 for 6 months. 1893— The *Rustler* suspended publication 20 December 1893.

1894–1897—*Lyons Topics*—There are no issues or microfilm available for this paper. 1896—*Lyons Topics*—E. B. Lollar, proprietor. Established 1890—weekly. $1.50/year

1898–1899—*St. Vrain News*—No issues or microfilms available at the University of Colorado or Colorado Historical Society.

1899–1900—*Lyons Herald*—No issues or microfilms available at the University of Colorado or Colorado Historical Society.

1900 March 26, 1943—*The Lyons Recorder*
'24 Jan 1901— *The Lyons Recorder* — Lyons has three newspapers. The "Windy Wonder", published by the Literary society, Editor Mike's paper and the "Recorder," Won't us editors have a good time now. Saying mean things about each otherÖEditor Mike thinks there should be but one newspaper in Lyons, and that should be Mikes. Also there should be but one editor, and that should be Mike. Also there should be but one store, and that should be owned by MikeÖ"

20 Jun 1901—*The Lyons Recorder*—The newspaper was reduced in size to save expenses.

1904—*The Lyons Recorder*—H. C. & O. A. Knight, Editors and Proprietors

1919—1922 —*Lyons Recorder*—Walter Spencer, Editor and Publisher.

24 November 1939—"*Lyons Recorder* Sold to M. W. Downie"
    "After this issue *The Lyons Recorder* will be under the management and editorship of Mr. M. W. Downie, who purchased the paper last week from L. T. Hartcorn.
    Mr. Downie comes to Lyons from Brainard, Minnesota, where he has been employed in the newspaper business. He is a young man with a pleasing personality and with the valuable newspaper experience he has had will undoubtedly give Lyons the best paper it has ever had.
    "We have enjoyed our stay here and wish to thank each and every one who has helped in any way to make it pleasant as well as profitable."

1947–1967—Lyons did not publish a local newspaper.

1967–*The Lyons Recorder*—Ada Lou Hammans, editor

Birth of a Quarry Town

05 Feb 1976—C N Brust became editor and manager of *The Lyons Recorder*. H.C. and M.C. Knight continued as owners. Mr Brust came from the east, settled in Denver for a short period, worked on a newspaper in Golden; and then moved to Lyons in 1976.

Office located on 2nd floor of a building located at the corner of Main and 4th.

?–1982— *The Lyons Recorder*—Jack Branscom of Iowa, owner and publisher.

1982–2000— *The Lyons Recorder*—Walt Kinderman, editor.
'19 Oct 2000—"Farewell" by LaVern M. Johnson
We have to say a fond farewell to Walt Kinderman, who has operated the Old Lyons Recorder the past eighteen years.

"A town newspaper is a 'must,' as there was no newspaper in Lyons for many different years in the town's life of 120 years. There was no Lyons newspaper from 1947 to 1967, when Ada Lou Hammans started the Recorder. She sold to Jack Branscom from Iowa, who then sold it to Walt. At one time, Walt sold the paper to James Hansen, then took it back a year later."

November 2000–present *The Lyons Recorder*,
owned and operated by News Media Corporation out of Chicago, Jim Woods, director, Jacque Watson, editor.

In 1998 the Lyons area became the recipients of a second local newspaper,
Redstone Review providing news from the Greater Lyons Area. Susan de Castro McCann, publisher/editor. The paper was originally created to allow the local citizens an alternative editorial opinion. The paper has continued on a bi-monthly basis with color photographs covering, people, places, and activities in the greater Lyons area.

News from the
Long's Peak Rustler
Lyons, Colorado

The office of the *Long's Peak Rustler* was located on the second floor of the Scanlon and Brice Store. Ben Durr was the Editor and Proprietor during 1890 and 1891. The paper sported the motto: Sic Semper Trantual. The pen is mightier than the gun, 'cept in' for a grizzly"

1890

Advertisements:
Lyons Townsite: Lots for Sale. T. G. Putnam, owner. For information call on W. P. Flanders, Room 2 over Pleasant Valley Dining Hall, Lyons, Colorado.

Daniels & Cole's Drug Store, Watches & clocks at bottom prices.

E. E. Patterson our jeweler is building a residence. Sleeping in a tent next to a coal oil barrel, don't exactly suit him.

Charles Bradford, Dealer in fine Whiskies, Wines, Cigars, & Imported Beer. Headquarters for Lemp's St. Louis Beer, a first class bar is kept, at which is to be had anything a man wants. Pool & Billiards.

Deckwith's Saloon
Herbert Eddy's, the first bar in Lyons is now May's Poker Room.

Jay's Place – Bar

Jay's Barber Shop, Geo. P. McIntire, Manager. Hot & Cold Baths.

O. M. Buchans, MD, Physician and Surgeon. Office at J. W. Daniels & Co.'s Drug Store.

Dell, Ramsey & Small. Groceries and Hardware.

Birth of a Quarry Town

Mrs. Carter's New Restaurant. First Class Meals at all Hours.

L. Martin, Furniture recently moved from Longmont to Lyons.

C. C. Foy. Hay, Grain, & Feed, Flour, meal, Graham, etc.

F. B. Fellows. Horse blankets, whips, gloves, mits. Repairs.

Dan Watt – Barber, Hair Cut, Shave and Shampoo

W. C. Watt–Livery, Sales & Feed Barn.

John Hindl. Boat & Shoe Maker. Repairs. Shop in back of Deckwith's Saloon.

J. W. Daniels – Drugs, Medicine.

Lyons Bakery. Richards & Drew's Fine Line of Confection ary.

Morey & Warner's Gents furnishings.

Mr. Eddy blacksmith sold his place to Mrs. Brown for a restaurant. He's going to Noland to open a first class bar.

Mrs. Woodbury of the Woodbury House – Good Food. Quail on toast, Stuffed Turkey.

Go to Dad for first class carpentering – Coffins made to Order.

News Clips:
Mrs. Carter takes the new Thorne building, and will open a Bon Ton Hotel.

A man got into a scrap with Dan Watt & Dan used a razor on him. A Fifteen Cent fine was made to the attacker.

E. T. Carlow & Smart have struck gold 4 miles from Lyons – a pay strike of 18 inches.

News from the Long's Peak Rustler

December 1890, Temperature is 85 in the sun and 66 in the shade.

1891

Advertisements:

Thorne & Lavridson – business General Merchandise.

A. A. Mathews has put up for sale all lots held in Noland. He is owner of most of the property.

F. B. Fellows found guilty of selling blankets, gloves, and mits for less than cost.

H. W. Richards has bought out Frank Drew's interest in the Lyons Bakery. C. D. Richards is manager. In a later issue, Frank buys out Richards.

F. H. Eich – House & Sign Painting

F. B. Fellow-Horse blankets, whips, gloves, mitts, etc.

J. L. Smith – Freight & Transfer Wagon

Jay's Barber Shop

John A. Donovan – Lumber, lath, Coal and Feed. Yard near Railroad track.

W. N. Hubbell – Livery, Feed stable and Estes Park Stage

Lyons Hotel near the depot is for sale with or without the furniture. 14 rooms. Apply to E. S. Lyons.

W. A. Rice, Attorney & J. J. Cartright, esq., Justice of the Peace are located in the old post office building.

Mrs. Carson's Restaurant next to J. A. May's Place and across from Charlie Bradford's.

Hotels: Burlington Hotel & Hotel Graham

Birth of a Quarry Town

15 cases of quarry shoes of various shoes of various sizes just received at Scanlon & Brice's. Come and see them.

H. N. Morey; R. J. Thorne–Notary Public

Odell & Ullery–Carpenters and Builders

News Clips:
McFadden is surveying the townsite.

To our constable. Next time he goes to arrest a dangerous character at 3:30 at night; without a gun, he must be sure the prisoner is alone, duly sober, and not under the impression he is being held up.

Ol' Mike broke a window and chandelier in Jay's Saloon with a 10 pound boulder.

O. E. Morey of Longmont completed four new residences in the most valuable part of town.

Dr. Matthews is in Noland to attend to all cases of the measles.

N. F. Hickston is drilling an artesian well at the SE corner of Nortonville.

Jim Costello has put up a stone building next to Dell, Ramsey, & Small for heavy mercantile.

Mr. Lyon moves post office into larger stone store. It is more centrally located. Post Office to have two mail delivers daily. There is a request that the post office be smoke free. Should be one place in town where you don't have to go through a cloud of smoke. The ladies of town and those with lung trouble desire this.

Miss Ida LaCook, schoolteacher was stabbed five times by an unruly student.

306

Charles Bradford can't vote in town. He lives on a ranch outside.

Mr. & Mrs. J. A. May have born a son, 8 pounds, February 25, 1891. J. A. May & Company has put up a magnificent Hotel.

A library is being organized for Noland.

Information taken from:
Colorado State Historical Society, Denver, Colorado. Microfilm of the*Long's Peak Rustler*, Lyons, Colorado, December 12, 1890-1891 Vol.1.

Societies in Town

Odd Fellow Lodge organized 1892.

Rebekah Lodge organized 1894. Ladies auxillary group of the Odd Fellows.

St. Vrain Lodge No. 102 I O O F; Meetings every Wednesday evening. J. L. Smith Noble Grand 1895

Excelsior Rebekah Degree No. 20 IOOF Meets 1st and 3rs Friday Evening. Each Month. Mrs. Minnie Smith Norble Grand, Miss Nettie Spaulding, Secretary 1895

Montezuma Tribe No. 34 Improved Order of Red Men. Meets every Thursday Evening. H. N. Morey Sachem, E. B. Lollar Chief of Records.

Long Peak Camp No. 233 Woodmen of the World Meetings 1st & 3rd Sat. Eve. M J Scanlon, Consul. R. B. Ground, Sec.

Ancient Order of Americans. Meets 1st Tuesday night after full moon. O M Burhan, Captain.

O. M. A. Alkoran Council 1758. Princes of the Orient. Meets in their Temple of Modern Wisdom whenever summoned or otherwise notified. J. C. Brodie, Grand Orient. L. H. Dieterich, Keeper of Parchment

Lyons Cornet Band; Practice every Thursday Evening. A. E. Howe, presidnet. L. C. Lyon, Secretary.

Lyons Hose Company No. 1. Meets 3rd Tuesday Evening each month. Theo McCall President. L. H. Dieterich, Secretary.

List of Some of The Quarries Now and Then
In the Lyons Area

Beach/Beach Hill
Bergquist, Axel, a small quarry in Noland
Blue Mountain Quarry
Breach & Giggley
Brodie Quarry
Burdick Quarry
Buster's Quarry
The Colorado and Nebraska Sandstone Company –
        D. W. Slaughter, Superintendent.
Cox Quarry
Craw & Co
Dewey & Pullman – quarry of pinkish/white sandstone.
South Fork of the St. Vrain. 1890.
Jacobsen-Lyons Stone Company
Alfred Jamison Quarry
Loukonen Quarry – started in 1954 by Leonard Loukonen.
The Lyons Rock and Lime Quarry Co. – E. S. Lyons,
Manager Manck & Kelley
McCall Quarries
The Murphy Red Sandstone Quarries – Hugh Murphy,
        Proprietor Nebraska Quarry
Noland Stone Quarry – F. H. Stickney, president.
        Ohline Quarry
Patrick Red Sandstone Company – Mr. Vreeland, failed
        January, 1891.
Phillips Stone Company
Pounders St. Vrain Quarries – John Pounder, Proprietor.
J. Fred Roberts Quarries – between Lyons and Noland
St. Vrain Red Sandstone Quarries – Sites, Buell and Ayres
Sites & Buell Stone Quarry
Sprague and Buster Quarry
Stone Mountain Quarry Wm. Thorne, Beech Hill
        purchased land for $1900 J/29/1897.
Tower Red Sandstone Quarries, H. A. Arefderhar, Prop.
Note: Smaller quarries were operated throughout

Boulder County Annual Superindent Reports
1881–1900

Year	Dis-trict	Census 6-21y	Actual Attendance	Teacher	Salary	Mths
1881	Lyons School built			E.S. Lyon & Hugh McDermott		
1884	47	34		Mrs. Adaline A. Lyon	$40	6
1885	47	54		Mrs. Adaline A. Lyon	35	5
1886	47	76		M. W. Richardson	45	2
1887	47	81	23	Dr. R. L. Leggett	50	3
				L. N. Smith	50	3
1888	47	80	26	Not recorded		
1889	47	139	32	L. C. Miller	50	6
				Mrs. L. C. Miller	30	3
1890	47	117	37	L. C. Miller	60	
				L. C. Miller	50	2
				Mrs. Emma Coberly	50	1
1891	47	238	162	Etta Day	60	
	53			G. E. Beavertine & Ruth Miller	40	
1892	47	170	170	Kitty Davis	65	1
				Date Newsom	40	6
	53	36	22	Kate Murphy	60	9
				W. L. Orr	60	9
1893	47	143	117	Kate Newsom	50	9
				Mary Thorne	45	7
	53	42	16	Alice C. Knight	60	9
1894	47	129	112	Katherine Davis	120	5
				Anna Morrison	75	9
				Alice C. Knight	60	9
	53	31	13	Mrs. Agnes C. Morris	65	9
1895	47	136	104	Mrs. Nevada Root	65	9
				Beatrice M. Arnold	55	9
	53	23	14	Bertha McKenney	45	4 3/4
1896	47	136	103/81	C. R. Dutro	50	9
				Anna Bailey	45	7
	53	16	14	Ida E. Stevens	45	9
1897	47	176	124	C. R. Dutro	45/55	7 1/2
				Sadie Mathews	45/49	7 1/2
	53	9	5	Edna Baily	45	7
1898	47	148	117	Maggie L. William	50	9

Superindent Reports for Lyons and Noland

Year	Dis-trict	Census 6-21y	Actual Attendance	Teacher	Salary	Mths
				S. W. Shenefield	50	9
				Nellie Mosteller	45	9
	53	15	8	Artes Cook	40	9
1899	47	173	142/93	T. J. Thomas	60	9
				Nellie Mosheller	55/33	3
				Agnes Dauford	60	6
	53	29	20	Artta M. Cook	40	9
1900	47	215	149	R. J. Thorne	60	9
				Anna Wilcox	50	9
				Grace Jamison	30	5
	53	32	21	Tillie Anderson	40	7

Superindent Reports, Annual Reports, located at State Archives;
     Denver, Colorado
     Roll #S82 1883 Arapahoe-1886 Weld
     Roll #S88 1899 Arapahoe-1900 Yuma

District   47   Lyons, Colorado
           53   Noland, Colorado

REFERENCES
AND
NOTES

REFERENCES

First People, Trappers and the Lost Hunter
The First People

Benedict, William L, Dr. Telephone Interview, 2001.

Boulder Genealogical Society Quarterly, Vol. 5, No. 3, August 1973.

Boyles, B. L. *The St. Vrain Valle.* Longmont, Colorado: St. Vrain
Valley Press, 1967.

Brackett, Frances Brodie, President Lyons Cemetery Association.
Personal interviews 1999–2001.

Denver Public Library, Western History Collection, Denver,
Colorado.

Keller, Douglas, unpublished paper for the Lyons Redstone
Museum.

Kingery, Eliner Eppich. "Lyons the Quarry Town." Monograph
Written in 1956. Lyons, Colorado: Lyons Redstone
Museum.

Knowlton, Lorna. *Weaving Mountain Memories.* Saline, Michigan:
McNaughton & Funn, 1989.

The Lyons Recorder, Aug 28, 1931, Sept. 4, 1931, Nov 25, 1938, and
several undated articles.

Trappers & Mountain Men

Boulder Genealogical Society Quarterly, Vol. 5, No. 3, August 1973.

Boyles, B. L. *The St. Vrain Valle.* Longmont, Colorado: St. Vrain
Valley Press, 1967.

_____. "Tales of the St. Vrain Valley."

Broadhead, Edward. *Ceran St. Vrain 1802–1870.* Pueblo,
Colorado: Pueblo County Historical Society, 1987.

Brown, Seletha. *Rivalry At The RiverÖIn Colorado's Fur Forts.*
Boulder, Colorado: Johnson Publishing Company, 1972.

*Colorado and Its People A Narrative and Topical History of the Centennial
State,"* ed. LeRoy R. Hafen, PhD & Litt. D., Executive
Director of the State Historical Society of Colorado,
Vol. 1. New York: 1948.

Grun, Bernard. *The Timetables of History.* 3rd Revised Edition.
New York: Simon & Schuster, 1975.

"South Platte River Trading Posts, Fort St. Vrain." *Colorado
Prospector,* Vol.9, No.8.

The Earliest Settlers

Billings, Clair, Personal Interviews, 1999–2000.

Billings, Norton A., Telephone and Mail Communication, 2000.

Boulder County Land Records, Boulder, Colorado.

Boulder County and Colorado State Census Records, 1860–
      1885.

Boulder County Treasurer's Ledger No. 39. Located at
Carnegie Branch Library, Boulder, Colorado.

"Boulder Genealogies." Boulder Genealogical Society Library
      at Carnegie Branch Libary, Boulder, Colorado.

Bracket, Frances Brodie, personal interviews, 1999–2001.

Estes Park Trail. Estes Park, Colorado newspaper, 12 Apr 1946, p2

Grant, Marcus, Gleichman, Mehls, Phillips, Velasquez. *Results
      of an Archaeological and Historical Inventory of Southern Rab
      bit Mountain & North Foothills Open Space Boulder County,
      Colorado.* USDI Bureau of Land Management Cultural
      Resources, 16 Dec 1996.

Grun, Bernard. *The Timetables of History*. 3rd Revised Edition.
      New York: Simon & Schuster, 1975.

Hygiene Cemetery Records, Hygiene, Colorado.

Johnson, LaVern, interview regarding John Reese.

Kingery, Eliner Eppich. *Lyons the Quarry Town*. monograph
      dated 1936. Located at the Lyons Redstone Museum.

Knowlton, Lorna. *Weaving Mountain Memories*. Estes Park,
      Colorado: Estes Park Historical Museum, 1989.

Longmont Daily Times-Call. obituaries and "Mountain Park
      Controversy." Weekend edition, 8-9 Dec 1984.

Lyons Cemetery Burial List 1888– 2001, Lyons, Colorado.
      Compiled By Diane Goode Benedict and Frances Brodie
      Brackett. Lyons, Colorado: Applications, Plus, 2001.

Longmont Ledger, 26 jan 1894, 27 april 1894, 18 May 1894,
      25 May 1894.

The Old Lyons Recorder, February 2, 1862, May 17, 1913,
      September 6, 1940, September 4, 1931, June 26, 1980 p6,
      and obituaries.

_____, "The Centennial Edition." September 26, 1991 p2.
      Johnson, Lavern, interview for The Lyons Recorder.

McRoberts, Mary, Boulder Genealogical Society Genealogist.
      Telephone Conversations, 1999–2001.

Montgomery, Donald. Personal interviews, 2001.

Obituaries found in newspapers and undated records in the
      Lyons Redstone Museum, Lyons, Colorado.

Birth of a Quarry Town

Rocky Mountain News, West. January 31, 1866:4 p1.
Weaver, Frank. *They Came by Covered Wagon.* Available at the
        Lyons Redstone Museum, Lyons, CO.
_____, Various contributions to the Old *Lyons Recorder*, most
        sources undated.
_____. Unpublished notes for the Lyons Centennial Book.

The Disappearance of
Aquilla Cook

Butman, Beverly, "Pioneer Hunter's Fate Never Known."
        Boulder Daily Camera, Boulder, Colorado. 18 January 1976.
Denver Public Library, Western History Department, newspaper
        index file, Denver, Colorado.
Kingery, Eliner Eppich, "Lyons the Quarry Town" a monograph.
        1956.
Rocky Mountain News, Daily. "Territorial News" 18 April 1871
        p1 C3, 26 March 1866 p4 C3, 02 May 1869 p4 C3.
Weaver, Frank, "They Came by Covered Wagon, A History of the
        Billings Family. The New Lyons Recorder, Lyons, CO 1977.

Lyons Ditch No. 1

Johnson, LaVern. Information submitted for publication.

Origins
The Origins Of Lyons, Colorado

Boulder County Land Records. Boulder County Courthouse,
        Boulder, Colorado.
Dunning, Harold Marion. *Over Hill and Vale*, Vol. I History of
        Northern Colorado. Loveland, Colorado: Johnson
        Publishing, 1956.
_____.*Over Hill and Vales*, Vol. III. Loveland, Colorado:
        Johnson Publishing, 1971.
Freudenburg, Betty D., *Facing the Frontier, The Story of the MacGregor
        Ranch.* Rocky Mountain Nature Association, 1998.
Kingery, Eliner Eppich, "Lyons the Quarry Town," monograph
        written in 1936. Lyons Redstone Museum, Lyons, Colorado.
Long's Peak Rustler. March 6, 1891.
Longmont Ledger, Longmont, Colorado, September 22, 1882,
        November 24, 1893.
Lyons, Edward S. "The Settling of Lyons, according to E. S. Lyon."
The Lyons Recorder, 1921. An angry response to the"Story of
        Lyons" written by Mrs. Lois Lamb-Hall. December 22, 1921.

316

The Lyons Recorder, Sept 13, 1900, 1922, Feb. 21, 1980 p5, March 3,
    1988 p1, Feb.27, 1997.
The Lyons Redstone Museum, Lyons, Colorado.
Tallant, MacDonald. Service, and Stauffer family interviews
    July 28, 1974. Estes Park, Colorado: Estes Park Historical
    Society.
That Beautiful Valley. Lyons, Colorado: *The New Lyons Recorder,* 1978.
_____. *The Came by Covered Wagon.* Available at the Lyons Redstone
    Museum.

Short Biographies
Of Lyons Pioneers

Brackett, Frances Brodie, Interview 07 November 2001.
Hall, C. Maurine. Genealogy given to Lyons Redstone Museum,
    18 August 1987.
"History of Hall family since late 1800's recalled." *The New
    Lyons Recorder.* 1 March 1979.
Lamb, Lois. "John Bigland Hall." Story of J. B. Hall in the Lyons
    Redstone Museum, Lyons, Colorado.
Longmont Ledger, Longmont, Colorado, 4 May 1923.
The Lyons Redstone Museum file on Blair. Undated photocopies of
    newspaper articles and Legal Notices, and a Family Group
    Sheet.
Melton, Jack R. and Lulabeth. Biography included in *Recollections of a
    Rocky Mountain Ranger* by Jack C. Moomaw. Estes Park,
    Colorado: YMCA of the Rockies. 1994.
Obituary, 20 April 1934. Unidentified photocopy of a newspaper
    article. Lyons Redstone Museum, Lyons, Colorado.
The Old Lyons Recorder, 16 January 1933, 8 October 1948,
    23 July 1987,p 18, 11 October 1998.
Photocopy of Obituary, "Monday Services Are Scheduled For
    Ranger Jack C. Moomaw, 82". Not referenced.
Weaver, Frank. Unpublished notes.

From Nebraska to Colorado

Beckett, Louise Aldinger. Unpublished paper on the story of
    Gotlieb Fredrick Aldinger and family in Lyons.
Middleton, Jim. Letter dated 05 September 2000 sent to Diane G.
    Benedict, editor of the *Boulder Genealogical Society Quarterly.*
_____, Several e-mail communications between Mr. Middleton
    and Ms. Benedict.

The Nortonville Addition
Boulder County Land Records. Boulder Courthouse, Boulder,
    Colorado.
Longmont Ledger, 05 Jan 1894, 19 Jan 1894.
Lyon, E. S. "the Settling of Lyons, According to E. S. Lyon."
    The Lyons Recorder, January 1922.

Life in a Quarry Town
Business on Main & High Streets

The Arcade Saloon
419 Main Street
The Denver Times. 02 November 1898, 03 November 1898.
The Old Lyons Recorder, 22 December 1904, Arcade Saloon Ad.
Newspaper article, unidentified (probably *The Old Lyons
    Recorder*) from the Lyons Vertical file at the Carnegie
    Branch Library, Boulder, Colorado.

McAllister Saloon
450 Main Street
Double Gateway to the Rockies, Lyons Historic sites map secured
    from the Lyons Redstone Museum, Lyons, Colorado.
Packet of Information including Title searches found at the
    Lyons Redstone Museum.
West, Elliott, *The Saloon on the rocky Mountain Mining
Frontier.*University of Nebraska Press. 1979.

The Golden Rule Store
Main Street
The Denver Post. "Contemporary Section," 29 October 1978.
Evert, Jack, Interview with the grandson of M. J. in 1993 by the
    Lyons Elementary third grade class.
Long's Peak Rustler, 19 December 1890, Vol.1, No. 2, p2.
The Lyons Recorder, 06 November 1902, 20 July 1978.
Weaver, Frank. "A Look Back at Lyons." *The LyonsRecorder,*
    15 April 1976, 21 August 1980, an updated photocopy of a
    newspaper from Carnegie Branch Library for Local
    History, Boulder, Colorado.
_____. "The Scanlon Family." A typewritten study of the family
    found in the files of the Lyons Historical Museum, Lyons.

The Men of Main Street
Frank Brothers

Bureau of Land management, General Land Office Records,
US Government. Internet search.

Weaver, Frank, series of undated *Lyons Recorder* articles found
in the files of the Lyons Redstone Museum, Lyons,

Weaver, Frank, "A Look Back At Lyons." *The Lyons Recorder* 2 Oct
1980 p11, vertical files at Carnegie Branch Library, Boulder,
Colorado.

The Old Stone Church
High Street & Fourth

Brackett, Frances Brodie. Telephone Interview 23 October 2001.

The Cornerstone, a Quarterly Newsletter. The Old Stone
Congregational Church. October, 2001.

Holts, Bud. Personal Interview with one of the workmen on the
refurbishing project for the house. 23 October 2001.

Longmont Ledger, "Dedication of the Congregational church at
Lyons", 18 Sep 1894.

Lyons and Surrounding Area, Double Gateway to the Rockies.
Lyons, Colorado: the Lyons Centennial-Bicentennial
Committee under the auspices of the Town Council of
Lyons, Colorado.1977.

The Old Lyons Recorder, undated photocopy in the Lyons Vertical File
at Carnegie Branch Library of Local History, Boulder,
Colorado. 04 September 1980, p.9.

Hamilton, Cindy, "History Cut In Stone." *Redstone Review*.
April, 2000.

United States Department of the Interior National Park Service
National Register of Historic Places Inventory Nomination
Form, July 02. 1976.

The Stone House
426 High Street

The Denver Post, 12 March 1919.

Land Records. Boulder County Court House Records, Boulder,
Colorado.

Newnan, John, Paper written 26 Apr 1989. Found in the files
Of the Lyons Redstone Museum, Lyons, Colorado.

Birth of a Quarry Town

Ralston , Steve. Telephone Interview 19 Oct 2001.

Lyons Redstone Museum
340 High Street
Daily Times-Call," Community Review." Longmont, 1978.
Lease Agreement from the St. Vrain Valley School District to the
    Lyons Historical Society, Inc. 1977.
The Lyons Redstone Museum, tri-fold informational sheet. 1979.
The Old Lyons Recorder, 22 Nov 1979, and an undated article.

Seward Street
"Lyons Colorado Historic District." Pamphlet Celebrating Lyons
    Centennial Year, June 1981–June 1982

History of the
Lyons Cemetery
Brackett, Frances Brodie, President of the Lyons Cemetery
    Association. Personal Conversations, 1999-2001.
Lyons Cemetery, Lyons, Colorado 1888–October, 2001. Compiled
    By Diane Goode Benedict and Frances Brodie Brackett.
    Lyons, Colorado: Applications, Plus, 2001.

Shootout at Charlies' Bar
The Boulder County Herald, Boulder, Colorado: 28 December
    1892, Vol.13 #266 p6; January 11, 1893, Vol. 13, #28 p8; May 3,
    1893, vol. 14, #63 p5; May 10, 1893, Vol. 14, #69 p5.
The Boulder News, Boulder Colorado: 29 December 1892;
    May 4 1893; May 4, 1893; May 10, 1893.
The Daily Camera, Boulder, Colorado: December 20, December
22, December 23, December 25, December 27 December 28, 1892;
    January 6, January 7, January 13, January 17, 1893; May 2,
    May 3, May 5, May 6, May 9, 1893,April 21, May 28, 1896.

Soiled Doves
Farrar, Harry, "Citizens move to beautify Lyons Cemetery,"
    The *Denver Post,* "Contemporary Section", 28 Oct 1978,
    Carnegie Branch Library, Boulder, Colorado.
Guided tour of Pagosa Springs, Summer, 2001.
Interview with George Murphy at the Off Broadway Coffee
    Shop, 2000.

The Long's Peak Rustler, 1891. Cut out article found at the Lyons
Redstone Museum, Lyons, Colorado.

Doctors and Undertakers
Longs Peak Rustler, Lyons, CO, February 06, 1891. Vol. 2
The Lyons Cemetery Burial List 1888-2001. Compiled by Diane
Goode Benedict and Frances Brodie Brackett. Lyons, CO:
Applications, Plus. 2001.
The Lyons Recorder. Various ads and small notices found in older
issues of the various Lyons newspapers.
Weaver, Frank. Unpublished notes

Albert E. Howe
Boulder Daily Camera, 30 July 1959.
Colorado Prospector, "Two Stages Run Daily From Lyons",
25 June 1899, Vol. 11, No. 3, Colorado Territory, Price,
Four Bits.
Department of the Interior Notice #04394
McRoberts, Mary. Family Group Sheet compiled July 1990.
University of Colorado Archives, CU campus, Boulder, Colorado.
A. E. Howe papers dealing with the Howe Mortuaries.

Sanitariums,
to Resorts
Berg, Denise, Telephone Conversation, October 31, 2001.
_____, personal interview, December 20, 2001.
Boulder Daily Camera, 17 June, 1897; 28 May 1938:8.
Colorado Cultural Resource Survey, Colorado Historical
Society, Burlington Hotel, March 27, 1981.
Dunning, Harold Marion. *Over Hill and Vale, Vol. I & II.*
History of Northern Colorado. Boulder, Colorado:
Johnson Publishing, 1956, 1962.
Evert, Helen Scanlon. "History of the Welch Resort by a Family
Survivor." Paper in the files of the Lyons Redstone Museum.
Undated.
Information sheet from the Lyon's Den Bed & Breakfast, Lyons, CO.
"Icibenda Bloomfield, hostess with mostest." *Longmont Daily
Times-Call*, December 14, 1976.
Letter. Plymouth Meeting Historical Society. January 23, 2001.
Longmont Ledger, 09 Feb 1894, 06 Apr 1894, 13 Apr 1894,19 Apr 1894.
Long's Peak Rustler, Vol.1 32 p2 1890.
The Lyons Recorder, June 13, 1901, 17 March 1904.

Mogan, Hilda and the Lyons Historical Society. "The History of the Welch Resort ." *The Lyons Recorder,* from the Lyons Vertical File at Carnegie Branch Library for Local History, Boulder, Colorado. Probably written from *History of the Welch Resort.* 2-typed pages found in the files at the Lyons Redstone Museum, Lyons, Colorado.

Newby, Betty Ann, "Thorne made Mark on Lyons,"*Longmont Daily Times-Call* July 2000.

Nofsinger, Rita. "Welch Resort Has Varied History." *Longmont Daily Times-Call,* 24 March 1971, p. 4A.

Olinger Crown Hill Cemetery, Denver, Colorado. Telephone Interview with Joan. October, 2001.

RhodesScholarship.org. Longmont Public Library Reference Desk January 29, 2002. "The Rhodes Scholarship Program began in 1902 after the death of Cecil Rhodes. The first American recepient was in 1904."

Shikes, Dr. Robert H., lecture at the Colorado Historical Society, Denver, Colorado, Thursday February 14, 2002.

Undated, unacknowledged photocopy of a newspaper article in the Grade school publication, "Lyons Years Ago, 1944.

Weaver, Frank. "A Look Back At Lyons." The Lyons recorder, December 4, 1980 p24.

_____, unpublished notes for the Lyons Centennial Book.

Welch Resort, March 27, 1981. *The Daily Camera,* 17 June 1897 last page, Boulder, Colorado.

Whitemarsh Township Residents Association (WTRA). "Erdenheim Farm Development. Agreement Marks Significant Progress for Open Space Preservation in Whitemarsh." http://www.wtra.org/farmdevelopment.html.

Too Much Water

The Boulder Daily Camera, June 2, 1894.
Longmont Ledger. 01 June 1894, 22 June 1894.
The Old Lyons Recorder, September 11, 1910, 1903.

Of Roads and Rails

The Stage

Arnold, Anne Morrison, Bliss, Elliott, Gooch, and Stapleton, *Steads Ranch and Hotel: Echoes within the Moraines."* Elyse Deffke Bliss, Bellvue, Colorado. 2000.

Colorado Prospector, Vol. 11, No. 3, *The Denver Times.* Colorado

Territory. Price Four Bits, March 1980.
James, Ted on Transportation, Estes Park Historical Society
       Oral History Interview 6-16-1983. Estes Park Library.
Kingery, Eliner Eppich., "Lyons the Quarry Town." *The Old
       Lyons Recorder, 1956.*
Knowlton, Lorna. *Weaving Mountain Memories. p. 8–9*, Estes
       Park Area Historical Museum; Estes Park, Colorado:
       McNaughton and Gunn 1989.
Lyon, E. S. "The Settling of Lyons." *The Lyons Recorder,* 1922
Merriott, Jim, "Two stages Ran Daily from Lyons." *The Old
       Lyons Recorder,* Lyons, Colorado, 9 Aug 2001 p18.

The Railroad

The Boulder News. Boulder, Colorado, January 15, 1891.
The Boulder News. Weekly, 28 Aug 1890:4.
Boyles, B. L. *The St. Vrain Valley.* Longmont, Colorado: St.
       Vrain Valley Press, 1967.
The Denver Times. "Colorado Prospector." Vol. 11, No. 3,
       Colorado Territory, Price, Four Bits, March 1980.
The Daily News, Denver, Colorado September 28, 1885 p. 6 c. 1-2.
U S. Government Land Patent Records. Internet Search.
Longmont Ledger, Longmont, Colorado, August 28, 1885.
The Lyons Recorder, 01 September 1977
_____ "A Look Back At Lyons by Frank Weaver," Wednesday,
       December 24, 1980 p. 8
_____, "Lyons Country." undated article found at the Lyons
       Redstone Museum.
_____, "A Touch of NostalgiaÖ", undated article found at the
       Lyons Redstone Museum.
Ramey, John, Conversation at Kokopeli's CafÈ in Lyons,
       Colorado, 09 January 2001.
Rowe, Michael A. of Boulder Colorado, a research paper sent to
       LaVern Johnson of the Lyons Redstone Museum, July 2 1996.

Lyons Railroad Depot

Daily Times-Call, Longmont, Colorado. 12 April 1973, 14 March
       1974, 16 April 1974 02 February 1975.
State Historical Society of Colorado files, Denver, Colorado.

The Lyons Road

Brown, Dick, Estes Park Car Club, Interview 9 September 2001.
Dunning, Harold M. *Over Hill and Vale.* "A Murder in Estes Park" –

Birth of a Quarry Town

undated newspaper article.
Knowlton, Lorna. *Weaving Mountain Memories*. Estes Park,
Colorado: Estes Park Historical Museum. 1989.
Lyons Recorder. 12 May 1904 & 25 November 1938.
Pickering, James H. *Mr. Stanley of Estes Park*, 101–107. Maine
and Estes Park, Colorado: The Stanley Museum, Inc.
Kingfield, 2000.

Lyons And Estes Park Toll Roads

The BoulderDaily Camera. 31 July 1945.
Boulder Harold Weekly. 29 May 1895:5 & 5 June 1895:6.
Boulder News. 30 May 1895:4.
Kingery, Eliner Eppich, "Lyons the Quarry Town." Monograph,
1956. Located at the Lyons Redstone Museum, Lyons.
Knowlton, Lorna. *Weaving Mountain Memories*. Estes Park,
Colorado: Estes Park Historical Museum, 1989.
Longmont Times-Call, "St. Vrain Valley Pioneer Recalls Lyons
Tollhouse." 15–16 March 1975.
The Lyons Recorder, 26 July 1900, 13 December 1900, 25 November
1938.
Obituary Index at Carnegie Branch Library, Boulder, Colorado.

The Quarries
Geology of Lyons

Benedict, Audrey D., *A Sierra Club Naturalist's Guide: The
Southern Rockies*, Sierra Club Books, 1991.
Braddock, W.A. and others, Geologic map of the Lyons
Quadrangle, Boulder County, Colorado, Geologic
Quadrangle Map GQ-1629, U.S. Geological Survey, 1988.
Eicher, Don L. & McAlester, A. Lee, *History of the Earth*,
Prentice-Hall, Inc, 1980.
Natural History of the Boulder Area, Hugo G. Rodeck, Editor,
University of Colorado Museum, Boulder, Colorado Leaflet
No. 13, August 1964.
Pace, Al, "Denver geologist explains origin of local sandstone."
Interview with Jack Murphy, curator of geology for the
Denver Museum of Nature and Science.
Walker, T.R. & Harms, J.C., 1972, Eolian Origin of Flagstone Beds,
Lyons Sandstone (Permian), Type Area, Boulder County,
Colorado. The Mountain Geologist, v. 9, nos. 2-3, p. 279-288.

324

Noland, Colorado
Quarry Town to Ghost Town

Boulder News. From the vertical files of the Denver Public
Library No dates or other references on the photocopy.
Brackett, William. "History of Noland." *Boulder News*,
26 September 1889, Boulder, Colorado.
Brodie, Mary, "Notes made on life in Noland."
Colorado Prospector, Vol. 11, No. 3. "Price, Four Bits," undated.
Hygiene Cemetery records downloaded from the internet at
spot.colorado.edu/~Wasson.
Kingery, Eliner Eppich. "Lyons the Quarry Town" 1956,
typewritten monograph.
Longmont Daily Times-Call, 13 August 1959, 04 May 1978 p. 5.
The Longs Peak Rustler, 27 February 1891, 25 February 1909.
Lyons Cemetery Records, compiled by Diane G. Benedict and
Frances Brodie Brackett, Applications, Plus. 2002
The Lyons Recorder, 26 December 1890, 23 Jan 1891, 2 April 1903 in
About Town, 18 July 1907, 3 March 1927, 4 August 1977,
"The Innertube," a Supplement, 26 November 1980,
15 November 1984, 16 June 1994.
McRoberts, Mary. Telephone Interview 23 October 2001.

Beech Hill

Boulder Camera. "Stone Exhibit at the World's Fair."
January 1, 1893 p1. Boulder, Colorado.
Johnson, Edwin. "Beech Hill" an unpublished paper.
Kingery, Eliner Eppich. "Lyons the Quarry Town" 1956,
typewritten monograph. Located at the Lyons Redstone
Museum, Lyons, Colorado.
Pace, Al, Telephone Interview to his home in Longmont, October,
2001.

Hugh Murphy
And The Murphy Quarries

Kingery, Eliner Eppich, "Lyons, The Quarry Town," 1936.
Monograph held at the Lyons Redstone Museum, Lyons.
Longs Peak Rustler. Vol.1 32 p2 1890, February 6, 1891.
The Lyons Recorder. March 18, 1909, April 1, 1909, June 13, 1941.
St. Vrain Red Sandstone Quarry Company. Archival box located in
Norlin Library, University of Colorado Archives. Box #1
holding 1904-1907 correspondence, vouchers, and payroll
sheets for the St. Vrain Redstone Quarry Company, Lyons. C

John Campbell Brodie
And The St. Vrain/Brodie Quarry

Boulder County Historic Landmark Nomination Form,
        "Brodie Quarry Blacksmith shop and Cistern, St. Vrain Quarries,"
        January 4, 2001.
Brackett, Frances Brodie. "Brodie St. Vrain Quarries." Brodie
        family history. Given to author by Mrs. Brackett.
Encyclopedia of Biography, p282-283.
"Genealogy of the John Campbell Brodie Family"by Frances
        Brodie Brackett, *Boulder Genealogical Society Quarterly,*
        Vol.33 No.2 May 2001.
Jenkins, Jewel Maret, "Historic Brodie Quarries Still in Operation
        After 73 Years."
Longmont Ledger, undated article sent to author.
The Lyons Recorder, 1904 issue, 26 Aug 1927, 13 April 1934,
        03 Jan 1936, 13 Jan 1936, 25 Dec 1942.
Pace, Al, wrote several interviews for *The Lyons Recorder,*
        documenting the remembrances and activities of present day
        quarry owners and stonecutters. 2000.
Unknown source, photocopy of picture and short paragraph
        on the Sayer-Brodie Mansion, Denver, Colorado.

Lyons Limestone Quarry And Kiln

Colorado Cultural Resource Survey, "Inventory Record."
        Boulder County Historical Site Survey, March 27, 1918.
The Denver Times. 20 June 1900.
Dunning, Harold M. *Over Hill and Vale,* Vol. II. Boulder, Colorado:
        Johnson Publishing Company, 1962.
Pace, Al. Telephone Conversation, 10 Nov 2001.
The Old Lyons Recorder. 7 Jun 1900, 21 June 1900.
Sullivan, Berene. Personal Conversations and Telephone Interviews.

McConnell Family

Johnson, LaVern. Personal Conversations and Telephone Interviews.
Sullivan, Berene. Personal Conversation and Telephone Interviews.
Weaver, Frank. Unpublished notes.

Note: In March, 1932 on the day of JA's funeral, the two-story farmhouse on the Reese Farm caught fire in the flue. The home burned to the ground. Young Bernie McConnell and his family moved uptown to the Van Sickle House until a new homes could be built.

Bertha sold the Sites property and moved to a new home in 1946. Shed died in 1958.

Blacksmiths

Colorado Business Directories, 1885 &1887 from the Denver Public Library, Western History collection.
Neville, Katherine. *The Magic Circle*. New York:.Ballentine Book. 1998 p400.
Various newspaper references from Lyons and Longmont.
Weaver, Frank. Unpublished notes.

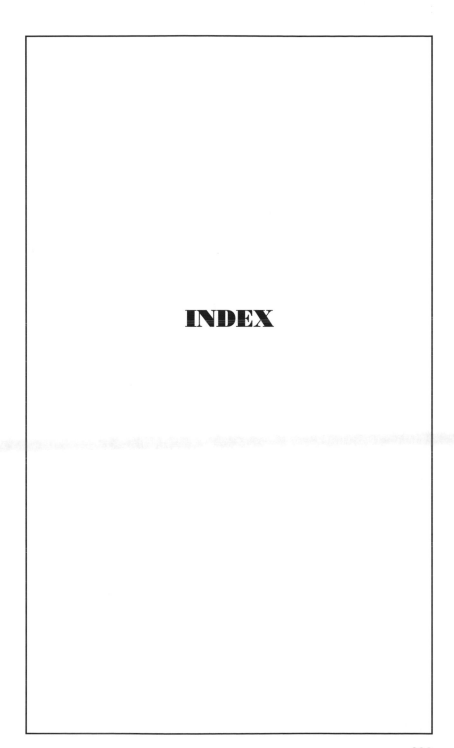

INDEX

A

A' Hearn, Thomas **188**
A. Hearn, Thomas 99
Adams, Judge 99
A'Hearn, Thomas 81, **185**
Alabama 57
Albert, Bertha Jane Reese **183**
 Elizabeth **183**
 Ethel **183**
 James **183**
 John 8
 Orville **183**
Aldinger
 Fred 76
 Gotlieb Fredrick 60, 66, 121
 Minnie Schwilke 66
Allen, Dr. Orfilo 40
Allenspark Town Company 61
American Car and Foundry
 Company **175**
Amick, Dr. 111
Ancestral Rockies 149
Anderson 121, **180**
Angelos, Cris 76
Antelope Park 57, 106
Apple Valley 149
Apples
 Apple Valley 18
 Orchard 18
 Wolf River 15
Arapahoe 5, 10, 14
Arbuckle 126
 Frank P. 128
Arbuckle Resort 126
Arcade Saloon 23, 78, 79, 80
Archie, James 126, 128, 138
Arizona 58
 Bisbee **184**
Arkansas River 4
Arnold, Anne Morrison 126
 Ralph B. 137, 138
Atkinson, John 106

Avenue
 Third 30

B

B. & M. R. R 135
Baker, Edward 97
 Jim 8
 Melinda Jane 17
 William 16, 17, 166
Baker School 16
Ballinger, Henry Franklin
 47, **190**
Bancroft, Dr. 134
Barber, W. H. 100
Barrett, Caroline Evangeline 36
Barry, James 9
Battles, Lee 100
Baughman, Lizzie 53
Bavaria, Lohr 51
Baxtor, William 97, 98
Beach Hill 61, **172**, **174**
Beach Hill Quarry **167**
Beach/Beech Hill **168**
Beaubien, Charles 9
Beckwith, Elmer 78, 79
Beckwourth, Jim 8
Bedell, Maude Frances Grace 27
Beech Hill
 45, **155**, **157**, **169**, **170**, **185**
Beech Hill quarries. 130
Benedict, Dr. William L. 3
 Robert James 145
Bent Brothers 10
Bent, Charles 8, 11
 George 9
 John 11
 William 8, 11
Bent, St. Vrain, & Company 9
Bent's Fort 4
Berg, Denise 116
Berger, Mr. 94
Bergman, Dan 47, 190
Bergman Family **190**

Ft. Morgan Times 57
Fuller, Dad 131

G

Gaddis, A. B. 89
Gallacher, P. **174**
Gammon , Dr. George W.
   98, 107, **207**
Garrigues, District Attorney 100
Gateway to the Rockies 13
Gauss, Robert 129
Gecke, William 133, 134
General Land Office 14
Geology
  Ancestral Rockies 149
  Cretaceous Dakota group 150
  Cretaceous period 150
  Flatirons 149
  Fountain 149
  Front Range 150
  Ingleside Formation 149
  Jurassic 150
  Limestone kiln 150
  Lower Permian 149
  Lyons sandstone 149, 150
  Morrison formation 150
  Pennsylvanian 149
  Permian 150
  Precambrian 149
  Quaternary 150
  Sandstone 150
  Silver Plume granite 149
  Steamboat Mountain 149, 150
  Stone Canyon 150
  Triassic Lykins formation 150
Germany 110
  Felbach, Wurtenburg 60
  Luxembourg 81, 82
Gibson, Charles 92
Gifford , Catherine (Kate) 19
Gilcrest 9
Gilfflin, J. H. 88
Gilfillan, J. H. 76

Gilger, U. S. 83, 84
  U. G. 37, 121
Gilroy, Theresa 27
Globeville Smelter **185**
Goddard, Charles M. 15
Golden Andesite Rock Company
  48, 144
Golden Rule Store
  37, 76, 77, 90, **154**, **185**
Goode, Rev. W. H. 10
Goodwin, Ella 82. *See also*
  Frank: Nicholas
Gordon, Barbra Summer 52
Gordon, C. F. 53
  Charles Fullerton 52, **207**
  J. C. R. 53
Gordon Family **207**
Gordon property 30
Gorter, Tim 31
Goss, John **183**
Graham, E. L. 101
  Eva R. 105
Grand Junction News 129
Grant, General 22
Grant, J. Q. **158**
  Q. **157**
  William 102
Great Lakes 54
Green , Deputy Sheriff Hank 99
Griff Evans Stage Stop 126
Griffith
  Dora 34, 36, 41
  Dora Thomas 51
  Harriet F. 41
  William 41
  William O. 41, 42
Griffith , William Family **208**
Grocery Store
  C. P. Wilcox Grocery 77
  Gaddis and Robson 62
  Frank Brothers 72
  H. N. Morey 60
  Lyons Golden Rule Store 62

ABOUT THE AUTHOR

Diane Goode Benedict is a graduate of the University of Colorado in Boulder, Colorado and the recipient of two advanced degrees from Wayne State University in Detroit, Michigan.

She is the editor of the Boulder Genealogical Society Quarterly and a free-lance historical writer for the *Lyons Recorder.* She is the member-at-large on the Boulder County Historic Preservation Advisory Board and an active member of Historic Boulder in Boulder, Colorado.

Two recent publications are:

LYONS CEMETERY BURIAL LIST 1888–2001 Lyons, Colorado,
    Compiled by Diane Goode Benedict and Frances Brodie
    Brackett.

LYONS CEMETERY, LYONS, BOULDER COUNTY,
    COLORADO 1888 to the Present. Documentation of interments in the Lyons Cemetery. Sources include obituaries, funeral home records, Census records, Coroner files, family interviews, tombstone readings, and plot measurements.

Diane is working on two new books about Northern Boulder County, as well as compiling documentation on burials in the Hygiene Cemetery, Hygiene, Colorado.